MACROMEDIA FLASH MX MAGIC

By Matthew David

Mark Baltzegar, Véronique Brossier, Jim Caldwell, John Dalziel, Aria Danika,

Robert M. Hall, Andreas Heim, Jason Krogh, Jessica Speigel, Glenn Thomas,

Helen Triolo, Joe Tripician, and 2Advanced Studios

New Riders

201 West 103rd Street, Indianapolis, Indiana 46290

MACROMEDIA FLASH MX MAGIC

International Standard Book Number: 0-7357-1160-7

Library of Congress Catalog Card Number: 20-02104045

Printed in the United States of America

First Printing: April 2002

06   05   04   03   02   7   6   5   4   3   2   1

Interpretation of the printing code: The rightmost double-digit number is the year of the book's printing; the rightmost single-digit number is the number of the book's printing. For example, the printing code 02-1 shows that the first printing of the book occurred in 2002.

Trademarks

Warning and Disclaimer

Publisher
David Dwyer

Associate Publisher
Stephanie Wall

Executive Editor
Steve Weiss

Production Manager
Gina Kanouse

Managing Editor
Sarah Kearns

Acquisitions Editors
Theresa Gheen
Elise Walter

Senior Development Editor
Jennifer Eberhardt

Copy Editor
Amy Lepore

Product Marketing Manager
Kathy Malmloff

Publicity Manager
Susan Nixon

Manufacturing Coordinator
Jim Conway

Cover Designer
Aren Howell

Interior Designers
Steve Gifford
Wil Cruz

Compositor
Wil Cruz

Proofreader
Debra Neel

Indexer
Lisa Stumpf

Media Developer
Jay Payne

CONTENTS AT A GLANCE

ABOUT THE AUTHORS

Matthew David has been developing Flash-based applications for more than six years. (That makes him very old in this business!) Examples of his work can be found at his web site, **www.matthewdavid.ws**, or you can email him directly at **mdavid@email.com**. Matthew's most recent publications include content for *Flash 5 Magic* and *Inside Dreamweaver 4*. You can also see him popping up in many online magazines such as Sitepoint.com, Windowatch.com, and UDzone.com.

ACKNOWLEDGMENTS: There are only four people I need to thank: my three kids—Jake, Emma, and Liam—and my beautiful wife. I could not do any of the things I do without you. I love you all.

Mark Baltzegar is an award-winning art director and interactive designer at Terra Incognita, bringing eight years of experience in working with video, print, and animation. Mark's work has been awarded the NY Films International Festival Gold Medal, has won Telly and Emmy awards, and has been recognized in *HOW* magazine. Like the other members of Terra Incognita's team, Mark has a strong background in the liberal arts. Mark attended the Louisiana Scholars' College, where his concentration was in the humanities and social thought. Mark is also a contributing author to *Step-By-Step Digital Design*.

ACKNOWLEDGMENTS: My wife and son, for their generous support; the Terra Incognita family, for their generous support; the Institute of Human Origins, for the generous use of imagery and audio from the *Becoming Human* interactive documentary.

Véronique Brossier currently works independently, developing games and web interaction design. A technology and art enthusiast, her work aspires to transcend programming and design and to engage the user. Today, Véronique teaches "Interactivity in Flash" in the same program where she received her M.A. when the Internet was in its infancy, the Interactive Telecommunications Program of New York University. Upon graduating from NYU, she worked for the American Museum of National History, designing and programming exhibition kiosks. Afterward, she joined the design studio Funny Garbage, where for three years she held the position of technical director in the animation department. Originally a French import, she has made New York City her home for many years.

Jim Caldwell is a self-taught and ambition-driven creative developer. His background lies within corporate surroundings, working for communications giants such as BellSouth and MCI WorldCom. At present, he is a senior applications developer with MCI WorldCom. Although he has been responsible for the company's intranet applications, his passion is creating new benefits and uses within Flash. His design studio, Innovative FX, LLC (**www.innovativefx.com**), contributes to his success by allowing him to serve clients such as Cisco Systems, Inc. Jim has always been a large part of the design community, moderating at forums such as Ultrashock (**www.ultrashock.com**), We're Here (**www.were-here.com**), and Flashmove (**www.flashmove.com**). Jim is the author of *Instant Macromedia Flash 5* (Osborne McGraw Hill).

ACKNOWLEDGMENTS: I'd like to thank my wonderful wife, Mary, for all the help and support she has given me. I owe the world to her.

John Dalziel is the U.K. correspondent for *FlashMagazine*. He has written tutorials on date and time for Ultrashock.com and tinkers with his own Flash projects at crashposition.com. He came to Macromedia Flash from a background in game design and is currently working for Pogo Technology, building Flash interfaces for mobile devices. John lives in London with his starfish.

ACKNOWLEDGMENTS: I'd like to thank my wife, Emma, and my parents for their support; Andrew Gibson for his wonderful photograph; Tom, Gary, and Andy for their inspiration; Jensa and Miko for letting me loose; and Bill Hicks for squeegee-ing my third eye.

Aria Danika is a web designer/developer for BBCi based in London, a moderator at **www.flashkit.com**, and a member of the Hypermedia Research Centre at Westminster University, where she currently pursues a graduate degree in hypermedia studies and interactive design. Aria comes from an arts background and was trained in photography and multimedia. She enjoys working with mixed media across various platforms and also works with Flash at a personal level for experimenting with her art and digital photography. When she is not Flashing or rollerblading, she can be found over at FlashKit.com or actionscript.com, talking all things Flash with the rest of the community.

ACKNOWLEDGMENTS: There are many people I would like to thank for their time, support, and encouragement and for sharing their skills and knowledge. Many thanks to David Emberton for the opportunity and the inspiration. Also to Mark Fennell, John Starkey, David Petley, Jeremy Carney, Sven Goewie (thanks for all the support guys), and everyone at FlashKit for the opportunity to learn, experiment, and share with other developers our common passion whilst having great fun in the process. Finally, my parents and especially my mom. Thank you!

Robert M. Hall, a native of Fort Lauderdale, Florida, is currently the senior developer for mCom LLC (**www.mcom8.com**) located in Philadelphia, Pennsylvania. Robert architects projects and develops ATM machine interfaces, award-winning Internet banking software, and wireless device applications. Prior to mCom, Robert was a consultant at Citicorp and a web developer for USABancshares.com. When Robert is not enjoying the outdoors with his girlfriend, he can be found listening to music, reading, tinkering with electronics, and trying out new technologies. Usually a piece or two of his experiments will wind up on his personal web site: Feasible Impossibilities, **www.impossibilities.com**.

ACKNOWLEDGMENTS: Thanks to Mike Chambers, Anna Marie Pises, and Niamh O Byrne of Macromedia; Phillip Torrone of Fallon & Flashenabled.com; Steve "Leo" Leone of NexusGroup; Daniel Taylor and my friends at mCom LLC; and all the folks who post to Flashcoders. Special thanks to David Dwyer and Theresa Gheen and the rest of the New Riders family for this opportunity; my friends Scott, Bill, and Chuck; my brother, Jimmy; my parents; and my girlfriend, Melissa, for all their support and inspiration.

Andreas Heim is from the small town of Hattenhofen, close to Stuttgart in Germany, a center of German car engineering. Originally intending to become a professional soccer player, his education took him into the area of media studies and programming. After creating an interactive CD-ROM, his focus shifted from film and video to interactive media. His school required him to do a six-month internship, which brought him to Smashing Ideas, where being a soccer-playing-and-beer-drinking German intern was highly respected. He had so much fun in Seattle that he extended his stay to one year before deciding to stay permanently. Andreas currently works on all kinds of cutting-edge digital-media projects, including bringing Flash to devices, while enjoying his time outside of work, snowboarding, and playing soccer.

ACKNOWLEDGMENTS: Thanks to the Flash team for creating the most excellent version of Flash yet, to Troy Parke for his help with designing Flatzee, and to Anna Hall for her support and for feeding me during the nights of writing.

Jason Krogh operates zinc Roe design, a small shop that specializes in advanced Flash development and training. He is actively involved in the Flash community and is a regular contributor to Ultrashock and the Flash Forward conference series. Under Jason's direction, zinc Roe has established itself in the world of children's new media. The company has developed projects for Canada's leading children's broadcasters, including the Family Channel, Teletoon, and TVOntario. Jason has been teaching advanced Flash techniques for more than three years and offers regular ActionScript workshops in Toronto.

ACKNOWLEDGMENTS: Thanks go out to Allan Kennedy for his help in reviewing this chapter, to Dave Yang and Sam Wan for putting up with my questions about OOP techniques, and to David Colquhoun, Jerrold Connors, and Anne-Sophie Brieger for their ongoing support. I would also like to thank all my students—past, present, and future—for their questions, curiosity, and inspiration.

2Advanced Studios
Over the past four years, 2Advanced Studios has flourished from its humble beginnings as the personal portfolio experience and digital canvas of renown motion-graphics designer Eric Jordan into its present form as a leading full-service interactive design and multimedia agency. Based out of Dana Point, California, 2Advanced Studios services a wide array of clients and industries worldwide in the disciplines of web design, interactive multimedia, custom video, and audio production, as well as 3D rendering and traditional print design. For *Macromedia Flash MX Magic*, contributing 2Advanced authors Eric Jordan and Stephanie Novak have combined their collective design and development expertise to deliver a rewarding presentation of both form and function.

Jessica Speigel co-founded We're Here Forums (**www.were-here.com**), a haven for knowledge-seeking Flash users and the largest privately owned and operated Flash resource site. Jessica began her career as a designer creating web sites for high-profile jewelry designers. Realizing Flash's power for dynamic content, she took a position with PersonalGenie developing unique personalization web applications using Flash as the front end. During this time, Jessica created the front-end to applications for Fortune 500 companies such as Procter & Gamble. Jessica has also contributed Flash-related articles to sites such as CNET's Builder.com, and she has been a contributing author on *Flash 5 Studio*, *New Masters of Flash: The 2002 Annual*, and *Flash MX: Application Design & Development*. In her spare time, Jessica enjoys painting, pottery, and secondhand-furniture shopping and restoration.

Glenn Thomas is one of the founders of Smashing Ideas, a leading digital media services company. Smashing Ideas' projects include the Madonna "Music" Shockwave Single, Email Chess, webcasting the Sydney 2001 Paralympics, Pocket PC games, and web animation shows such as Zombie College. He has been involved with Flash since its inception and has spoken at numerous industry conferences. He authored the book *Flash Studio Secrets*, which details innovative ways to use Flash in the real world.

Helen Triolo is the owner of i-Technica, a web design shop in the Washington, D.C. area. An electrical engineer turned programmer turned web designer, she became fascinated with Flash after obtaining a copy of Flash 4 and discovering its limitless possibilities for programmable animation and database integration. Addicted ever since, she has used Flash in a variety of client web sites and CDs, has posted an archive of Flash Q&A's (**http://i-technica.com/flashlist**) and ActionScript tutorials (**http://actionscript-toolbox.com**), and teaches and writes about ActionScript whenever possible. You can find more of Helen's work at **www.i-technica.com** (business site) and **www.action-script-toolbox.com** (Flash ActionScript samples and reference).

ACKNOWLEDGMENTS: My thanks to Theresa, Matthew, and Dave Yang for providing me with the opportunity to work on this book; to my husband, Paul, for providing endless technical support and encouragement; to Nic and Sarah for being willing to cook their own mac-and-cheese when Mom's too busy to cook dinner; and to the many Flashmeisters at the chinwag, flashmacromedia, and flashcoders email lists, from whom I've received a ton of inspiration and support.

Joe Tripician is an Emmy-award-winning producer/writer/director whose work has been broadcast on network and cable television across America, Europe, and Japan. His humor book, *The Official Alien Abductee's Handbook*, was published by Andrews and McMeel in 1997. Joe is also the author of several feature-film screenplays, including a script optioned by veteran producer Ben Barenholtz. In 1998, Joe co-founded iStreamTV, a streaming media technology company based in New York.

ABOUT THE TECH EDITORS

Patricia Geneva Lee Hall is a web software developer from way back…at least as far back as 1998. She has two cats (working on more), one husband (one's enough), and an ever-growing extended family. When not busy tech editing, policing her husband's mad-scientist hobbies, or building random pieces of web software, she finds court TV shows strangely amusing. Everyone needs to have a vice, don't they?

Jennifer Hall is senior technology officer for JPMorganChase and is also teaching Flash and Director for Multimedia Enterprise. She has been a contributing author for *Flash 5 Magic* and *Flash 5 Visual Insight*. Jennifer has worked with leading multimedia companies including Top Drawer (Human Code [Sapient]), Thought Interactive (Meritage Technologies), Cortex Interactive, and Eyeland Studio for clients including Disney, Prentice Hall, Nokia, Lycos UK, and Holt, RineHart, and Winston. In her spare time, Jennifer eats, reads, runs, sits, rock climbs, dances, loves, and lives. Visit her at **www.jennifershall.com**.

Laura McCabe is a freelance Flash designer and developer currently living in Baltimore, Maryland. Her eclectic interests have led her through an undergraduate degree in psychology, studies in art and design at the Maryland Institute College of Art and the University of Baltimore, and, ultimately, to Flash. In six years of internet experience, she's honed her skills in web production, information architecture, design, and development while working with clients such as AARP. Her Flash designs have been featured at the collaborative site **www.poemsthatgo.com**, and her personal playground is **www.stolenglance.com**. In her spare time she is a photographer, writer, trainer, editor, and recovering book junkie.

Chrissy Rey is the vice president of education and a senior developer at digitalorganism. She is also the founder and webmaster of FlashLite and the founder of the Baltimore Macromedia Organization (BAMMO). A Maryland native, Chrissy graduated from the University of Maryland with a degree in zoology (of all things). After a brief stint as a zookeeper, and then as an animal technician in a genetics lab, Chrissy discovered Flash and Generator. At digitalorganism, she uses her experience to lead internal, private, and public education efforts. She also leads digitalorganism's development efforts by capitalizing on her extensive array of knowledge.

A Message from New Riders

As the reader of this book, you are our most important critic and commentator. We value your opinion and want to know what we're doing right, what we could do better, in what areas you'd like to see us publish, and any other words of wisdom you're willing to pass our way.

As Executive Editor at New Riders, I welcome your comments. You can fax, email, or write me directly to let me know what you did or didn't like about this book—as well as what we can do to make our books better. When you write, please be sure to include this book's title, ISBN, and author, as well as your name and phone or fax number. I will carefully review your comments and share them with the authors and editors who worked on the book.

Please note that I cannot help you with technical problems related to the topic of this book, and that due to the high volume of email I receive, I might not be able to reply to every message. Thanks.

Fax:	317-581-4663
Email:	**steve.weiss@newriders.com**
Mail:	Steve Weiss
	Executive Editor
	New Riders Publishing
	201 West 103rd Street
	Indianapolis, IN 46290 USA

Visit Our Web Site: www.newriders.com

On our web site, you'll find information about our other books, the authors we partner with, book updates and file downloads, promotions, discussion boards for online interaction with other users and with technology experts, and a calendar of trade shows and other professional events with which we'll be involved. We hope to see you around.

Email Us from Our Web Site

Go to **www.newriders.com** and click on the Contact Us link if you…

- Have comments or questions about this book.
- Want to report errors that you have found in this book.
- Have a book proposal or are interested in writing for New Riders.
- Would like us to send you one of our author kits.
- Are an expert in a computer topic or technology and are interested in being a reviewer or technical editor.
- Want to find a distributor for our titles in your area.
- Are an educator/instructor who wants to preview New Riders books for classroom use. In the body/comments area, include your name, school, department, address, phone number, office days/hours, text currently in use, and enrollment in your department, along with your request for either desk/examination copies or additional information.

INTRODUCTION

The first thing you are going to notice is that the name has changed. Macromedia Flash MX is not just an upgrade from Flash 5. Flash MX is a pivotal product in the evolution of Flash. The last five versions have created a tool that is second to none for control over animation and ubiquity across the Internet. Flash 4 and 5 introduced a powerful programming language called ActionScript. Flash MX has taken great strides to extend the functionality and control and increase the speed needed to complete Flash projects. You will find improvements with almost every aspect within Flash, from the panels receiving a welcome makeover to better compression with final .swf movies to enhanced scripting control. It is a new generational step for Flash, and so we have a new name.

You will also see that there is a new structure to this book. When you are developing a web site, there are certain tools you need. You need tools to manage your site, additional tools to dynamically add content, and still other tools to manipulate the presentation of the content. With this in mind, we have divided the book into these four sections:

1. Fundamentals
2. Scripting Tools
3. Site Management
4. Advanced

The focus of *Macrmedia Flash MX Magic* is to highlight the strongest new features in projects you will actually need to use in the real world. Solutions such as dynamic charting and polling are key to the vision of *Macromedia Flash MX Magic*. Now, no matter where you are in the process of developing a Flash-driven web site, you will have the tools you need to deliver a high-impact transaction between you and your customers.

WHO WE ARE

Macromedia Flash MX Magic is the creative vision of its lead author, Matthew David. Matthew is heavily involved with the Flash community, having contributed to many Flash 5 and MX books, web sites, and magazines. He believes strongly that Macromedia Flash is the technology to deliver next-generation web sites. You can find out more about Matthew at his web site, **www.matthewdavid.ws**.

No book can be written by just one person. This is even more the case with *Macromedia Flash MX Magic*. Some of the most talented Flash developers in the world contributed their time and energy to projects in this book. Among them are Mark Baltzegar, Véronique Brossier, Jim Caldwell, John Dalziel, Aria Danika, Jennifer Hall, Patricia Hall,

Robert Hall, Andreas Heim, Eric Jordan, Jason Krogh, Laura McCabe, Stephanie Novak, Chrissy Rey, Jessica Speigel, Helen Triolo, Glenn Thomas, and Joe Tripician. Each person is a great asset to the Flash community. These people know what can be done with Flash and are not shy about sharing their knowledge with us all.

WHO YOU ARE

Whether you've been using Flash since before it was a Macromedia product or you just picked it up yesterday, there's something for everyone in *Macromedia Flash MX Magic*. Primarily though, the book is targeted at web developers who want to leverage Flash more effectively in the production process.

This book does not cover the basics of the Flash authoring environment or the .swf file format. It does cover basic to advanced examples of object-oriented scripting, Flash application development, client/server interaction, rich media content development, and of course, animation.

You can be either a linear or nonlinear reader and get equal enjoyment from *Macromedia Flash MX Magic*. It is built around projects and integrated techniques rather than individual features of Flash, so don't feel as though you need to start at the beginning.

WHAT'S IN THIS BOOK

The *Macromedia Flash Magic* books have always pushed the boundaries of Flash as a technology, and this book continues to do so. The projects in this book range from fundamental Flash movies to a complex understanding of ActionScript and interaction with databases and web servers.

As you move through the book, you will find that almost all of the new scripting features and design tools are covered. This is a brief list of some of the new tools covered:

- Using Components
- Scripting Components
- Templates
- Accessibility
- Audio Control
- Loading External .jpg and MP3 Files
- JavaScript Integration
- PHP and ASP Integration
- Scripted Drawing Methods
- Object-Oriented Programming

The table of contents at the front of this book contains a complete list of the Flash MX technologies used.

THE CD-ROM

As you would expect, the accompanying CD-ROM has all of the files used in the projects throughout the book, together with links to great Flash web sites and demonstration software. While you are surfing, check out our official *Macromedia Flash MX Magic* web site at **www.flashmxmagic.com**.

To view the contents on the accompanying CD-ROM, all you have to do is insert the disc into your CD-ROM drive. The CD-ROM should begin to play automatically. A welcome screen will pop up, enabling you to choose to view either the .fla files used in the book, demonstration software from Macromedia, or links to web sites.

CONVENTIONS USED IN THIS BOOK

Most of the techniques in this book direct you to enter code or ActionScript into the start files or the Flash files that go along with each technique. This code is set apart from the first column of text into the second column (where most of the figures are) in a screened box. The code you will be asked to enter will be set in a colored box.

Some of the lines of code featured in this book's techniques are too long to fit on one line. Wherever you see the ➥ symbol, this indicates that the line of code has been wrapped around. In other words, when you enter a line of code with the wrap-around symbol, enter it as one line without the wrap-around symbol included.

INTRODUCTION TO ACTIONSCRIPT

Flash MX ActionScript is used extensively throughout this book to create richly interactive movies once considered impossible with anything other than Director or Java. The creators of Flash have managed to create an accessible, powerful authoring environment, but it is not without idiosyncracies. This short introduction will try to prepare you for possible pitfalls while giving a general overview of the ActionScript language in its latest incarnation.

If You're New to Flash

Although the examples and techniques in this book are explained as thoroughly as possible within the scope of the *Magic* series, it will definitely help to have at least some familiarity with basic programming principles if you are to fully understand the ActionScript code you are inputting.

ActionScript can be characterized as intelligent glue, enabling you to combine various elements of a project programmatically and to create movies that go far beyond simple linear animation. ActionScript, based on JavaScript's standardized parent language ECMAScript, exposes a lot of the raw power of the computer to you, so you can use Flash as a simplified Visual Basic or other program development tool. The advantage is that Flash has a media engine already built in, so all you have to do is create the various elements (graphics, animations, audio) and then use ActionScript coding to control them.

If You're Already a Flash User

If you have used previous versions of Flash, you're probably already fairly familiar with what ActionScript is all about. Flash MX incorporates a vastly superior—and therefore more challenging—version of ActionScript that comes close to matching the power and flexibility of JavaScript used in conjunction with a web browser. Along with a strong object-oriented focus, ActionScript includes standard flow-control mechanisms, math functions, operators, and even XML support.

Flash MX ActionScript supports all previous Flash 5 actions. However, it comes complete with a new JavaScript-like syntax, or way of writing things, and seasoned Flash 5 users might need time to come to grips with it. Also, a number of operators and actions that were commonly used in the past are now deprecated. This essentially means that although they're still supported, it is recommended that you start migrating to their newer replacements just in case they are dropped in the future.

HAPPY FLASHING

If you're new to programming, learning ActionScript in Flash MX can be a daunting task. We hope this book will make the task much easier and more rewarding. Furthermore, we hope you will find the techniques in this book more applicable to your everyday job requirements. Although the art resources in this book are not freely available, you're certainly welcome to use the code featured in the book for your own projects (as if we could stop you). Soldier through it, and have fun!

Some of the most exciting tools in Flash MX are the new Components. *Components* are drag-and-drop elements that you can place onto the stage to make it easier to build complex movies. You will find that Components can consistently help you with your projects.

Almost all of the projects in this book use Components at one point or another to reduce the amount of development time you would ordinarily spend. The bottom line is this: If you want to get it done right and fast, you have to learn how to use Components. You will be very glad you did.

1

COMPONENTS

by Matthew David
with animations by Steve Leone

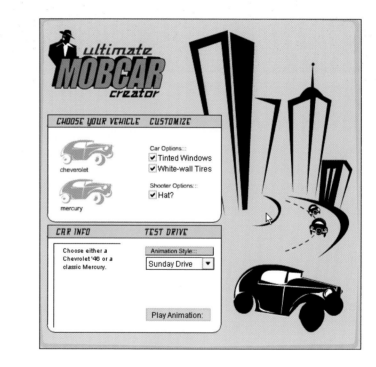

Difficulty Rating: ★★★★

Made With: Macromedia Flash MX

Final File Size: 38KB

Modem Download Time: 30 seconds

Development Time: 1 hour

IT WORKS LIKE THIS

Throughout this project, you will learn to leverage Flash MX Components within a movie. You'll build a movie in which users can design their ideal mobster car. In particular, the focus is on three different Components: `MenuList`, `PushButton`, and `CheckBox`.

These Components enable users to choose elements in a custom animation they will build. The first is a check box option that determines whether the final animated vehicle has white or black tires. The second is a drop-down window that presents different backgrounds. Finally, the `PushButton` Component takes the options chosen and builds the final animation.

With this project, you will be able to reduce the development time needed to build complex interactive movie clips through the use of Components. It is possible to re-create the movie without the Components because, after all, the Components themselves are just images with a lot of ActionScript applied to each one—and that's the benefit. Macromedia has already developed each Component.

Finally, each Component's design is in and of itself an object within the ActionScript programming language hierarchy. With this in mind, properties and methods in each Component can be programmatically modified with your ActionScripts. This enables you to create your own Components. You'll learn more about this in later chapters.

PREPARING TO WORK

Before starting, you'll need to copy the **01_Components** folder onto your hard disk, start Flash, and open the **Components.fla** file.

SETTING THE STAGE

Although Flash MX Components are new, the technology is based on the same foundation as all Flash movies. That is, you place Components onto the stage and control them in much the same way as you control other objects. Before adding the Components, the movie itself must be set up. You will have the basic layout of the movie, together with all of the layers. The movie is two frames long.

Macromedia Flash MX: Components are based on the smart clip technology introduced with Flash 5. The evolution of smart clips to MX is so great that the technology has been renamed to identify it as something altogether new and much better.

Components are drag-and-drop modules that you can place onto the stage. In many ways, they are similar to a cross between objects and behaviors used in Macromedia Dreamweaver. Seven Components come with Flash MX. You will notice that these Components are all form related. This is largely due to Flash 5 and earlier versions being limited to only text field form elements. On the web, forms are comprised of menus, check boxes, and radio buttons. These are needed in the Flash environment.

Note: The structuring of each Component demonstrates Flash's range of flexibility. Small details, such as forcing a menu list to be a specific width, cannot be done with HTML. Other details, such as modifying the visual appearance of each Component, enable a designer to easily synchronize the visual layout of the form Components with the movie. Again, this is hard to achieve with HTML. Cascading Style Sheets give you some design control, but you cannot easily change the presentation of elements such as a check box in the same way that Flash can.

The mobster car settings are configured in frame 1 and presented in frame 2.

1 Select frame 1 from the **Labels** layer. Open the Property Inspector, noting that the properties for frame 1 on the **Labels** layer are highlighted. Add the label **info**.

2 Select frame 2 from the **Labels** layer and set the label to **animation**.

These two frame labels will be used in your ActionScript later on.

3 Open the Library, expand the **car** folder, and double-click the movie clip called **man** to open it in edit view. To make navigating through the **man** movie clip easier, label the first frame **hat** and the second frame **no_hat**.

As you can see, the movie clip is two frames long. The second frame is the same man without a hat. Later, you will add a Component that enables a user to choose whether he or she wants to see the man with or without his hat.

4 Drag the instance of the movie clip **man** onto the second frame of the main movie and into the **Animation** layer.

Three more movie clips will be configured in the same way as the **man** movie clip.

5 From the Library, expand the **car** folder. Open the **tint** movie clip into edit view. Label the first frame **tint** and the second frame **white**. Open the **wheels** movie clip into edit view and label the first frame **white** and the second frame **black**.

6 Open the **animation** movie clip from the Library. Label the first frame of the **animation** movie clip **1** and the second frame **2**.

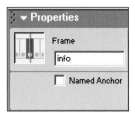

The Property Inspector gives you fast access to common properties for an object such as a frame.

The movie clip of the man will be configured by the user.

This movie clip is longer than the others. The user will choose which animation he or she wants as the background to the final movie. The movie clip contains two different animations: a blank animation and one with a mobster car driving up at high speed.

7 Navigate back to the main movie. Select frame 2. Select the **Tint** layer and drag an instance of the **tint** movie clip onto the stage and into the **tint** layer. Select the **shooterCar** layer and drag instances of the **shooting car** and **wheels** movie clips onto the **tint** movie clip. Finally, drag an instance of the **animation** movie clip onto the stage and into the **Animation** layer.

The first frame of the **animation** movie clip is blank. A single white dot will identify where the movie clip is on the stage.

The main movie is now set. Each movie clip has been configured with the correct labels.

The animation elements will be controlled by a combination of buttons and ActionScript.

THE COMPONENTS

With the stage set, you will now use three Components: CheckBox, ComboBox, and PushButton. Each Component is similar to the HTML form elements you see on many web sites. Each Component has its own custom settings, and the Property Inspector will change to reflect which settings can be modified.

▼ Properties				Properties	Parameters
Component	Editable	false			
cars	Labels	[Mercury,Chevrolet,Audi,VauxHall]			
	Data	[]			
W: 100.0 X: 107.3	Row Count	8			
H: 17.6 Y: 211.6	Change Handler				

The ComboBox Component adds web-like drop-down menus to a movie clip. The properties of the Component can then be modified by the Property Inspector.

1 Drag an instance of the `CheckBox` Component onto the stage under the **Car Options** label in frame 1 of the **Components** layer of the main movie. Use the Property Inspector to set the instance name to **tinted**, the Label to **Tinted Windows**, and the Initial Value to **true**.

The Property Inspector lets you modify the settings for the `CheckBox` Component. You need to set the instance name so that you can refer to this instance of the Component with ActionScript later on.

2 Drag a second instance of the `CheckBox` Component onto the stage. From the Property Inspector, name this instance **tires**, add the Label **White-wall Tires**, and change the Initial Value to **true**. Add these Components to the **Animation** layer.

3 Drag a third instance of the `CheckBox` Component onto the stage under the label **Shooter Options**. Name this instance of the `CheckBox` **hats**, add the Label **hat**, and set the Initial Value to **true**. If this `CheckBox` is selected, the final movie will show the mobster with a hat on.

4 Drag an instance of the `ComboBox` Component onto the stage. You will immediately see that the Property Inspector is different than in the `CheckBox`. Again, add this to the **Components** layer. Place it below the **Animation Style:::** label on the stage.

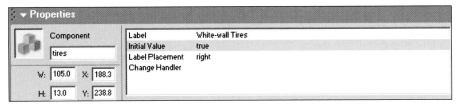

The properties of the **tinted** `CheckBox` Component.

The properties of the **tires** `CheckBox` Component.

The properties of the **hats** `CheckBox` Component.

The `ComboBox` Component has different properties than the `CheckBox`.

Note: You must name each instance of a Component on the stage for ActionScript to successfully interact with it. In this way, you can treat Components the same as movie clips. In many ways, Components are just very complex movie clips. The beauty is that the ActionScript used to build them has been completed for you.

5 Name the instance of the ComboBox **animation_style**. Select the Labels property and click the magnifying glass icon from the Property Inspector. In the Values window, add these two values: **Sunday Drive** and **Shoot 'em up!** Click OK to close the Values window.

A ComboBox works in the same way that a drop-down menu does within a web form. For the ComboBox to be effective, you need values from which a user can choose. To add a new value, select the + icon.

6 Because the **animation_style** ComboBox is not the same width as the button above it, use the Property Inspector to change the width of the ComboBox to 110px.

It is now perfectly aligned with its label. The next step is to add the button that will enable you to move from the first screen to the next one. As you might guess, there is another Component you can use to do this.

7 Drag an instance of the PushButton from the Components Panel onto the stage. Place it in the bottom-right corner of the movie in the **Components** layer.

The PushButton Component has only a couple of properties that can be modified.

8 From the Property Inspector, change the Label of the PushButton to **Play Animation:::**. Name the instance of the PushButton **play_button**.

The values will be dynamically added to the ComboBox.

Note: The ComboBox is similar in appearance to the traditional dropdown menus used in web pages. The relationship stops at this point. A ComboBox is essentially a very smart, ActionScript-programmed movie. This allows for great flexibility within your designs.

One feature of the ComboBox worth mentioning is the Editable property. The value for the Editable property can be set to either true or false. Selecting true allows a user to write directly into the ComboBox when being played as a .swf movie. This is useful if you are creating a form in which a user can choose from a list of options (such as favorite colors) and add the option he or she is looking for if it is not listed. This relieves developers of having to add a second text field to accommodate alternative selections.

Properties for the PushButton instance **play_button**.

You will see the label of the `PushButton` change on the stage. Finally, the Click Handler controls how the user will interact with the button. An `onClick` event has to be written within the Property Inspector, so enter the text **onClick** as the Click Handler property. When a person clicks on this `PushButton`, it will execute an ActionScript.

9 Select the second frame in the **Componenets** layer and add a new `PushButton`. The button Label and instance name are **Reset**, with **onClick** for the Click Handler.

The **Reset** `PushButton` properties.

MODIFYING COMPONENT "SKINS"

As you have seen, Components offer more flexibility than conventional web forms in that you can integrate them seamlessly within your Flash movies. A further enhancement comes with the visual presentation of the Component, including the color.

All of the visual elements for the Component in the Library are in a folder called **Flash UI Components**. An additional folder inside of this one, called **Component Skins**, stores the visual elements used for each Component.

All of the ActionScripting needed for the Component is separate from the "skins." The `PushButton` skins are saved in the folder **FPushButton Skins**. Four movie clips are used to create the visual effect of the `PushButton`.

1 From the Library, expand the **Flash UI Components**, **Component Skins**, and **FPushButton Skins** folders. Open the movie clip **fpb_disabled** for editing.

The clip can be edited exactly the same as any other movie clip.

The `PushButton` Component is placed in the Library as a Component with a separate subfolder storing the "skin," or visual appearance, of the object.

2 Double click on the gray square in the center of the icon to edit the image and change the color of the square to #D8D418. Do the same for **fpb_down**, **fpb_over**, and **fpb_up**.

When you preview the movie clip, the color of the button will be changed to the new color scheme.

Note: Each visual element of a Component can be modified. For instance, you can change a radio box to the shape of a heart. This enables you to match the Component with the style of your movie.

ADDING INTERACTIVITY

The final step to complete this movie is to add the ActionScript that will join the choices made by the Components with the movie clips. This will enable each Component to execute a choice or action made by the user. For instance, the CheckBox will let you choose whether you want the hat on the man in the final animation.

1 Select frame 1 on the **Scripts** layer. Add this code:

This ActionScript initializes the default values for the objects in the movie. The PushButtons placed on the stage are triggered by this ActionScript. For instance, when the PushButton named **play_button** is clicked, it sends the user to the frame labeled **animation**. When the PushButton named **Reset** is selected, it returns the user to the frame labeled **info**.

```
initValues();
// push button control
function onClick(btn) {
    if (btn == play_button) {
        setAnimation();
        gotoAndStop("animation");
    } else if (btn == Reset) {
        gotoAndStop("info");
    }
}
```

The ActionScript controls where the movie will move to when a PushButton is pressed.

9

2 Add this code below the onClick function:

Components need to be told how to work. First, you set up the Components, such as the CheckBox **Hat**, to have a value. With the **Hat** Component, it was to see if you wanted the hat on or not. When the option has been chosen, that value must be captured. Flash needs to know how to do this. Enter ActionScript. With this code, you capture the value of the **Hat** CheckBox and then convert it into a variable. This variable, called hat_value, can now be used by the animation in the second part of the movie. As you can see, the whole thing is not exactly magic, but what it gives you is great control over how the value of the Component is interpreted.

```
function setValues() {
        tinted.setValue(tinted_value);
        tires.setValue(tires_value);
        hats.setValue(hat_value);
        animation_style.setValue(animation_value);
}


function setAnimation() {
        tinted_value = tinted.getValue();
        tires_value = tires.getValue();
        hat_value = hats.getValue();
        animation_value = animation_style.getSelectedItem()
➡.label;
}
```

The CheckBox and MenuList Components allow you to make choices. The value of those choices is then passed onto the ActionScript. The ActionScript is then able to programmatically change the final movie using the user's choices.

3 To stop playback of the movie to enable users to make their choices, add this to the end of the ActionScript:

```
stop();
```

4 The values for each setting are now known. From the Library, edit the **man** movie clip, which can be found in the **car** folder. In frame 1, add this code:

Here is a simple if…else statement looking for the value that hat_value is set to on the root of the movie. If the value is set to true (that is, the check box is selected), the man will have a hat on his head, and the movie will go to and stop on the frame named **hat**. Otherwise, the movie will go to the frame named **no_hat**.

```
if (_root.hat_value == true) {
    gotoAndStop("hat");
} else {
    gotoAndStop("no_hat");
}
```

5 The same trick needs to be applied to the **tint** and **wheels** movie clips in the Library. Here you will take the values of the variables created in the first frame and use them to determine the construction of the final animation.

The ActionScript for the **tint** movie clip is added to frame 1 of the **tint** movie clip:

```
if (_root.tinted_value == true) {
    gotoAndStop("tint");
} else {
    gotoAndStop("white");
}
```

The ActionScript for the **wheels** movie clip is added to frame 1 of the **wheels** movie clip:

```
if (_root.tires_value == true) {
    gotoAndStop("white");
} else {
    gotoAndStop("black");
}
```

The ActionScript is using the variable `tires_value` to determine which animation should be played.

6   Open the **animation** movie clip in the Library. Select frame 1 and add this script:

This final ActionScript controls which background animation is played. As with the previous movie clips, the ActionScript is attached to frame 1 of the **animation** movie clip. Instead of an `if...else` statement, as in Step 4, you use an `if...else if` statement. This allows for two or more values to be matched.

```
if (_root.animation_value == "Sunday Drive") {
    gotoAndStop("1");
} else if (_root.animation_value == "Shoot 'em Up!") {
    gotoAndPlay("2");
}
```

7   Preview your work. Now you can custom design the mob car of your dreams.

How to Improve

Components have enormous potential. For instance, if you are developing a game, you can use Components to enable a user to custom design the hero he or she would like to play as well as the weapons he or she would like that hero to use. The Components are designed to make it easier to build forms. These forms can then, in turn, be used to send data to and from a database or XML source.

Sometimes you get creatively blocked. In some cases, Flash MX can help break that block. Flash MX has pre-packaged templates, movies that contain graphics, ActionScript, and everything you may need to design many types of movies. When you use one of these templates, all you need to do is plug in your content.

This project will use a template to make a presentation and then we'll go one step further and make the presentation accessible to users with visual disabilities. Of the nearly half billion people who surf the web today, 22 million are blind. Flash movies must be made available to these users, else we risk alienating a large percentage of our audience. We will use Flash MX accessibility features that will enable screen reader software to "read" the presentation.

TEMPLATES AND ACCESSIBILITY

by Matthew David
with images by Bromide73

Difficulty Rating: *
Made With: Macromedia Flash MX
Final File Size: 354 Kbps
Modem Download Time: 3 seconds
Development Time: 1 hour

It Works Like This

Flash MX comes prepackaged with a number of templates designed to get you up and running quickly. In many ways, you can think of them as similar to templates in Microsoft PowerPoint. But it is almost unfair to compare Flash MX templates to PowerPoint. Powerpoint is only for creating slideshow presentations and Flash MX templates go way beyond slideshows. Take a quick look at the list of templates you can choose from. You'll see that Flash MX offers you a lot of great options:

- **Ads.** There are ten different ad templates that enable you to develop Flash movies that follow the standards of the Interactive Advertising Bureau (IAB).

- **Broadcast.** The single broadcast template enables you to design a Flash movie for broadcast over television. The layer guide gives you directions for where to place text and images for optimum viewing on a television.

- **Menus.** Using an external XML source, you can quickly create menus for your site.

- **Mobile devices.** Both Nokia's phones and Pocket PC devices support Flash 5. These templates give you guidelines to developing for these platforms.

- **Photo slideshow.** This is a movie that enables you to quickly build slideshows.

- **Presentation.** Flash has long been a solid standby for creating presentations, so why not use a template with four different styles that enables you to do just that?

- **Quiz.** You can create a quiz from three different styles.

You will use one of the presentation templates and create a slideshow about web site accessibility. The presentation templates have ready-made graphics, navigation buttons, ActionScript to advance the frames, and even ActionScript for printing a slide.

You can choose from up to 25 different templates.

OPENING A TEMPLATE

All of the templates are easily available. You can get to them by selecting File > New From Template.

1   Select New > New From Template. The New Document template window opens.

2   Choose Presentation from the Category window and then style 4 from the Category Items window. Click Create.

A new movie is opened up in Flash. The new movie is automatically drawn at 640×480 pixels. The size of the movie is predefined in all of the templates.

The first thing you will notice is that across the entire movie is a layer with instructions. This layer is a guide and will not be seen in the final presentation. You can hide the layer by selecting the show/hide layers icon. Do not delete this layer because it is useful to refer to later.

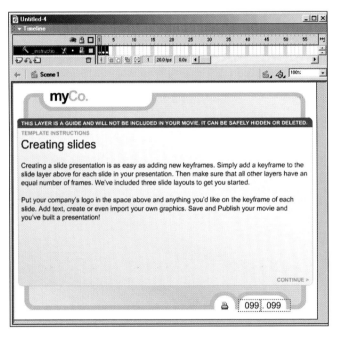

The instructions for the template are placed in a layer guide. They will be hidden in the final presentation.

14

Adding Content

The first frame of the movie is the title screen. Here you add the title of the presentation, the name of the presenter and, possibly, a quote. Adding content to the template is simple: For every slide you want to produce, add a new frame to the movie and replace the default graphics and text with your own.

1   Select frame 2 of the **Slides** layer.

This frame is already populated with content. You don't want the content, but you want to keep the layout. You need to make copies of this frame so that you can use it as a layout design for adding your own content.

2   Press F5 to add a new frame, and then right-click that frame and choose Convert to Keyframe to create a new keyframe. Move to frame 3, which is now a complete replica of frame 2. Press 5 12 more times.

This step sets up all of the frames needed for the presentation. This is the total number of frames you need for your presentation.

3   Remove the final frame of the movie by selecting the frame through all of the layers of the movie and choosing Modify > Remove Frames.

4   Save the movie as **accessibility.fla**.

When you preview the movie, you will see that with the ActionScript added to the movie, you can navigate from frame to frame with the arrow buttons. You can print any frame and see both the current frame number and the total number of frames displayed in the dynamic text boxes in the bottom-right corner.

Note: For this presentation, you will be using content from the W3C web site on accessibility. You can find the complete presentation at **www.w3.org/Talks/WAI-Intro/slide1-0.html**.

Note: The textual content from each slide of the W3C's presentation on web accessibility has been copied into the Flash MX template. Each slide from the W3C presentation will be placed into a different frame from the 12 you just created.

One of Flash's strengths is that anything that works in Flash can be added to a template. You can add movie clips, load sound files, and add your own interactive forms. The downside is that importing text can be a real pain. When you cut and paste, you lose formatting such as bullet points. When you paste text into your template, take the time to go through the content and reformat it. What might be better is to import rich text files (.rtf) into Freehand or Illustrator and then import the .fh or .ai files into Flash.

Adding Accessibility

If you read over the W3C presentation used in this project, you will see that a number of countries, including the United States, now have a law that mandates that all web sites must be accessible to people with disabilities.

Macromedia has taken this requirement very seriously. All of its web software programs are being developed to be accessible. MX movies can be made accessible to Windows platform screen reader software. Unfortunately, there is not a reader for the Mac platform.

You can add keywords and descriptions to objects in a Flash MX movie. When screen reader software detects these keywords, it reads them aloud to the user. Movies made with previous versions of Flash are only seen as blank, descriptionless graphics. There is no way for a screen reader to know what is there. Because of the keywords and descriptions, Flash MX movies now have meaning to people who use screen readers.

Use the presentation created with the template as an example of how to make a movie accessible to visually impaired users. The first step will be to turn on the accessibility features of this movie. The accessibility features are located in the main movie properties.

1   With **accessibility.fla** open, click the eye icon in the timeline inspector to hide all of the layers. The Property inspector will change to show the main movie properties.

2   On the far right side of the Property inspector is a blue button with a white star. This is the Accessibility button, select it.

3   In the Accessibility panel, give the main movie object a name and a description. Select the eye icon again to display all of the movie content. Hide the **_instruction** layer.

Note: Macromedia Flash text is not automatically accessible to screen readers and must be made accessible like any other graphic. Screen readers interpret Macromedia Flash text as graphics, so it is vital to duplicate the text in accessibility descriptions, much like ALT tags on graphical text in HTML.

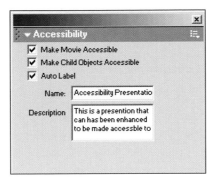

The Accessibility panel allows you to add a textual description of an object on the stage.

This information will be picked up by the screen reader software. As with anything, the more information you provide, the greater the information that can be shared with the user.

The next objects that will be made accessible are the navigation arrows.

4   Double-click the right navigation arrow to select it. The Property inspector displays this button's information.

Again, to the far right of the Property inspector is the Accessibility inspector icon.

5   Open the Accessibility inspector. You'll notice that this time the inspector is displaying three fields: Name, Description, and Shortcut. Buttons can be assigned a keyboard shortcut accessibility property, which makes it possible for visually impaired users to navigate through the movie. Fill in these values in the Accessibility inspector for the right button instance:

Name: **Right Arrow**

Description: **Right arrow navigates to the next frame**

Shortcut: **<SPACE>+R**. The <SPACE>+R shortcut will trigger a mouse click event on the right navigation button when a user presses the space bar and the R key at the same time.

Buttons can have keyboard shortcuts added to them.

Note: The shortcut is only available to users with screen reader software. If a shortcut is not specified, the software will automatically add one.

6 For the left navigation button, add the following settings:

Name: **Left Arrow**

Description: **Left Arrow navigates to the previous frame**

Shortcut: **<SPACE>+L**

7 Text can also be made accessible. The one caveat is that static text cannot be made accessible. All of the text in this presentation is static. To make it available to the Accessibility panel, change the text from static to dynamic text in the Property inspector. Now a description can be added to each and every text box. I would use the text used in the presentation as the Accessibility descriptions.

Your movie is now accessible to a whole new audience with screen reader software.

> **Note:** There are a number of objects that, by default, can be made accessible. Those objects are dynamic and input text fields, buttons, movie clips, and entire movies.

Summary

Could you build every Flash movie from scratch? Sure you could. But why not be up and running in little to no time by leveraging a predesigned template? In this project you have seen how easy it is to use a presentation template. The resulting effect is to create a Microsoft PowerPoint-style presentation. The huge bonus you have, though, is that no one needs to have PowerPoint installed to view this presentation.

Using the template was the first of two parts in the project. The second part was to make the content in the presentation accessible to visually impaired viewers. You can easily take most of the content in a movie and make it available to anyone accessing the Internet with screen reader software. This must be a key element to any Flash movie you create.

How to Improve

This project covered only one Flash MX standard template. As you saw at the beginning of the project, there are a number of other possibilities to choose from. Experiment with the other templates. The ones that I find engaging are the templates that are specifically designed for PDA's and broadcast. I have to admit that the closet marketer in me also finds the templates for online ads a good alternative to flashing animated .gifs.

In addition, this project only scratched the surface of Flash MX accessibility. All movies, graphics, and text should be made accessible. This will increase the accessibility your site has to a growing market.

The .swf file format is top notch for streaming

animation, but as more and more Flash

designers and developers create full web sites

in Flash, the need to preload content effectively

as well as efficiently gets much more important.

In this project, you'll deconstruct a Flash web

site that offers downloadable wallpapers and

employs a modular site structure with separate

.swf files for each main section and external

.jpg images for each wallpaper.

3

PRELOADING

by Jessica Speigel

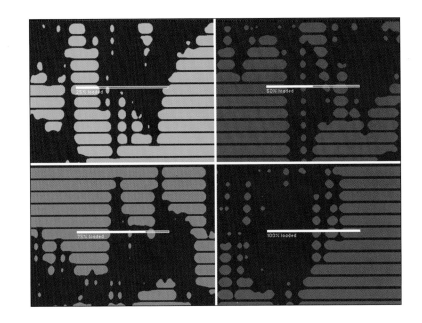

Difficulty Rating: ★★ and a half

Made With: Graphics created using Adobe Photoshop and Macromedia Flash MX

Final File Size: 45KB

Modem Download Time: 16 seconds

Development Time: 4 hours

It Works Like This

This project will use a common preloader for all sections that need to be preloaded, so you don't need to duplicate code and graphics throughout the site. After all, that wouldn't be very modular! When a new .swf needs to be loaded, all the necessary information will be passed to a function that will first load the .swf and then invoke the preloader. This functionality will be contained in a movie that also loads and displays the additional content movies.

The necessary .swf files (home page and navigation) will be preloaded first, and each subsequent section selected by the viewer will be preloaded on demand. To enable visitors to view the wallpapers before downloading, you'll extend the preloader's functionality to preload externally loaded .jpg thumbnails of each wallpaper!

The MovieClip object has two very handy built-in methods that you'll be harnessing with your modular preloader, `getBytesTotal()` and `getBytesLoaded()`. Like their names imply, these methods fetch the total size of the loaded file in bytes and the amount downloaded in bytes. .jpg images loaded via the `loadMovie()` method are treated as movie clips, so these methods will work on them as well.

You're also going to take advantage of an action new to Flash MX, `setInterval()`, which enables a function to be executed every so many milliseconds until the interval is destroyed using the companion `clearInterval()` action. The functionality this provides is much like executing actions using an `enterFrame` clip event in Flash 5. The `setInterval()` function is more flexible, though, allowing the interval to be stopped and started at will, along with not being dependent on a movie clip symbol or the frame rate of the movie. You'll tie everything together with a generic preload function that can preload any number of specified objects at once.

Macromedia Flash MX: In the old-school days of Flash 3, developers normally practiced the ancient art of preloading using the `ifFrameLoaded()` method, except it was called `If Frame Loaded/End If Frame Loaded` back then. This method is now considered to be deprecated, meaning it isn't recommended for use, and future support for the action could be limited.

Flash 4 introduced two properties to replace `ifFrameLoaded()`, `_framesloaded`, and `_totalframes`. These were a big step forward, enabling specific movie clips to be preloaded individually.

Flash 5 introduced the `getBytesLoaded()` and `getBytesTotal()` methods to the movieclip object. Although they might seem extremely similar to the properties Flash 4 introduced, they were the first actions that let developers track download progress using file size. Also, they allowed for the creation of much more accurate percentage preloaders because the status could be assessed using file size rather than frame info. In my humble opinion, the `getBytesLoaded()` and `getBytesTotal()` methods are much more flexible than all of them combined.

Now comes the important part—what Flash MX introduced. What might seem like a small addition can go very far, adding support for the `getBytesLoaded()` and `getBytesTotal()` methods to all objects that can download external data, be it in the form of media assets or information.

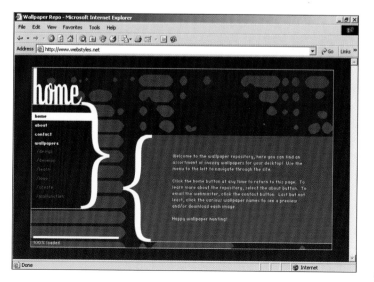

PREPARING TO WORK

Before you can get started, you'll need to copy the **02_Preloading** folder onto your hard drive from the accompanying CD-ROM. If you take a look through this folder, you'll notice the **Assets** folder, which contains all the wallpapers for all the different image sizes of the finished web site. Also notice that only two of the project source files (**preload** and **wallpapers**) have start and final files included. The other movies are merely one-screen movies containing a bitmap background graphic and a content screen with some prewritten copy. The navigation movie is the only one containing any ActionScript at all, but none of it pertains to preloading. For brevity's sake, you won't waste time with these movies, but they make the preloader so much more fun, especially with the large bitmap graphics.

Each project movie has been exported to an .swf format already for testing purposes during the project. In the case of movies that you'll be working on, the start file has been exported.

Also, this project makes use of the Standard font family, a pixel font developed especially for use with Flash by Craig Kroeger. The family can be downloaded from **www.miniml.com** and is free for noncommercial use. Any font can be substituted if you would rather use a different typeface.

START WITH A SIMPLE PRELOADER

First let's build a bare-bones preloader that will grow into a super modular preloader by the end. The bare-bones preloader contains enough functionality to load one file. It also contains a progress indicator and reports the percentage of the file that has been downloaded.

1 Open **preload_start.fla** and save it as **preload.fla** in your project folder.

2 Choose Insert > New Symbol or press Ctrl+F8/Cmd+F8 to create a new movie clip symbol. Name the new symbol **mc preloader**.

   After you click OK, Flash should automatically open the symbol for editing.

Note: The point behind preloading is generally to make the wait as short as possible. This example, however, is making a point of preloading that enables you to fudge a bit with big bitmap graphics so you'll have time to admire your work in the end. After all, it's not the content you're worried about for this example, it's your beautiful preloader!

Note: The Miniml fonts must be positioned on a whole pixel to remain aliased when viewed. For example, if a text field using the font were placed at X: 5.5 and Y: 5, the type would be blurry unless the X position were changed to either 5 or 6. Also, the font must be used at the intended point size of 8 (or multiples of 8) for optimal results. A guide is available online at **www.miniml.com/flash/fonts/guide.pdf**.

Creating a new symbol.

3 Rename the initial layer in the timeline to
Preloader. Select the empty keyframe on the
Preloader layer and drag an instance of the gr
preloader graphic symbol from the **Assets** folder
found in the Library onto the stage. Set both the
X and Y positions for the graphic to 0 in the
Property Inspector to position the upper-left
corner of the graphic at the center point of the mc
preloader symbol.

4 Select the Text tool and draw a new dynamic text
field directly below the preloader graphic at X: 0
and Y: 5. Be sure the new text field is wide enough
to display 100% loaded without cutting off any
of the text. In the Property Inspector, set the font
to Standard 07_54 at a point size of 8 and then set
the font color to white. Type **0% loaded** in the
text field.

5 With the new text field still selected, enter **display** in
the Instance Name field.

This enables you to manipulate the text field via
ActionScript.

Next you need to embed the outlines of the font in
the .swf file so that viewers that don't have the font
installed can still view the status indicator.

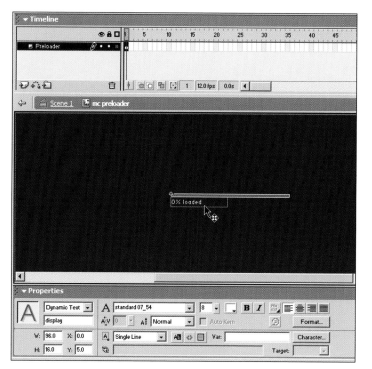

The display text field properties.

23

6 Select the display text field (the text field you just created) and click the Character button on the bottom-right side of the Property Inspector. Select the Only option, select Numerals, and then enter **% loaded** in the And These Characters field. Click Done.

This embeds only the outlines for numerals and the characters you need in the .swf file. You could just select the All Characters option, but this method saves on file size so that the preloader can start up quickly without having to load 30KB of font information first.

Now you need to create a status indicator that will display a graphical representation of the loading progress.

7 Choose Insert > New Symbol or press Ctrl+F8/ Cmd+F8 to create a new movie clip symbol. Name the new symbol **mc percentage bar**. Drag an instance of **gr percentage bar** from the **Assets** folder in the Library onto the stage and position it at 0,0 coordinates like you did for the **mc preloader** movie clip.

8 Reopen the **mc preloader** movie clip symbol for editing and create a new layer named **Percentage Bar** in the timeline above the **Preloader** layer. With this layer selected, drag an instance of the **mc percentage bar** movie clip you just created onto the stage and position it at 0,0 coordinates so that it's right on top of the preloader graphic. Then set the instance name of the **mc percentage bar** movie clip's instance to **bar** in the Property Inspector.

Embedding the font outlines into the movie.

The **mc percentage bar** movie clip instance properties.

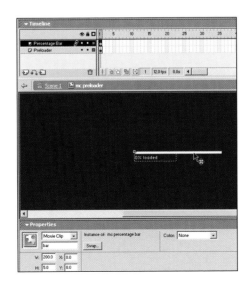

24

That's it for the symbols that the preloader requires; the finished preloader movie clip should look like the one shown here when you are complete. Now you have to write a bit of code to get it working!

The completed **mc preloader** movie clip.

WRITING THE ACTIONSCRIPT

Now it's time to write the ActionScript to make the preloader work. This is where the `setInterval` function discussed earlier comes into play. The preloader requires two functions: one to initialize the preloader and one to update the display every time the interval passes or the preload status changes.

1   Navigate to the main timeline of the movie and, with the **Preloader** layer selected, drag an instance of the newly created **mc preloader** movie clip onto the stage. Give it an instance name of **preloader** and position it in the lower-left corner of the stage.

The **mc preloader** movie clip instance properties.

2 Select the first blank frame in the **Functions** layer and launch the Actions panel by choosing Window > Actions or by pressing F2. Add this code:

Note: The editor also can be launched by Alt+double-clicking the keyframe.

First, the **preloader** movie clip is initialized. The visibility property of the movie clip is set to true (1), the x scale property of the **percentage bar** movie clip is set to 0, and the display text field's text is set to "0% loaded". The last line of code sets an interval to execute the preloadCallback() function (which you'll write next) every 10 milliseconds, storing the interval ID that you'll use to delete the interval later. Also, one parameter is passed to the preloadCallback() function, a reference to the object passed to this function as a parameter; that's what you're going to preload.

3 Add this code after the preload function:

The function first creates three new local variables using var to track the loading progress. The first variable will hold the total download size. The second variable will contain the size of the information currently downloaded. The third variable will contain the current percentage loaded.

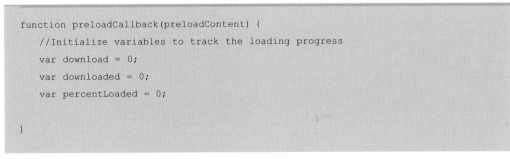

```
function preload(preloadContent) {
    //Turn on and initialize the preloader
    preloader._visible = 1;
    preloader.bar._xscale = 0;
    preloader.display.text = "0% loaded";
    //Set an interval to update the loading progress
    intervalId = setInterval(preloadCallback, 10, preloadContent);
}
```

The preloader initialization function.

```
function preloadCallback(preloadContent) {
    //Initialize variables to track the loading progress
    var download = 0;
    var downloaded = 0;
    var percentLoaded = 0;

}
```

The function to update the preloader display.

4   Add this code after the local variables are set:

Then, using the `preloadContent` argument passed to the function from the `setInterval()` action, the total and loaded bytes are stored in their respective variables, and the percentage loaded is calculated.

```
//Grab the loaded and total bytes of the preloadContent
download = preloadContent.getBytesTotal();
downloaded = preloadContent.getBytesLoaded();
percentLoaded = Math.ceil(downloaded / download * 100);
```

Updating the variables used to track download progress.

5   To update the display of the preloader graphics, add this code at the end of the function:

The display text in the preloader is updated with the `percentLoaded` value, and the x scale of **bar** is set to the `percentLoaded` value.

The `updateAfterEvent()` function is used to refresh the screen each time the function is called. This is important because the function will be executing more quickly than the frame rate of the movie; using the `updateAfterEvent()` function ensures that the display updates fast enough.

```
//Update the preloader display
preloader.display.text = percentLoaded + "% loaded";
preloader.bar._xscale = percentLoaded;
updateAfterEvent();
```

Updating the display of the preloader.

6   The last code you need to add to the function checks to see if the download is complete.

The `if` statement checks to see if the download is complete by comparing the `download` and `downloaded` variables, also making sure that the download is larger than 0 bytes. This is important because `getBytesTotal()` sometimes requires a bit of time to compute with externally loaded data, so you want to make sure that has happened before moving on. If the download is complete, the interval is cleared so that the callback function won't continue to execute when it's not needed and the **mc preloader** is hidden from view.

```
//See if we're finished
if (downloaded == download && download > 0) {
    //Delete the interval and turn off the preloader
    clearInterval(intervalId);
    preloader._visible = 0;
}
```

Checking to see if the download is complete.

The last thing you have to do before testing your preloader is give it something to preload. If you were to test the movie now, it would preload too quickly because the only assets you have make up the preloader. I've included the bitmap background used in the home movie in the Library for just this purpose.

7 Insert a blank keyframe in frame 2 of the **Preloader** layer of the main timeline and drag the home bitmap from the Library onto the second keyframe and place it in the upper-left corner of the stage. You also need to call your `preload` function. Select the first frame on the ActionScript layer on the main timeline and add this code:

```
preload(this);
```

This calls the `preload` function, passing a reference to the current object (the main timeline in this case).

8 Enter Test Movie mode by choosing Control > Test Movie or by pressing Ctrl+Enter. Now choose View > Show Streaming or press Ctrl+Enter (yes, again) to simulate loading the file over the connection speed specified under the Debug menu.

You can change the connection speed under the Debug menu to see how the movie behaves at different download speeds. The Bandwidth Profiler (accessible from the View menu) is also very useful for testing preloaders because you can see the size of each individual frame in the movie.

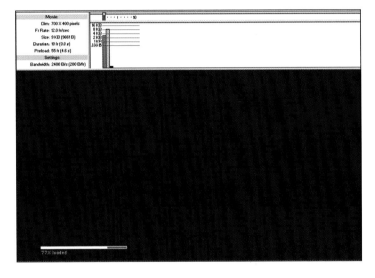

Testing the preloader with the Bandwidth Profiler.

EXTENDING THE SIMPLE PRELOADER

Now that your preloader is functioning, it's time to extend its functionality so that it can preload multiple objects at once. Luckily for you, this is pretty easy to accomplish. All you need is a little array and some `for` loops.

1 Select the keyframe in the **Functions** layer on the
main timeline and launch the ActionScript editor.
Then replace the `preloadCallback()` function
with this code:

The main change to the function is the type of data it
expects to receive in the `preloadContent` variable.
Instead of just a single object reference, it now
expects an array containing any number of object
references. Most of this code is pretty similar to the
original function, so let's just dissect the new parts
shown in bold.

The first new block of code initializes a `for...in`
loop to iterate over each item contained in the
`preloadContent` array. The immediately following
`if` statement checks to see if the current object exists
in the Flash Player by checking the file size. If the
object passes this test, the loaded and total bytes are
calculated by adding the values onto the existing
`download` and `downloaded` values instead of
replacing them like the original function.

The second block of new code loops through each
item in the `preloadContent` array and uses the
`gotoAndStop()` method to send the playhead
of that timeline to a frame labeled **run**. Of course,
this will only function as expected if the object is a
movie clip. Otherwise, it will be ignored because the
`gotoAndStop` action is a method specific to
the `MovieClip` object. Luckily for you, that behavior
is perfect. This action lets you easily initialize any
movies that need it; any movie not containing a **run**
label will ignore this action.

```
function preloadCallback(preloadContent) {
    //Initialize variables to track the loading progress
    var download = 0;
    var downloaded = 0;
    var percentLoaded = 0;
    //Loop through each object passed to the function
    for (var i in preloadContent) {
        //Make sure the object exists, if not, exit the function
        if (preloadContent[ i] .getBytesTotal() > 0) {
            //Grab the total and loaded bytes
            download += preloadContent[ i] .getBytesTotal();
            downloaded += preloadContent[ i] .getBytesLoaded();
        } else {
            return;
        }
        //Update the preloader display
        percentLoaded = Math.ceil(downloaded / download * 100);
        preloader.display.text = percentLoaded + "% loaded";
        preloader.bar._xscale = percentLoaded;
        updateAfterEvent();
    }
    //See if we're finished
    if (downloaded == download && download > 0) {
        //Initialize the preloaded movies
        for (var i in preloadContent) {
            preloadContent[ i] .gotoAndStop("run");
        }
        //Delete the interval and turn off the preloader
        clearInterval(intervalId);
        preloader._visible = 0;
    }
}
```

The complete `preloadCallback` function.

2 Notice that this file already contains the labels
   needed for the new and improved preloader to work,
   so all you have to update is the call to the `preload`
   function on the first frame of the **ActionScript**
   layer. Replace the existing code with the following:

```
var preloadContent = new Array(this);
preload(preloadContent);
stop();
```

3 Test the movie again to make sure nothing
   got broken.

PRELOADING THE CONTENT MOVIES

Now that your modular preloader is complete, you can start loading different content
movies. Rather than loading the various content movies into levels, you're going to
load them into target movie clips. Levels are a bit touchy to preload with a generic
function because they aren't actually present in the Flash Player until data is loaded into
them. Instead of dealing with all that, you'll emulate levels by creating empty movie
clips to load each content movie into at runtime. The first thing you need to do is
clean up the preloader movie.

1 Delete the **Preloader** layer on the main timeline.

   You don't need the background bitmap to test
   any longer, and you're going to put the **preloader**
   movie clip on the stage at runtime using the
   `attachMovie()` method. You need to do this so
   that you can keep the preloader above other loaded
   movies. To use the `attachMovie()` method,
   you have to set up the Linkage of the **preloader**
   movie clip.

2 Right-click/Cmd-click the **mc preloader** symbol
   in the Library and select Linkage from the context
   menu. Select the Export for ActionScript and Export
   in First Frame options, and enter **preloader** as the
   Linkage Identifier.

Linkage Properties

Identifier: preloader

Linkage: ☑ Export for ActionScript
☐ Export for runtime sharing
☐ Import for runtime sharing
☑ Export in first frame

URL:

[OK] [Cancel] [Help]

Preloader movie clip Linkage Properties.

3   Now you need to write a new function to initialize this movie. Enter this code onto the **Functions** layer above the two existing functions:

The first block of code takes care of attaching and positioning the **preloader** movie clip. A new generic object is created, and the properties you want the **preloader** movie clip to inherit are set. Then the movie clip is attached onto the main timeline at a depth of 6 (the highest in this project) so that it will remain above the other movies. The object you created is passed for the initObject parameter of the method.

Then five empty movie clips are created on the stage, one for each content movie in the project. The movies needed for the site to display initially are loaded first, an array containing references to these first three objects is created, and the preload function is called.

The last line of code stores a reference to the home movie clip in a variable that will be used while switching sections within the site.

```
function init() {
    //Load the preloader
    var obj = new Object();
    obj._x = 5;
    obj._y = 379;
    obj._visible = 0;
    this.attachMovie("preloader", "preloader", 6, obj);
    //Create holder movieclips for the different sections
    this.createEmptyMovieClip("navigation", 5);
    this.createEmptyMovieClip("home", 1);
    this.createEmptyMovieClip("about", 2);
    this.createEmptyMovieClip("contact", 3);
    this.createEmptyMovieClip("wallpapers", 4);
    //Load the movies we need to start
    navigation.loadMovie("navigation.swf");
    home.loadMovie("home.swf");
    //Make an array containing the paths to the objects we want to preload
    var preloadContent = new Array(this, navigation, home);
    //Call the preload function
    preload(preloadContent);
    //Store the first section used in a variable
    lastSection = home;
}
```

A function to initialize the project.

4   Now modify the ActionScript on the first frame of the **ActionScript** layer to call the init function rather than the preload function. The code that creates the array for the preload function should be removed now as well.

```
init();
stop();
```

The modified ActionScript.

31

5   Speaking of switching sections, that's the last piece of code you need, so add it now. Insert the following code on the **Functions** layer beneath the `init` function:

This function is pretty self explanatory, but there's one important thing to note about it. It takes one parameter, `section`, which is a string containing the section name (such as home, navigation, and so on). The function reuses this variable to load the section into the appropriate empty movie clip by evaluating the string using the array access operator, forcing Flash to evaluate the string as an object. This is handy because your empty movie clips are named the same as the sections.

Now you're ready to test it out again with the content movies in place. One important thing to note is that the Show Streaming setting in Test Movie mode doesn't simulate streaming for externally loaded content, so don't be surprised if the loading finishes very quickly. After the loading completes, each movie preloaded should jump to its respective **run** labels, showing the navigation and home pages. If you run into problems with the preload section, compare your finished file with the final file in the **Project** folder.

```
function switchSection(section) {
    //Unload the last section used
    lastSection.unloadMovie();
    //Load the new section into the appropriate target
    this[ section] .loadMovie(section + ".swf");
    //Update the lastSection variable with the new section
    lastSection = this[ section] ;
    //Preload the new section
    var preloadContent = new Array(this[ section] );
    preload(preloadContent);
}
```

A function to switch between sections in the project.

BUILDING THE WALLPAPERS SECTION

You're finally ready to create the wallpapers section of the site, and it can take advantage of your modular preloader as well.

Note: While ShowStreaming will simulate the download speed of your movie, it does not simulate the download speed of movies that are loaded using the loadMovie method. So to fully appreciate the preloader, you should test your files online.

1   Open **wallpapers_start.fla** from the **Project** folder and save it as **wallpapers.fla**.

Notice that the timeline has already been set up for you with the appropriate labels and artwork in place in each frame. The symbols needed for this section also have been created already. All you have to do now is write the code to make it all work together.

2   Start with the `init` function specific to this movie. Add this code to frame 1 of the **Functions** layer on the main timeline:

First, a new array is created and populated with the names of your wallpapers. Then a `for` loop enables the six wallpaper buttons in the navigation movie; these were initially disabled and dimmed by the `init` function contained in the navigation movie. Finally, the `buildWallpaperView()` function is called to generate a page of thumbnails and preload them.

```
function init() {
    //Make an array containing the wallpapers
    wallpaperContent = new Array("design", "develop", "learn", "love",
    ➥"create", "malfunction");
    //Turn on the wallpaper buttons in the navigation section
    for (var i = 0; i < wallpaperContent.length; i++) {
        _root.navigation["wp" + i].enabled = 1;
        _root.navigation["wp" + i]._alpha = 100;
    }
    //Build the page of wallpaper thumbnails
    buildWallpaperView();
}
```

A function to initialize the wallpapers section.

3   On the **ActionScript** layer, select frame 2 (the frame that corresponds to the run label) and add a call to the `init` function.

This will call the `init` function after the entire wallpapers movie is preloaded.

```
init();
stop();
```

The ActionScript in the first keyframe of the **ActionScript** layer.

4 Because you turned those wallpaper navigation buttons on, you have to turn them off when they aren't needed anymore. Enter the following ActionScript right below the `init` function:

This code redefines the movie's `onUnload` event so that it turns off the buttons in the same fashion in which they were turned on.

```
this.onUnload = function() {
    //Turn off the wallpaper navigation buttons when this movie unloads
    for (var i = 0; i < wallpaperContent.length; i++) {
        _root.navigation["wp" + i].enabled = 0;
        _root.navigation["wp" + i]._alpha = 35;
    }
}
```

The ActionScript executed when the movie is unloaded.

5 Before you write the `buildWallpaperView()` function, take a look at the content of the frame labeled `wallpaperView`, which contains the interface for that screen.

6 These movie clip instances will eventually hold your loaded wallpaper thumbnails. You'll take a closer look at this symbol after you write the `buildWallpaperView()` function.

Instance of mc wallpaper.
Instance name: wp1.

Instance of mc wallpaper.
Instance name: wp0.

Instance of mc wallpaper.
Instance name: wp2.

The wallpaper view screen.

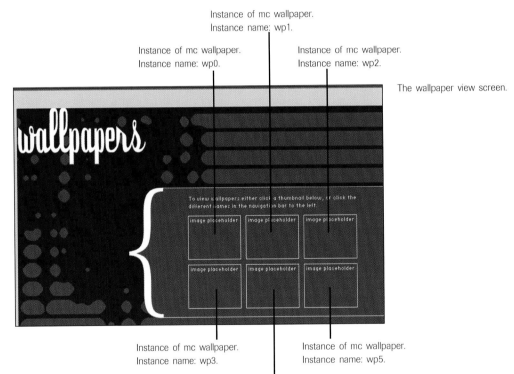

Instance of mc wallpaper.
Instance name: wp3.

Instance of mc wallpaper.
Instance name: wp5.

Instance of mc wallpaper.
Instance name: wp4.

7 With the first keyframe of the **Functions** layer selected, open the ActionScript editor and insert the following code after the `init` function:

The function first sends the playhead to the appropriate frame label and then creates a new array object to hold the list of objects to be preloaded. A `for` loop iterates over each entry in the `wallpaperContent` array (defined in the `init` function) to generate each thumbnail image. First the wallpaper name associated with the image is stored in the movie clip, and then the thumbnail version of the wallpaper is loaded into a movie clip named **image** contained in the **wallpaper** movie clip. The last line in the `for` loop adds the current object to the end of the `preloadContent` array. Lastly, the `preload` function is called to preload the thumbnails.

```
function buildWallpaperView() {
    //Send the playhead to the wallpaperView frame
    gotoAndStop("wallpaperView");
    //Initialize an array to hold the movie clips to preload
    var preloadContent = new Array();
    for (var i in wallpaperContent) {
        //Store the current movie clip's wallpaper name in the instance
        this["wp" + i].myWallpaper = wallpaperContent[i];
        //Load the appropriate image
        this["wp" + i].image.loadMovie("Assets/" + wallpaperContent[i] +
        ➥"_thumb.jpg");
        //Add the current movie clip to the preload array
        preloadContent.push(this["wp" + i].image);
    }
    //Preload the images
    _root.preload(preloadContent);
}
```

A function to build the thumbnail view of wallpapers.

8 Now let's take a look at what makes up each wallpaper thumbnail. Open the **mc wallpaper** symbol in the Library for editing.

There are two symbols that make up the **wallpaper** movie clip. The first symbol is a holder movie clip named **image** that the `buildWallpaperView()` function loads the thumbnail into, replacing the text already contained in the symbol. On the layer above this is the second symbol—a button that will take the viewer to a detailed view of the wallpaper. The button contains a rectangle that's the same size as the thumbnail. In the Up state of the button, the rectangle's alpha is set to 0% to let the thumbnail show through. Then it's changed to 35% in the Over state to dim the image slightly when it's rolled over with the mouse.

The mc wallpaper symbol.

Instance of mc imageholder. Instance name: image.

image placeholder

Instance of bn wallpaper. Instance name: bn.

9 Select the button in the **mc wallpaper** movie clip and attach the following ActionScript to the instance:

This calls the `buildDetailView()` function (which you'll write next), passing the `myWallpaper` variable as a parameter.

```
on (release) {
    _parent.buildDetailView(myWallpaper)
}
```

The ActionScript attached to the instance of bn wallpaper.

Note: If you find it difficult to select the instance of the button, click on its outline.

---

10 Now navigate back to the main timeline so that you can take a look at the `detailView` frame.

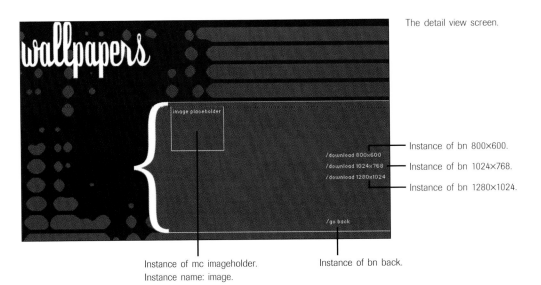

The detail view screen.

Instance of bn 800×600.
Instance of bn 1024×768.
Instance of bn 1280×1024.

Instance of mc imageholder.
Instance name: image.

Instance of bn back.

11 Insert the following ActionScript on the **Functions** layer beneath the other functions:

The playhead is first sent to the `detailView` label, and the currently selected wallpaper is stored in a variable for future reference. Then a larger thumbnail image of the wallpaper is loaded into a second image-holder movie clip and is preloaded.

```
function buildDetailView(wallpaper) {
    //Send the playhead to the detailView frame
    gotoAndStop("detailView");
    //Store the current wallpaper in a variable
    currentWallpaper = wallpaper;
    //Load the wallpaper image
    image.loadMovie("Assets/" + wallpaper + ".jpg");
    //And preload it
    var preloadContent = new Array(this.image);
    _root.preload(preloadContent);

}
```

A function to build a detail view of the specified wallpaper.

12 The last thing you need to do is write a function to fetch the appropriately sized wallpaper for download. Enter the following ActionScript on the **Functions** layer:

All this function does is create a filename from the wallpaper name and size passed, and then it uses the getURL action to load the image into a new browser window. Easy! The last thing you have to do is add the appropriate ActionScript to the various buttons on the detail view screen.

```
function downloadWallpaper(wallpaper, size) {
    //Fetch the specified wallpaper at the specified size
    getURL("Assets/" + wallpaper + "_" + size + ".jpg", "_blank");
}
```

A function to download the specified wallpaper at the specified size.

13 Select the instance of the go back button on the detail view screen and attach the following ActionScript to the instance:

This simply calls the buildWallpaperView() function when the button is clicked.

```
on (release) {
    buildWallpaperView();
}
```

The ActionScript to take the viewer back to the thumbnail page.

14 Select the 800×600 button and attach the following code to the instance:

This calls the downloadWallpaper() function, passing the currentWallpaper variable (you knew that variable would come in useful) for the wallpaper name and 800×600 as the size.

```
on (release) {
    downloadWallpaper(currentWallpaper, "800x600");
}
```

The ActionScript to download the current wallpaper at 800×600.

15 Attach the same ActionScript to the other download buttons, changing the size to the appropriate value for each button (1024×768 for the second button and 1280×1024 for the third).

That's it! All you have to do now is export it to .swf so that you can test it in context.

16 Choose File > Export Movie and overwrite the original **wallpapers.swf** file in the project folder. Launch the preload movie if it's not still open and test it out. If you run into problems with the wallpapers section, compare your finished file with the final file in the project folder.

Note: To thoroughly test out the modular preloader, you really need to upload the .swf files to the web. I've included an **index.html** file in the project folder that's all prettied up and ready to use. Remember to upload the **Assets** folder as well so that you can check out how the external .jpgs are loaded into movie clips and preloaded.

SUMMARY

In the beginning of the project, I talked briefly about preloading different types of objects. Flash MX added support for the `getBytesTotal()` and `getBytesLoaded()` methods to objects that can import external data or media. The following objects can use these methods:

- MovieClip
- LoadVars
- XML

These objects will be more than enough for most people, but if you happen to be into OOP, you can also create your own new object using any of the preceding objects listed as a prototype, and the new object will inherit the methods as well.

After taking this into account, it's obvious that this preloading project is even more flexible than it looks at first glance. If you wanted to extend this project in the future to load the list of wallpapers from an .xml file, you could preload that information just as easily as preloading a section of the site without changing any of the ActionScript. All you would have to do is pass a reference to the XML object that the file is loading into in the `preloadContent` array. It can't get easier than that!

What time is it?

This question has been mulled over by the world's greatest minds since the dawn of civilization. The answer is complex and raises more questions than it answers. The current time is the crucial variable in any dynamic web site. This project is going to explore the ActionScript Date object, and along the way, you'll discover a bit more about the history and politics of timekeeping.

4

TIME ZONES

by John Dalziel
with original images by d74

Difficulty Rating: ★★

Made With:

    Graphics created using Macromedia Flash

    Stock sourced from the Internet

Final File Size: 105KB

Modem Download Time: 24.2 seconds (56K)

Development Time: 1.5 hours

IT WORKS LIKE THIS

In this project, you're going to look at the differences between local time and Coordinated Universal Time (UTC) and illustrate these differences by building an interactive map of the world's time zones.

The twin concepts of date and time (and the tools used to measure them: calendars and clocks) are human inventions. They are used to rationalize, sequence, and measure the events of our lives. Although often bundled together, these twinned elements function very differently. Time, as measured by a clock, is a cyclical system that repeats every 24 hours. Dates are part of the calendar system and stretch backward and forward in time forever, never repeating themselves.

In Flash, an ActionScript Date object is used as a convenient way to group date and time variables into one package. After an ActionScript Date has been defined, it can be expressed in either local or Coordinated Universal Time.

> **Note:** The advent of mass transportation (and its requisite timetables) at the end of the nineteenth century brought about a requirement for a unified system of time. The United States was the first territory to adopt the time-zone system in November of 1883. In the following year, the International Meridian Conference applied the same system to the rest of the world.
>
> The earth is longitudinally (pole to pole) divided into 24 time zones spaced 15 degrees apart. The lines separating these time zones have been adjusted to avoid passing through the middle of territories. The areas within each zone observe a local or "civil time" one hour earlier than the zone immediately to the east.

In this project, you are going to build a Flash application that is driven by the properties and methods of the Date object. By the end of this tutorial, you will have done the following:

- Centered the world map on the viewer's location
- Compared Coordinated Universal Time with the local time in other zones
- Added and subtracted dates and times
- Built a real-time analogue clock for each zone

> **Note:** Both ActionScript and the study of timekeeping are laden with their own technical jargon. I will not avoid using the proper terms, but I will try to explain anything unusual as you progress. It's all part of the learning process, so good luck and stick with it!

The properties and methods of the Date object can be expressed in either local time or Coordinated Universal Time.

Preparing to Work

The base file for this project is a map of the world rendered in Cartesian projection. Overlaid on the map is a series of buttons covering each of the world's time zones. You will be adding `Date`-driven ActionScript to these assets to make them interactive. Before you can get started, you'll need to copy the **04_Time_Zones** folder onto your hard disk, start Flash, and open the **timezones.fla** file.

Take a few minutes to familiarize yourself with the structure of the movie.

1 Press Click+Enter to test the Flash movie.

If you pan your mouse over the map, you'll notice that each of the world's time zones is displayed. This graphical feedback is currently the only form of interactivity in the movie. You'll also edit an external ActionScript file that will drive the time and clocks at the bottom of the screen.

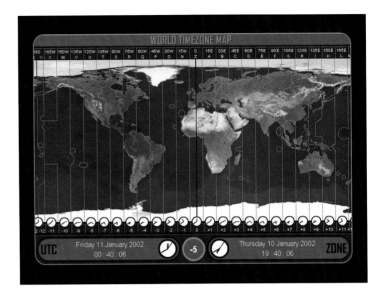

Using #include to Load ActionScript from a Text File

How many times do you write the same old scripts? Wouldn't it be great to write a script once and be able to reuse it again and again across multiple movies and projects? This is exactly what `#include` will let you do. When you compile a Flash movie containing an `#include` statement, Flash replaces the statement with ActionScript loaded from an external text file. Notice that the syntax for this statement does not include a trailing semicolon.

1 In the Flash MX editing environment, select the **maps** movie, and then open the ActionScript window. You'll notice that it contains a single line of code:

```
#include "timezones.as"
```

The Flash MX code window.

Next you're going to examine the file **timezones.as** in a text editor.

2　Start up your favorite text editor.

3　Load the file named **timezones.as** into the editor.

> **Note:** An ActionScript file is merely a text file saved with an .as extension.

The **timezones.as** file in a text editor.

RUNNING CONDITIONAL CODE WITH ONCLIPEVENT

A clip event enables you to add a unique block of code to an instance of a movie clip. You can also define the conditions under which the code will be run. The command syntax is made up of two sections. The keyword, contained within parenthesis, defines when the code or "statement block" within the curly brackets will be run.

Look at the text file in your editor. You'll notice that it currently contains two empty clip events. Any code you add within the body (the area between the curly brackets) of the onClipEvent (load) section is run when the movie clip first appears. This is where you will put your function definitions and any initialization code.

Code placed within the body of the onClipEvent (enterFrame) section, however, will be run on the second frame and every subsequent frame thereafter. Although loads of conditions for clip events exist, these two are the most common.

THE TIME ZONE BUTTON LAYER

To get you started, I've already added some basic interactivity to the time zone map. To understand how this works, you're going to dig down a few layers and see what's going on.

1   Click anywhere on the map to select it. Right-click (Ctrl-click on Mac) and select Edit in Place.

    Inside the map movie, you will notice that there are actually three maps of the world side by side. These are all instances of the same movie. Having them side by side enables you to scroll the map right and left.

2   Click anywhere on Map2 (the one in the middle) to select it. Right-click (Ctrl-click) and select Edit in Place.

    Here you will find the map graphics and a blue-colored layer called **timeZones**. This layer contains a movie that's also called **timeZones**. This is the movie you are going to investigate next.

3   Right-click (Ctrl-click on Mac) the **timezones** movie and select Edit in Place.

This movie contains a jigsaw of interlocking buttons, one for each possible time zone. If a button has a hit area but no graphics, it shows up in the editing environment as a transparent blue shape.

4   Select any button you like and examine the code in the ActionScript window. The code should look similar to this:

```
on (rollOver) {
    _root.zone = -5;
}
```

Note: Each zone is allocated a letter and is referred to by that letter's military call sign. For example, the letter for the prime meridian is Z; thus, UTC is sometimes referred to as "Zulu" time. There are only 24 time zones, yet all 26 letters of the alphabet have been allocated. Although they lie within the same zone, each side of the international dateline receives a letter (M and Y). The remaining letter, J, is used to refer to the current local time of the observer.

Note: The biggest irony of all time is this: For millennia, well-meaning emperors, astronomers, politicians, and popes have tinkered with the calendar system in the pursuit of astronomical accuracy. This work has led us to an atomic measurement of time that is now even more accurate than the earth itself.

In 1972, UTC superceded Greenwich Mean Time (GMT) and became an International Standard (SI). UTC is calculated by the addition or subtraction of leap seconds from International Atomic Time (TAI). These leap seconds keep UTC in sync with the rotation of the earth.

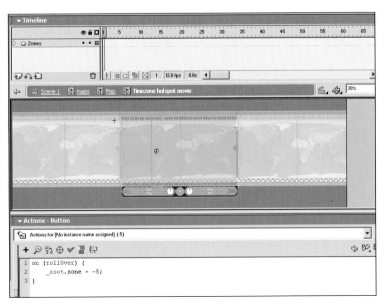

The rollover code for each zone.

Each zone has a button, and each button has code similar to this. The prefix _root refers to the top level of the movie hierarchy. Rolling over the button will set the value of a variable called zone in the main timeline. The value being set is the difference in hours between the time in the zone and the UTC. This is what is commonly called the *time zone offset*.

USING FUNCTIONS TO REPEAT COMMON TASKS

Okay, that's enough looking around—it's time to get coding! Because the value of zone is updated every time the user rolls over a new zone, the map is already interactive. With a little cosmetic alteration, you can take the value of zone and display it onscreen as the user pans around the map.

This tutorial is going to make good use of functions. A *function* is a block of code that is designed to be frequently reused. Some functions take parameters, some return values, and others do neither. Also, every function needs to be defined before it can be used, which is why you place them within the onClipEvent (load) section.

Note: The black zigzag line on the map is the international dateline. This line is exactly 180 degrees east of the prime meridian (the straight line) that runs through Greenwich in London. The line itself is a little ragged because each territory along the border has arbitrarily chosen which side of the dateline it wants to be on. Travelers crossing this line going eastward must set their calendars back by one day. Westward travelers must set their calendars forward by one day.

1 Go back to your text editor and add this code below the FUNCTION LIBRARY title of the onClipEvent (load) section.

This first function takes an integer and creates from it a string called TimezoneOffsetString. The code inside a function can be as long or as short as you like; in this case, it is a single if condition. If the value of zone is negative, the returned string is identical. If the value of zone is positive, the string is returned with a preceding plus sign.

```
// FUNCTION: to create timezone offset string
function setTimezoneOffsetString(zone) {
    if (zone > 0) {zone = "+" + zone};
    return zone;
}
```

Creating the timezone offset string.

2 Place this function call within the `onClipEvent` (`enterFrame`) section.

This code ensures that the `TimezoneOffsetString` is constantly updated by placing the function call within the `onClipEvent` (`enterFrame`) section and feeding it the current value of `zone`.

3 Save your text file.

```
// Set Time Zone Offset String
TimezoneOffsetString = setTimezoneOffsetString(_root.zone);
```

Formatting the offset string.

```
onClipEvent (load) {

    // --------------------------------------------------------
    // FUNCTION LIBRARY
    // --------------------------------------------------------

    // FUNCTION: to create timezone offset string
    function setTimezoneOffsetString(zone) {
        if (zone > 0) {zone = "+" + zone};
        return zone;
    }

    // --------------------------------------------------------
    // INITIALISE
    //

}

onClipEvent (enterFrame) {

    // Set Time Zone Offset String
    TimezoneOffsetString = setTimezoneOffsetString(_root.zone);

}
```

4 Back in Flash MX, test your movie.

If you pan around the map with your mouse, you should see the time zone offset displayed in the middle circle at the bottom of the screen. Congratulations, you've made a start!

So far, you have used purely fixed values to demonstrate the difference in time between UTC and each zone. This approach limits you to only showing comparisons. To show the actual time in each zone, you must now introduce the `Date` object.

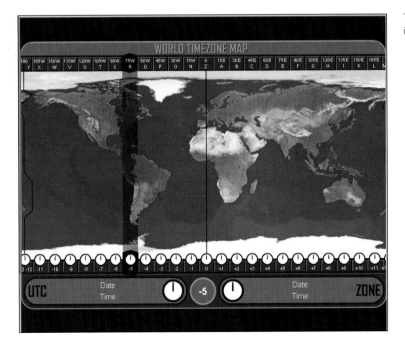

The published movie in Flash MX.

46

KEEPING TIME WITH THE ACTIONSCRIPT DATE OBJECT

The `Date` object is a convenient package within which you store a unique set of date and time variables. There is enough information in each `Date` object to pinpoint any single moment in time. Internally a `Date` object distills down to a value in milliseconds before or after 1st January 1970. This is a common epoch among operating systems and programming languages.

1 Go back to your text editor and add this code below the `INITIALISE` title in the `onClipEvent (load)` section:

This line creates a new instance of a `Date` object called `now`. When you use the `Date` constructor, you have the option of passing it variables for the year, month, day, and so on. If you don't pass any parameters, the new `Date` will default to the current date and time. As with any object, once created you can examine its properties.

You use the `Date` property `.getTimezoneOffset()` to return the difference in time between UTC and the viewer's own time zone. Next, you are going to make use of this value to center the world map on the viewer's location.

2 On the next line, add this code:

These first two lines are comments, which act as reminders and guideposts to help you understand the code in its context after you've finished. The last line finds the viewer's time zone by checking the `.getTimezoneOffset()` property. This property is always returned in minutes, so you divide it by 60 to convert it to hours.

Note: Unlike the SI unit of time, there is no international body to regulate the world's time zones. The offset from GMT/UTC is determined entirely at the whim of the governing body of the region. This has given rise to some strange situations. For example, if you pan around the zones on the map, you'll discover that some territories have elected to offset their clocks by halves of an hour.

```
// Create new Date object
now = new Date();
```

Creating a new instance of `Date`.

Note: It's worth noting that although time zones generally are offset in hours, the `.getTimezoneOffset()` property is returned in minutes. The name of this property is fairly misleading because its value also contains an offset for daylight savings time (DST).

```
// Create timezone offset value
// Convert mins to hours and express as negative
now_timezoneOffset = -(now.getTimezoneOffset() / 60);
```

Finding the user's timezone.

3 On the next line, add this code:

The resulting variable `now_timezoneOffset` becomes your initial or default offset zone. This value can then be passed through the function you created earlier to display it onscreen.

```
// Create timezone offset string
TimezoneOffsetString = setTimezoneOffsetString(now_timezoneOffset);
_root.zone = now_timezoneOffset;
```

Setting the offset zone.

4 On the next line, add this code:

The last piece of code centers the map on the viewer's world position by adjusting the x coordinate of the map. The x coordinate is calculated from the viewer's time zone offset and the width of a single time zone. The formula to calculate the width of a zone makes use of a handy new object called `Stage`. This object returns the dimensions and scale of the movie stage. Although not used here, the `Stage` object also has a very useful `Listener` method, which can be used to react to the resizing of the browser.

```
// Set map x-coordinate to users timezone
zoneWidth = Stage.width / 24;
this._x = (-now_timezoneOffset * zoneWidth);
```

Setting the map's position.

The initialization code.

```
onClipEvent (load) {

    // ---------------------------------------------------------------
    // FUNCTION LIBRARY
    // ---------------------------------------------------------------

    // FUNCTION: to create timezone offset string
    function setTimezoneOffsetString(zone) {
        if (zone > 0) {zone = "+" + zone};
        return zone;
    }

    // ---------------------------------------------------------------
    // INITIALISE
    // ---------------------------------------------------------------

    // Create new Date object
    now = new Date();

    // Create timezone offset value
    // Convert mins to hours and express as negative
    now_timezoneOffset = -(now.getTimezoneOffset() / 60);

    // Create timezone offset string
    TimezoneOffsetString = setTimezoneOffsetString(now_timezoneOffset);
    _root.zone = now_timezoneOffset

    // Set map x-coordinate to users timezone
    zoneWidth = Stage.width / 24;
    this._x = (-now_timezoneOffset * zoneWidth);

}

onClipEvent (enterFrame) {

        // Set Time Zone Offset String
    TimezoneOffsetString = setTimezoneOffsetString(_root.zone);

}
```

DEFINING FUNCTIONS FOR A REAL-TIME DISPLAY

A common misconception with the `Date` object is that it is a pointer to the current time. This is incorrect. The properties of a `Date` object are static. They only hold the date and time values given to them at the moment of their creation. If you check those values later, they will be unchanged. Before you build yourself a real-time clock, you are first going to prepare a few functions.

1 Go back to your text editor and add this code next to the other functions in the `onClipEvent(load)` section:

This first function is really a little helper for the next two. As a rule of thumb, if you use a block of code more than once, you should turn it into a function. In this case, you're going to be parsing some dates and times into a readable format, and this function will really help with that.

It takes a number parameter and, by adding a preceding zero if the number is less than 9, returns a double-digit string. The important command here is `return`. Whenever a function encounters the `return` statement, it terminates and returns a value to wherever it was called from.

```
// FUNCTION: to return a number as a double digit string
function doubleDigits(val) {
        if (val > 9) {return val} else {return "0" + val}
}
```

Returning a double-digit string.

2 Add this code below the other functions in the `onClipEvent(load)` section:

This function makes use of the above function to format the hours, minutes, and seconds of a `Date` object. You access these individual elements using the `.get` methods of the `Date` object.

```
// FUNCTION: to return the time formatted with zeros
function timeString(inDate) {
    return  doubleDigits(inDate.getUTCHours()) + " : "
        + doubleDigits(inDate.getUTCMinutes()) + " : "
        + doubleDigits(inDate.getUTCSeconds());
}
```

Formatting the time.

For example, to find the `Hours` value for a `Date` object called `inDate`, use the syntax `inDate.getHours()`, which returns the number of hours in the local time. To find what the value of `Hours` was, unadjusted for time zones and DST, use the syntax `inDate.getUTCHours()`.

This function checks these time properties in turn and returns a string in the familiar colon-separated, double-digit format of digital clocks everywhere.

3   Add this last function below the other functions in the `onClipEvent(load)` section:

This third function does for the date what the last function did for time. More experienced readers will notice, though, that this function is making calls to two `Date` properties that don't actually exist! Don't panic. This is okay because you're going to add them in a minute.

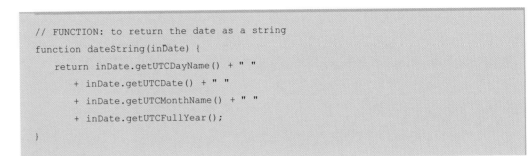

```
// FUNCTION: to return the date as a string
function dateString(inDate) {
    return inDate.getUTCDayName() + " "
        + inDate.getUTCDate() + " "
        + inDate.getUTCMonthName() + " "
        + inDate.getUTCFullYear();
}
```

Formatting the date.

USING PROTOTYPE TO EXTEND THE DATE OBJECT

ActionScript is based on ECMA-262, the same standard used by JavaScript. Consequently, the ActionScript and JavaScript `Date` objects and methods are almost identical. There are, however, several useful `Date` methods that, mainly due to localization issues, don't exist in either language. The names of the months and weekdays are a good example. Next you're going to add these new methods to the `Date` object.

This next function declaration will be slightly different from previous ones. This one makes use of the `.prototype` method to extend the `Date` object. In layman's terms, this syntax enables you to add your own function calls to an existing ActionScript object. Once applied, these can be called just as you would any object method.

50

1   Insert this code into the function declaration section:

When called, this function returns the name of the weekday. First, the function creates a temporary array called `daynames` to store the names of all the days of the week. When any variable is preceded with the `var` statement, it is deemed to be local and only exists for the duration of the function. The `return` line for this function takes the `Date`'s existing `.getUTCDay()` method and uses it to access the correct day within the `daynames` array.

```
// FUNCTION: to return the weekday name
Date.prototype.getUTCDayName = function() {
    var daynames = new Array('Sunday', 'Monday', 'Tuesday', 'Wednesday',
    ➡'Thursday', 'Friday', 'Saturday');
    return daynames[ this.getUTCDay()];
};
```

Returning the weekday.

2   Insert this code into the function declaration section:

This last function uses a similar array lookup technique to return the name of the month. When you understand the syntax of these extensions, you'll find them very easy to write. They are also very simple to translate into other languages.

```
// FUNCTION: to return the month name
Date.prototype.getUTCMonthName = function() {
    var monthnames = new Array('January', 'February', 'March', 'April', 'May',
    ➡'June', 'July', 'August', 'September', 'October', 'November',
    ➡'December');
    return monthnames[ this.getUTCMonth()];
};
```

Returning the month.

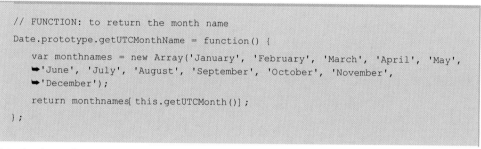

Date and time formatting functions.

UPDATING IN REAL TIME

With all the supporting functions in place, it's finally time to create the "real-time" clock. The properties of a Date object are static, so you keep them up-to-date by refreshing the object every frame. All the code within the curly brackets of the onClipEvent(enterFrame) section is run every frame, so if you create a new Date object called now within this section, it will constantly be refreshed with the current time.

1 Insert this code in the onClipEvent(enterFrame) section:

The first line after the comments creates a new Date object called now. The next two lines pass the now object into your new formatting functions. The variables created by these functions have already been assigned to text fields at the bottom of the map.

```
// Set UTC Date object
now = new Date();
nowDate = dateString(now);
nowTime = timeString(now);
```

Refreshing the Date object for UTC time.

2 Save your ActionScript text file.

3 Go back to Flash MX. Recompile and test your movie.

It is important to save the text file because Flash includes this code when it compiles. If all goes well, you should now see the days, hours, and minutes tick over in real time!

UPDATING THE MOUSE TIME ZONE

The next batch of code will do for the mouse zone time what the previous batch did for UTC time. The two blocks are almost identical, except for some Date modifications that tweak the Date to compensate for the time zone offset.

1 Back in your text editor, add this code to the onClipEvent (enterFrame) section:

```
// Set Zone Date object
Mousezone = new Date();
Mousezone.setMinutes(now.getUTCMinutes() + (_root.zone * 60));
MousezoneDate = dateString(Mousezone);
MousezoneTime = timeString(Mousezone);
```

Refreshing the Date object for mouse zone time.

Note: This is where the beauty of the Date object finally shows itself. If you try doing any calendar calculations using multiple individual variables, you'll soon go slightly mad. The biggest advantage to Date object mathematics is that it takes care of all the rounding stuff for you. For example, if you add 610 minutes to a Date, it knows to add 10 hours and 10 minutes, correct for new days, leap years, and all the other potential pitfalls. It's worth it!

You'll notice the modification in the third line. Here you take a new Date object called Mousezone and use .getUTCMinutes to add enough time to compensate for the time zone offset. The currently highlighted zone is converted to minutes by multiplying it by 60. It is then added to the current value of UTCMinutes to offset it. Once modified, the new Mousezone Date object can be interrogated as normal.

2 Save your ActionScript text file.

3 Go back to Flash MX and recompile your movie. Watch this time for the time difference as you pan around the map!

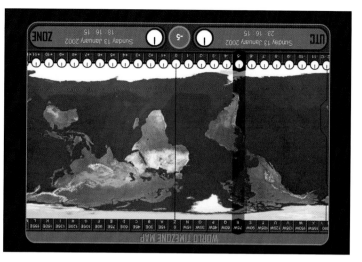

Real-time date and time.

SETTING AN ANALOGUE CLOCK

Although the properties of the Date object are returned as numbers, they don't have to be displayed as such. Next you're going to use these values to drive the hands of an analogue clock. The second hand of the clock movie is not visible by default. You want to show the second hand on the two large clocks, so the first line of code makes this hand visible.

1   Back in your text editor, add this code to the onClipEvent(enterFrame) section:

The clock hand movies have been drawn so that their registration point (the little cross that represents the origin) is located at the position where you would want to rotate it. With these pivot points already set, all you have to do to set the hands of the clock is change the _rotation property of each movie.

```
// Draw UTC clock
_root.UTCClock.Hands.Second_Hand._visible = true;
```

Displaying the clock hands.

2   Add this code immediately after the last block:

These three lines convert the value of the Date properties to a corresponding _rotation value in degrees. For example, in the case of seconds, you take a value from 0 to 59 and multiply it by 6 to give you a _rotation value in degrees between 0 and 354.

Strictly speaking, the second sections of each formula are not actually required. They are merely micro adjustments to smooth the transitions of the larger hands. You can use an almost identical block of code to drive the time zone clock.

```
_root.UTCClock.Hands.Second_Hand._rotation = (now.getUTCSeconds() * 6);
_root.UTCClock.Hands.Hour_hand._rotation = (now.getUTCHours() * 30) +
    (now.getUTCMinutes() / 10);
_root.UTCClock.Hands.Minute_hand._rotation = (now.getUTCMinutes() * 6) +
    (now.getUTCSeconds() / 10);
```

Adjusting the clock hands.

3 Add this code immediately after the last block:

```
// Draw zone clock
_root.ZoneClock.Hands.Second_Hand._visible = true;
_root.ZoneClock.Hands.Second_Hand._rotation = (MouseZone.getUTCSeconds() * 6);
_root.ZoneClock.Hands.Hour_hand._rotation = (MouseZone.getUTCHours() * 30) +
     (MouseZone.getUTCMinutes() / 10);
_root.ZoneClock.Hands.Minute_hand._rotation = (MouseZone.getUTCMinutes() * 6)
     + (MouseZone.getUTCSeconds() / 10);
```

Drawing the mouse zone clock.

```
// Create timezone offset string
timezoneOffsetString = setTimezoneOffsetString(now_timezoneOffset);
_root.zone = now_timezoneOffset;
// Set map x-coordinate to users timezone
zoneWidth = Stage.width / 24;
this._x = (-now_timezoneOffset * zoneWidth);
}

onClipEvent (enterFrame) {
// Set Time Zone Offset String
timezoneOffsetString = setTimezoneOffsetString(_root.zone);

// Set UTC Date object
now = new Date();
nowDate = dateString(now);
nowTime = timeString(now);

// Set Zone Date object
MouseZone = new Date();
MouseZone.setMinutes(now.getUTCMinutes() + (_root.zone * 60));
MouseZoneDate = dateString(MouseZone);
MouseZoneTime = timeString(MouseZone);

// Draw UTC clock
_root.UTCClock.Hands.Second_Hand._visible = true;
_root.UTCClock.Hands.Second_Hand._rotation = (now.getUTCSeconds() * 6);
_root.UTCClock.Hands.Hour_hand._rotation = (now.getUTCHours() * 30) + (now.getUTCMinutes() / 10);
_root.UTCClock.Hands.Minute_hand._rotation = (now.getUTCMinutes() * 6) + (now.getUTCSeconds() / 10);

// Draw zone clock
_root.ZoneClock.Hands.Second_Hand._visible = true;
_root.ZoneClock.Hands.Second_Hand._rotation = (MouseZone.getUTCSeconds() * 6);
_root.ZoneClock.Hands.Hour_hand._rotation = (MouseZone.getUTCHours() * 30) +
     (MouseZone.getUTCMinutes() / 10);
_root.ZoneClock.Hands.Minute_hand._rotation = (MouseZone.getUTCMinutes() * 6) +
     (MouseZone.getUTCSeconds() / 10);
}
```

The real-time clock code in place.

SETTING A ROW OF CLOCKS

You have one final flourish left. You're going to set all the analogue clocks along the bottom of each time zone. Because you'll be setting these clocks more than once, you're going to follow my earlier advice and build this process into a function.

The clock-hand drawing routines will use much the same technique as you used for the larger clocks. The main difference this time is that you're going to wrap your code within a couple of loops. The first of these loops will ensure that all three instances of the map movie (left, right, and center) are updated. The second loop will run through all 24 time zones, creating a new Date object for each. The properties of the object will then be used to drive the hands of the clock.

1 Add this code below the other function definitions in the onClipEvent (Load) section:

```
// FUNCTION: to set clock times
function setClocks() {

    // Cycle through maps
    for (var i = 1; i < 4; i++) {

        // Cycle through clocks
        for (var j = 1; j <= 24; j++) {

            // Get zone offset converted to minutes
            zoneOffset = (j - 13) * 60;

            // Apply zone offset
            zone = new Date();
            zone.setMinutes(now.getUTCMinutes() + zoneOffset);

            // Draw clock hands
            this["map" + i]["clock" + j].Hands.Hour_hand._rotation =
                (zone.getUTCHours() * 30) + (zone.getUTCMinutes() / 10);
            this["map" + i]["clock" + j].Hands.Minute_hand._rotation =
                (zone.getUTCMinutes() * 6) + (zone.getUTCSeconds() / 10);
        }
    }
}
```

Setting the time.

There's a lot going on in this routine, but each individual line is pretty straightforward. The two loops make sure that every clock on every map gets attended to. The important variable in all this is zoneOffset:

```
zoneOffset = (j - 13) * 60;
```

This is derived by removing 13 from loop j (the time zone loop) to generate a number between −12 and +12. This is effectively the UTC time zone offset in hours. When you multiply it by 60, you are converting it from hours to minutes.

```
zone.setMinutes(now.getUTCMinutes() +
    zoneOffset);
```

When you add this minute value to the current value of .UTCminutes, the new properties of the zone Date object will reflect the local time in that zone.

USING SETINTERVAL TO UPDATE THE CLOCKS

Trying to set 26 analogue clocks every frame would likely bring your processor to its knees. For this reason, you're only going to set them about once a minute. To do this, you're going to use a really useful new command called `setInterval()`. It takes two parameters: The first is a function to call (in this case, the brand-new `setClocks()` routine), and the second is a period in milliseconds. Once set, the named function will be called at the end of every period cycle.

1 Add this code to the end of the function definition section in the `onClipEvent(load)` section and save your ActionScript file:

```
// Draw map clocks every minute
setInterval(setClocks(), 60 * 1000);
```

Updating the clocks.

2 Return to the Flash MX authoring environment and test the movie for the last time.

You'll notice that the clocks along the bottom of the map are now all being set correctly. Congratulations, you made it!

Note: This application only attempts to display time zone offsets. It makes no attempt to compensate for DST within each region to show actual local time. Every attempt has been made to ensure that the time zone offsets for each territory are correct, but like everything in life, they are subject to change.

Note: Ben Franklin first posited the notion of daylight savings time (DST) in a humorous essay back in 1784. It wasn't until World War I, however, that it was finally introduced. The practice is not universally adopted (even within territories), but where it is, clocks are put one hour ahead of UTC time during the summer months.

As already explained, the `.getTimezoneOffset()` property returns the difference between UTC and local time. Despite its name, this value is actually a combination of the offset for the time zone and the offset for DST.

The Flash Player gets the values of UTC time and local time from the operating system on which it is running. It is worth being aware, though, that different combinations of Flash Player and operating system handle DST differently. Full details of how the Flash Player deals with these combinations are contained within the `Date` object specification in the ActionScript Dictionary.

THE PROLEPTIC NATURE OF THE ACTIONSCRIPT DATE OBJECT

The ActionScript `Date` object is *proleptic*, meaning it applies a fixed set of calendrical rules beyond the times when they historically existed. In general use this won't be a problem, but creating `Dates` in the past can be a bit of a minefield. Here are a few events to be aware of:

Daylight savings time (DST):

Introduced into several countries in Europe in 1916, it has been randomly applied and removed ever since. DST is the worst offender for anarchic application. Some territories have applied as little as 20 minutes and as much as 2 hours. In wartime, the United States applied DST all year round.

Time zones:

The time-zone system was introduced to the United States in November of 1883. The rest of the world followed in 1884. Territories adjust their offset and hop from one side of the dateline to the other with alarming regularity.

The Gregorian reform:

The Gregorian calendar originally replaced the Julian calendar by Papal Bull in 1582. At that time, 10 days were removed from the calendar to correct for astronomical drift. In effect, October 4, 1582, was followed immediately by October 15, 1582. Just to complicate matters, not everyone adopted the calendar straightaway, with many Protestant territories objecting on religious grounds. It was eventually introduced into England and its colonies in 1752 when Wednesday, September 2 was followed by Thursday, September 14.

When you consider this transition to be valid is a matter of debate, but `Dates` created earlier than it are effectively in the Julian calendar system. The only real difference with the Julian reckoning is that it does not apply leap millennia. The `Date` object (being Gregorian proleptic) does not correct for the missing days and will consequently return the wrong day of the week.

Although rendered somewhat irrelevant by the calendar changeover, it's also worth mentioning that any new `Dates` defined with fewer than three digits are set to 1900 + the year. To define years before the year 100, you need to use the `.setTime` method and set the value in milliseconds.

Going further back in time, before C.E. 1 (usually referred to as A.D. 1), reveals another feature of the `Date` object. It employs the astronomical convention of date recording by using negative numbers to represent B.C.E. dates. In this system, zero represents the year 1 B.C.E. and −1 represents 2 B.C.E. and so on.

Note: For more information, check out these books and web sites:

Standard C Date/Time Library by Lance Latham (ISBN 0-87930-496-0)

The Calendar by David Ewing Duncan (ISBN 1-85702-979-8)

Mapping Time by E.G. Richards (ISBN 0-19-286205-7)

www.crashposition.com/books/flashMXmagic

www.ultrashock.com/tutorials/flash5/date_ext.html

www.twinsun.com/tz/tz-link.htm

HOW TO IMPROVE

The combination of space and time offers up limitless possibilities for further enhancements, and I would be very interested in hearing from anybody who adds to this application. Here are a few ideas to kick off:

- Make the map "live" by centering it on the current noon time zone.
- Add shadows to differentiate night areas from day.
- Tie it into a daylight savings time database to display live local times.

SUMMARY

Thus ends your little sojourn through the delights of time zones, calendrical history, and the `Date` object. If I've done my job correctly, this tutorial will have done two things: made the `Date` object a little clearer to you and made the commonly accepted structures of timekeeping less so. It's always important to keep in mind that the procedures we follow in our lives are only human-made approximations. The"science" of computus is a veritable minefield of exceptions and kludges.

Everyone dreams of traveling to exotic places and meeting interesting people. Few among us, however, have the resources to consistently fulfill those dreams. With Flash, you can satisfy your thirst for adventure and bring the experience home to share with family and friends.

This project breaks the four boundaries of a browser's window and transforms them into a portal, transporting you into an immersive, hands-on learning expedition a continent away. Through the creative use of layered imagery and programmatic movement, guests can explore a remote environment half a world away.

5

IMMERSIVE PANORAMA

by Mark Baltzegar
Photographs © Donald Johanson and the Institute of Human Origins.

Difficulty Rating: ★★★

Made With:

    Original images courtesy of the Institute of Human Origins

    Images edited with Adobe Photoshop

    Graphics created with Adobe Illustrator

Final File Size: 240KB

Modem Download Time: 30 seconds

Development Time: 4 hours

IT WORKS LIKE THIS

The magic of this site begins when guests realize that they can venture forward and explore a virtual landscape. The person nearest them passes from view as another appears. The scenery is moving, too. Closer objects move faster than the distant horizon, which is barely moving. You can probably remember this same effect from gazing out of a car window as a child at a motionless horizon in the setting sun, with grass and trees nearby passing in a dizzying blur. With ActionScript, it is now simple to re-create this sensation in response to a guest's interactions with the screen.

In this project, you will build an interactive walkthrough with sample content from the interactive documentary *Becoming Human* (**www.becominghuman.org**). The experience is a panoramic 3D environment composed of many layers of bitmaps moving in parallax. Two navigational buttons control movement through the simulated space. Visitors can alter the speed of the experience at any time by pressing the up- or down-arrow key. They can also return quickly to a previously visited location with the browser's Back and Forward buttons.

PREPARING TO WORK

Before starting, you'll need to copy the **ImmersivePanorama** folder onto your hard disk, start Flash, and open the **dig_start.fla** file.

SETTING THE STAGE

The scene has two main parts: a landscape and the people who occupy it. The landscape consists of three mountain ranges. Farthest away is a distant mountain range shrouded in mist and dust. Nearer is an imposing peak tapering off into a meandering ridge of dirt and rock. Nearer still is a barren hillside of exposed rock and loose sand. Added to this landscape are the main characters: four scientists and a handful of local researchers intently searching for scientific clues among the rubble. These images are bitmaps, and many contain transparency. You will import them, organize them into layers, and individually position them to construct the scene.

1 Create a new layer and select File > Import. Import all of the images in the **assets/images** folder.

Conceptually, several of the individual images exist on the same plane and at the same distance from the viewer. You will eventually consolidate these images into single layers for convenience. But first, in Step 2, you'll separate all the images for easier handling.

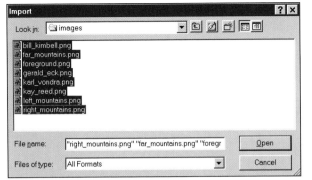

Import the images from the **assets/images** folder.

2 Choose Edit > Select All. Choose Modify > Distribute to Layers.

Each image now resides in its own layer. The layers are named with the file's name.

3 Delete the initial layer (which is now empty), being careful not to delete the **labels** or **action script** layers.

The Distribute to Layers command makes organizing assets into layers quick and easy.

4 Place the layers in the following order from top to bottom:

labels

action script

kay_reed

bill_kimbell

karl_vondra

gerald_eck

foreground

left_mountains

right_mountains

far_mountains

> **Note:** If file extensions are visible in your operating system, Flash names the layers using the filename plus the extension. In this project, it is assumed that the extensions are absent from the layer names.

5 Select the **bill_kimbell.png** image from the **bill_kimbell** layer and select Edit > Cut. Then, with the **kay_reed** layer selected, Edit > Paste the image, positioning it at X: 420, Y: 32 in the Property Inspector.

6 Select the **right_mountains.png** image from the **right_mountains** layer. Cut and paste the image into the **left_mountains** layer, positioning it at X: 610, Y: 33.

7 Delete these newly emptied layers, being careful not to delete the **labels** or **action script** layers.

Reordering the image layers.

8   Position the **karl_vondra.png** image at X: 0, Y: 87.

Move **karl_vondra.png** to X: 0, Y: 87.

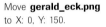

9   Finally, position the **gerald_eck.png** image at X: 0, Y: 150.

Move **gerald_eck.png** to X: 0, Y: 150.

Note: Use the Show/Hide and Lock/Unlock layer options for each layer to ease selection of hidden or obscured elements.

PREPARING ASSETS FOR SCRIPTING

At this point, you have imported your assets and organized them. Before you can move them programmatically, however, you need to convert each image into a movie clip and give it an instance name. A few of the assets also need to move in unison, so they'll be grouped inside a single movie clip.

Macromedia Flash MX: New to this version is creation-time control of the registration point's position. The registration point is the X: 0, Y: 0 (or origin) of the movie clip's internal coordinate system. Its position is especially important when movies are nested within each other. Programming the movement of a nested movie clip is often easier if the coordinate system of the nested movie clip is aligned to that of its containing movie clip. Because the stage's origin is at the top left, it's a good idea to create new movie clips with their origin at the top left also.

Prior to Flash MX, registration-point control was only achieved by repositioning the contents of a movie clip after its creation. This arduous process was especially painful if it was required for many movie clips. Fortunately, in Flash MX, once the registration is set, the same preference is applied to each successive movie clip created.

1   Select the **far_mountains.png** image and select Insert > Convert to Symbol.

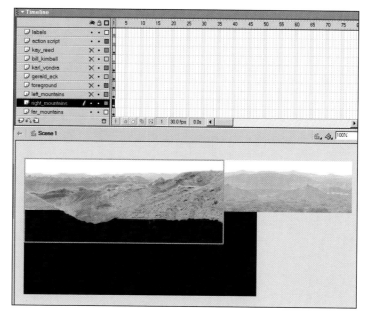

The visibility property makes selection of hidden elements easier.

2 In the dialog box that appears, set the Behavior to Movie Clip, the Registration to the top-left, and the Name to **slider1**.

3 In the Property Inspector, set the newly created movie clip's Instance Name property to **slider1**.

4 Select both the **left_mountains.png** and **right_mountains.png** images from the **left_mountains** layer and convert them to a new movie clip named **slider2**, setting its instance name to **slider2**.

5 Select the **foreground.png** image and convert it to a new movie clip named **slider3**, setting its instance name to **slider3**.

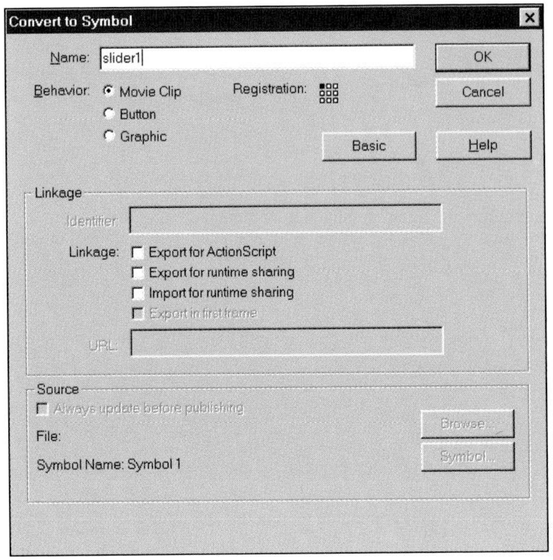

Converting **far_mountains.png** to a movie clip. Registration-point control has improved in Flash MX.

PREPARING ASSETS FOR SCRIPTING—PART II

All of the images, when layered together, form a complete picture of the landscape. The preceding three images naturally touch the top of the stage because of their larger size and placement as part of the background. Therefore, their top-left corners are located at X: 0, Y: 0. Many of the following images, however, are shorter than the stage height and belong to the foreground. They will be aligned to the bottom of the stage. Unfortunately, this poses a minor problem. Because these foreground images are not as tall as the stage, their top-left corners would not rest at X: 0, Y: 0 if they were converted to movie clips in their present form.

As you will see later, it's very important for the top-left corner of each of the six final movie clips to rest at the stage's origin so that one simple motion script can be applied to them all uniformly. You'll overcome this small problem starting with the next image, which is located at X: 0, Y: 150.

1   Select the **gerald_eck.png** image and convert it to a new movie clip named **eck**, setting its instance name to **eck**.

Using two different methods, you're going to create what I like to call placeholder movie clips. These invisible movie clips trick Flash into thinking the movie clips' dimensions are wider or taller than they would be otherwise.

2   While still in the **gerald_eck** layer, create a placeholder movie clip by drawing a 10-pixel square on the stage with its top-left corner at X: 0, Y: 0. Convert this square to a movie clip with its Registration set to the top left and a Name of **placeholder**.

You won't be moving this placeholder movie clip programmatically, so there's no need to give it an instance name.

Note: The color of the square is unimportant as long as it can be easily seen against the background images. Also, try setting the stroke to clear before drawing the square. This will prevent you from accidentally leaving the stroke behind when converting the selected square to a movie clip.

Note: As you create the following movie clips, set their registration points to the top left.

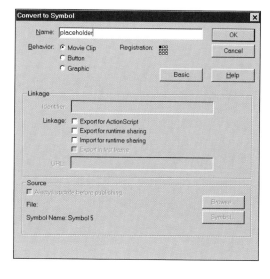

Placeholder movie clips maintain widths of nearly empty movie clips.

3 Apply the following code in the Object Actions panel to hide the square:

```
onClipEvent(load){
    _visible = false;
}
```

Setting the `visible` property of the movie clip to `false` in an `onClipEvent(load)` event handler hides the movie clip before it can render to the screen.

This prevents the placeholder movie clip from being seen in the final composition.

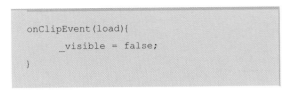

Hide the placeholder programmatically.

> **Note:** Alternately, you could write `this._visible = false`. Unless another path is specified explicitly, however, `this` is implied by default.

4 Select both of the newly created **eck** and **placeholder** movie clips. Create a new movie clip named **slider4**, setting its instance name to **slider4**.

5 Select the **karl_vondra.png** image and convert it to a new movie clip named **vondra**, setting its instance name to **vondra**.

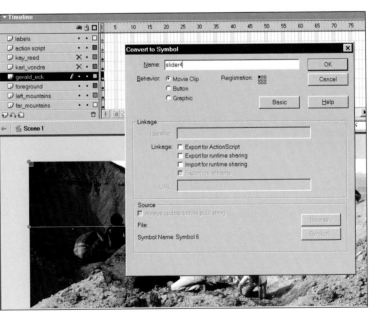

Convert both **placeholder** and **eck** to a single movie clip.

6 From Window > Library, place a copy of the previously created placeholder movie clip onto the stage at X: 0, Y: 0. Apply the hiding code shown previously in Step 3 to the movie clip.

Copy another placeholder from the Library.

7 Select both of the newly created **vondra** and **placeholder** movie clips and convert them to a movie clip named **slider5**, setting its instance name to **slider5**.

8 Convert both **kay_reed.png** and **bill_kimbell.png** into movie clips, giving them names and instance names of **reed** and **kimbell**. Convert both instances to a single movie clip named **slider6**, setting its instance name to **slider6**.

9 For clarity, rename the layers to match the movie clips within them, beginning with **slider1** at the bottom and ending with **slider6** at the top.

Note: Now it's easier to understand the purpose of the placeholder movie clips used in **slider4**. You added them to create a virtual width for the movie clip that contains the movie clip of Gerald Eck. If you had not taken this approach, you would have had to create a .png that was thousands of pixels in length. This approach, however, would have made the file prohibitively large. The solution is to cut out only what you truly need and trick Flash into thinking that the movie clip is wider than it truly is. Keep this technique in mind because you will use it several more times in this project.

Renaming the layers for clarity.

POSITIONING THE CAST

Three of the movie clips (**eck**, **vondra**, and **kimbell**) are temporarily positioned for convenience. Why temporarily? The reason is simple. Each movie clip's final X-axis position is many thousands of pixels offstage. Unfortunately, Flash MX imposes strict limitations on where you can physically position a movie clip. Were you to try, you wouldn't be able to move these movie clips to their correct locations. Add a few lines of code that will position the movie clips programmatically and extend the width of the movie clips that contain them.

> **Note:** Be aware that any shapes drawn with the `lineTo()` function will be rendered below content created with the authoring environment's drawing tools.

Earlier, you created and placed a placeholder movie clip by hand. You did this so that **slider4** and **slider5** would have a top-left corner at X: 0, Y: 0. You will need similar placeholders for the right side of several movie clips.

Macromedia Flash MX: Useful new additions to ActionScript in Flash MX include the `_global` object, the `createEmptyMovieClip()` function, and the `lineTo()` function.

The `_global` **object.** With the `global` identifier, you now have the capability *to* define a function or variable that can be accessed from anywhere in a movie. The `_global` object is a master object of sorts, containing the core ActionScript classes such as String, Object, Math, and Array. Methods and properties defined in the `_global` object can be referenced from anywhere in a movie and do not need identifiers such as `_root` or `_level`. Furthermore, unlike `_root` or `_level`, the `_global` object cannot be removed or over-written, so properties and methods of the `_global` object are safe from accidental erasure.

The `createEmptyMovieClip()` **function.** As its name implies, this function creates an empty movie clip. The function accepts two arguments. The first argument is the instance name of the movie clip that will contain the new empty movie clip. The second argument is the depth at which the empty movie clip will be attached. It is important to remember that the registration point of every empty movie clip created with this function will be located at the top-left corner.

In general, the `createEmptyMovieClip()` function is similar to the `attachMovie()` function, but it does not require that a movie clip be placed in the Library with an external linkage name.

The `lineTo()` **function.** This is a very simple function for drawing straight lines. The function accepts two arguments: the x and y coordinates that together represent the endpoint of the line segment to be drawn.

If an initial point has not been set with the `moveTo()` function, the initial point of the line segment is considered to be X: 0, Y: 0. Each successive call to `lineTo()` uses the previous call's x and y coordinates as the initial starting point of the new line segment. All lines are drawn using the current line style.

1 Select frame 1 of the **action script** layer and add this code in the Frame Actions panel.

An empty placeholder movie clip alone is not enough to change the width of its containing movie clip. The empty movie clip must be filled with a drawn shape or other visible element. Here you define a globally accessible function that will create an empty movie clip within the object that calls it. The function then fills this empty movie clip with a 1-pixel line and hides the entire movie clip.

```
_global.createPlaceholder = function(objRef, xPos){
    objRef.createEmptyMovieClip("right_placeholder", 1);
    objRef.right_placeholder.lineTo(0,1);
    objRef.right_placeholder._visible = false;
    objRef.right_placeholder._x = xPos;
    }
```

This function is globally accessible. It creates an empty movie clip inside the movie clip referenced by objRef, fills it with a 1-pixel line, hides it from view, and set its x position to the value of xPos.

This function programmatically creates placeholder movie clips.

2 Select the instance of **slider4** and add this code in the Object Actions panel.

This positions **eck** programmatically and changes the width of **slider4** without stretching its contents.

```
onClipEvent(load){
    _global.createPlaceholder(this,
    ➥2490);
    eck._x = 1100;
```

After **slider4** loads but before it is rendered to screen, this ActionScript creates a placeholder movie clip at X: 2,490 within **slider4**. It then moves the **eck** movie clip to X: 1100.

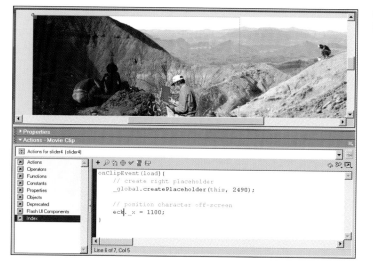

Programmatically position the **eck** movie clip.

3 Apply the same code to **slider5**, this time sending 3100 as the second parameter of createPlaceholder () and setting **vondra**'s x position to 750.

```
onClipEvent(load){
        _global.createPlaceholder(this, 3100);
        vondra._x = 750;
}
```

4 Do the same for **slider6**, but use 3880 as the second parameter of createPlaceholder () and set **kimbell**'s x position to 3557.

```
onClipEvent(load){
        _global.createPlaceholder(this, 3880);
        kimbell._x = 3557;
}
```

CHOREOGRAPHING THE MOVEMENT

Now your stage is set. Infuse the scene with life by allowing your guests to walk through the scene. You'll create two buttons: one to move left and one to move right. Also, you'll disable these directional buttons when the guest can go no farther. Along the way, you'll learn about external libraries, optimization techniques, and dynamically assigning functions to a variable.

1   Create a new layer named **nav** above the others.

2   Select File > Open as Library and open **library.fla**. Select **left_nav** and **right_nav** from the Library and place them on the stage at X: 40, Y: 260 and X: 520, Y: 260, respectively.

Note: Moving many full-screen images at once is processor intensive, so take advantage of any optimizations you can. The two navigational buttons are contained within another movie clip. They reside there because the two buttons share code in common, and each button's code should only run when its counterpart is idle. You achieve this by assigning a function to the variable `go` in the outermost movie clip. This function is called on every frame due to its inclusion in an `onClipEvent(enterFrame)` event handler. When the value of `go` is `null`, nothing happens because there is, in fact, no code to execute. When a guest rolls over a button, however, the button places its own custom version of the `go` function into the space reserved by the variable in the outer movie clip. When the guest rolls out of the button, the `go()` function becomes `null` once again. So, in effect, you have one function that acts like two, easing the overall processing load.

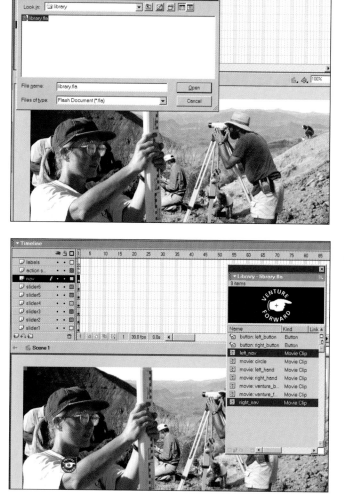

Open as Library the **library.fla** file in the **assets** folder.

Drag the **left_nav** and **right_nav** movie clips from the Library.

3 Select the instance of the **left_nav** movie clip, giving it an instance name of **left_nav**. To this instance, add this code in the Object Actions panel.

Place the `goLeft()` function on **left_nav**.

```
onClipEvent(load){
    function goLeft(){
        with(_parent){
            if (_parent.slider1._x >= 0) {
                // move sliders to starting point
                for(var i=2; i<=6; i++){
                    _parent.slider[i]._x = 0;
                }
            } else {
                // move sliders to the right
                _parent.slider1._x += .5;
                for(var i=2; i<=6; i++){
                    _parent["slider"+i]._x = _parent.slider1._x * multiplier[i];
                }
            }
            updateAfterEvent;
        }
    }
}


on(rollOver){
    _parent.go = goLeft;
}


on(rollOut){
    _parent.go = null;
}
```

When the mouse rolls over the movie clip, you assign the function `goLeft()` to a variable in the movie clip's parent. When the mouse rolls out, you then remove the same function. The `goLeft()` function moves all of the image layers to the right in parallax until **slider1**'s x is greater than or equal to zero.

4 Select the instance of the **right_nav** movie clip, giving it an instance name of **right_nav**. To this instance, add this code in the Object Actions panel.

Place the goRight() function on **right_nav**.

Briefly, what the goLeft() and goRight() functions do is simple. They both move the movie clip **slider1** a fraction of a pixel per frame. The fraction is determined by a speed variable that will be set in the outer movie clip.

Each remaining slider is moved by the same amount plus an additional percentage, which is computed from the difference in a given movie clip and **slider1**. This percentage will also reside in the outer movie clip.

The updateAfterEvent command causes a screen redraw each time the function is called. Without it, the screen would only redraw when the playhead moved to another frame. This, of course, is governed by the frame rate of the movie. This command often makes programmatic animation play smoother.

```
onClipEvent(load){
    function goRight(){
        with(_parent){
            if ((_parent.slider1._x <= ((sliderwidth - Stage.width) - 3) * -1 )){
                // move sliders to right end point
                _parent.slider1._x = ((sliderwidth - Stage.width) -3) * -1;
            } else {
                // move sliders to the left
                _parent.slider1._x -= .5;
            }
            // move other sliders
            for(var i=2; i<=6; i++){
                _parent["slider"+i]._x = _parent.slider1._x * multiplier[i];
            }
            updateAfterEvent;
        }
    }
}


on(rollOver){
    _parent.go = goRight;
}


on(rollOut){
    _parent.go = null;
}
```

When the mouse rolls over the movie clip, you assign the function goRight() to a variable in the movie clip's parent. When the mouse rolls out, you then remove the same function. The goRight() function moves all of the image layers to the left in parallax until **slider1**'s x is touching the right side of the stage.

5 Select both the **left_nav** and **right_nav** movie clip instances and convert them to a new movie clip named **nav**, giving it the instance name **nav**. To this instance, add this code in the Object Actions panel.

When your two navigational buttons load, you create an array of numbers that represent the difference in length of the different image layers. You also reserve space for a future go() function so that you can reference it from elsewhere in the movie. In every frame, you call the go() function, which for now does nothing. Then check to see if slider1 traveled to the extreme right or left of the panorama. If so, hide that direction's navigational button.

Here, **slider1** is forced to stop when its left or right edge meets the left or right edge of the stage.

The variable assignments on the outer movie clip compute the ratio used to offset each of the many layers by comparing two distances. The first distance is the distance each layer must travel before its right edge meets the right edge of the stage. The second distance is the distance **slider1** must travel to do the same. These ratios are stored in an array named multiplier.

Also, code in the outer movie clip hides a button when a guest can no longer travel in a particular direction.

```
onClipEvent(load){
    // initialize shared variables
    var sliderWidth = _parent.slider1._width;
    var go = null;
    var multiplier = new Array();

    // determine multiplier for each layer
    var baseDistance = sliderWidth - Stage.width;
    for(var i=2; i<=6;i++){
        multiplier[ i] = (_parent["slider"+i]._width - Stage.width) / baseDistance;
    }
}


onClipEvent(enterFrame){
    go();

    // turn off right button if we're at the right end
    _parent.slider1._x <= -243 ? right_nav._alpha = 0 : right_nav._alpha = 100;

    // turn off left button if we're at the left end
    _parent.slider1._x >= 0 ? left_nav._alpha = 0 : left_nav._alpha = 100;
}
```

6 Now is a good time to test the panorama. Select Control > Test Movie.

Note: Be sure to minimize the test window so that the stage is the correct size. Remember that the stage's width is dynamically computed into the `baseDistance` value usingFlash MX's `Stage.width` property.

Convert **left_nav** and **right_nav** to a new movie clip and place the parallax code on it.

Setting the Tempo

Visitors can now walk through the virtual landscape. However, they might each have widely differing experiences. At present, the pace of movement is tied to the frame rate, which in turn varies with the speed of the visitor's computer. To make the experience more uniform for everyone, tie the execution of code to the passage of time by using the new `setInterval()` and `clearInterval()` functions.

1 Before proceeding, eliminate the `go()` function call from the `onClipEvent(enterFrame)` event handler in the Object Actions panel of the **nav** instance.

You will use `setInterval()` to call the function instead.

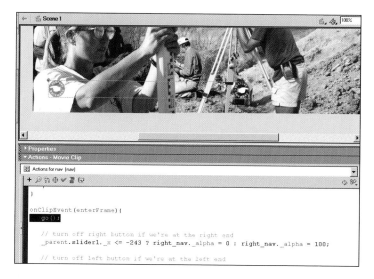

Remove the `go()` function from `nav`.

2 Create a variable named **intervalSpan** at the beginning of the `onClipEvent(load)` event handler of **nav** and set it to 10. This variable will be shared by both your left and right `go()` functions. Also, create a variable named **intervalID** to store the ID returned by the `setInterval()` function.

Macromedia Flash MX: The new `setInterval()` function repeatedly calls a function or object method that you specify at a given interval, stated in milliseconds. When the `setInterval()` function executes, it returns a unique ID. This ID can be captured by assigning the function call to a variable. The ID is needed to later stop the function call from repeating. One must pass the ID to the `clearInterval()` function as an argument to stop the function previously specified.

The `setInterval()` function takes either two or three arguments, depending on where the function you want to call resides. If the function is a method of an object, one must first pass in the object name, then the method name, then the delay in milliseconds, and then optionally an array of arguments. If the function is in the same scope as `setInterval()`, all you need to do is pass in the name of the function to be called and the delay time in milliseconds. Here, too, you can pass in an optional argument array if necessary.

```
onClipEvent(load){
    var intervalID;
    var intervalSpan = 10;

    ...
}
```

Here you are defining two variables that will be shared by the `goLeft()` and `goRight()` functions. `intervalID` stores the reference returned by the `setInterval()` function and `intervalSpan` is the amount of time in milliseconds before the function should execute.

Initialize the `intervalID` and `intervalSpan` variables.

3 Place the `setInterval()` call in the `rollOver` event handler of both the **left_nav** and **right_nav** instances within the **nav** movie clip and remove it with a `clearInterval()` call placed in both instances' `rollOut` event handlers.

When the mouse rolls over a navigational movie clip, `setInterval()` is applied to its parent's `go()` function for the duration specified in the `intervalSpan` variable. The ID returned by `setInterval()` is stored in `intervalID` so that it can later be passed to `clearInterval()` when the mouse rolls out of the navigation movie clip. With this code in place, the `go()` function executes only when the visitor's mouse is over a navigational button.

4 Test the movie again just to make sure everything still works. Remember to minimize the test window when testing the movie in the authoring environment.

```
on(rollOver){

    ...

    _parent.intervalID = setInterval(_parent.go, _parent.intervalSpan);

}


on(rollOut){

    ...

    clearInterval(_parent.intervalID);

}
```

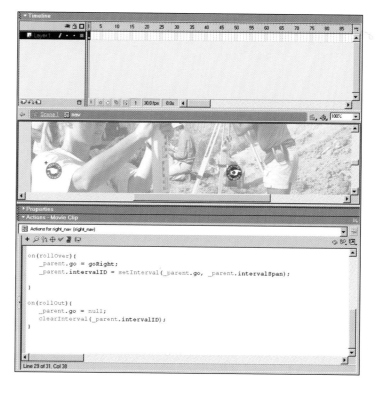

The `setInterval()` function is called when the mouse rolls over a button and stops when the mouse rolls out.

PROGRAMMING PARALLAX IN DEPTH

So how does this parallax thing really work? Basically, objects farther away from you move slower than those closest to you. The images start aligned left, so their speed is determined by the time it takes their right sides to align with the right side of the stage. If you make each layer progressively longer yet require that each layer's right side align itself at the same time, the longer the image is, the faster it will move to meet its goal.

You accomplish this programmatically by means of a multiplier. A given slider's multiplier represents the difference in the distance it must travel and the distance **slider1** must travel in the same time period. Take, for example, the difference between **slider1** and **slider2**; **slider1**'s width is 846 pixels, while **slider2**'s width is 1,124 pixels. If the stage is 600 pixels wide, **slider1** must move 246 pixels (the movie clip's width minus the stage width) to the left for its right side to align with the right side of the stage. **Slider2**, however, must travel 724 pixels in the same time period. The ratio you get when you divide **slider2**'s 724 pixels by **slider1**'s 246 pixels is 2.9. Therefore, for the right sides of both sliders to meet on the right side of the stage, **slider2** must move 2.9 pixels for every 1 pixel that **slider1** moves.

EMPOWERING THE VISITOR

Now that you are using setInterval() to control the speed of movement, it is simple to give the visitor more control over the pace of his or her experience. You will add keyboard support so that the visitor can regulate the walkthrough's speed with the up- and down-arrow keys.

1 Add this code to nav's onClipEvent(load) event handler, placing it below the variable declarations for intervalID and intervalSpan.

The concept of listeners is new in Flash MX. Listeners provide easy access to system events. In this code, you are implementing a Key event listener.

The built-in Key object broadcasts two system events: onKeyUp and onKeyDown. To receive these events, you must first create an object and register it with the Key object. In this case, your custom object is named speedListener and is created using the new Object() constructor.

```
function increaseSpeed(){
        clearInterval(intervalID);
        if(intervalSpan > 0){intervalSpan -= 10};
        intervalID = setInterval(go, intervalSpan);
}


function decreaseSpeed(){
        clearInterval(intervalID);
        intervalSpan += 10;
        intervalID = setInterval(go, intervalSpan);
}


var speedListener = new Object();

speedListener.onKeyDown = function () {
        if(Key.isDown(Key.UP)){ increaseSpeed()}
        if(Key.isDown(Key.DOWN)){ decreaseSpeed()}
}
Key.addListener(speedListener);
```

You register `speedListener` with the `Key` object by passing `speedListener`'s object reference as an argument to the `Key` object's `addListener()` method.

To work, your custom object must have a method with the same name as the event you are trying to receive. Therefore, you must add an `onKeyDown` method to your `speedListener` object. This method will execute when `speedListener` receives an `onKeyDown` event.

Upon execution, the `onKeyDown` method quickly determines which button was pressed. If the up arrow was pressed, the `increaseSpeed` function is executed, incrementing the `intervalSpan` variable. Alternately, if the down arrow was pressed, the `decreaseSpeed` function is called, decrementing the `intervalSpan` variable.

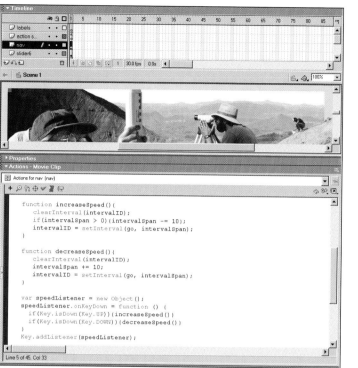

Place the `Key` event listener on **nav**.

```
function increaseSpeed(){
    clearInterval(intervalID);
    if(intervalSpan > 0){intervalSpan -= 10};
    intervalID = setInterval(go, intervalSpan);
}

function decreaseSpeed(){
    clearInterval(intervalID);
    intervalSpan += 10;
    intervalID = setInterval(go, intervalSpan);
}

var speedListener = new Object();
speedListener.onKeyDown = function () {
    if(Key.isDown(Key.UP)){increaseSpeed()}
    if(Key.isDown(Key.DOWN)){decreaseSpeed()}
}
Key.addListener(speedListener);
```

BOOKMARKING AND THE BROWSER'S BACK BUTTON

Even with control over the pace of the experience, walking through the landscape can take a while. A hurried visitor might want quick access to a section previously visited. Another visitor might want to bookmark a particular segment of the experience that he or she has found interesting. You can satisfy both visitors with Flash MX's new bookmarking feature.

Normally, allowing for bookmarks is easy. You simply add a label to a frame and check the corresponding Named Anchor box of the Property Inspector. Unfortunately, to work, named anchors require movement of the playhead across multiple frames. At first glance, this requirement seems to pose a problem for the panorama. Because it is programmatically driven, the entire experience takes place in only one frame.

As long as the sliders remain continuous across frames, however, it doesn't matter how many frames there are or where the playhead resides. You can programmatically move the playhead to different named anchors for each segment of the walkthrough. The reverse is also true. You can move the landscape in response to a change in frame location resulting from the Back button being clicked or a bookmark being loaded. Add the named anchors.

1 Select frame 40 in all of the layers. Select Insert > Frame.

Keyframe Spacing: The spacing between keyframes is arbitrary. As a matter of preference, I usually add a few more frames in between keyframes so that I can easily read the label names. Otherwise, one must roll over the keyframe and wait for a ToolTip to see the label's name.

2 Create five keyframes after frame 1 in the **labels** layer, naming them **reed**, **vondra**, **eck**, **afar**, and **kimbell** in the Property Inspector. Check the Named Anchor box for each.

Create five keyframes in the **labels** layer.

3 Create five keyframes in the **action script** layer,
corresponding to the keyframes in the **labels** layer.
Place this code in the Frame Actions panel for each
keyframe, replacing the null value of the
centeredX variable as follows:

reed	**0**
vondra	**-49**
eck	**-116**
afar	**-224**
kimbell	**-242**

```
var centeredX = null;
if(flag){
    slider1._x = centeredX;
    for(var i=2; i<=6; i++){
        this["slider"+i]._x = slider1._x * nav.multiplier[i];
    }
}
flag = true;
stop();
```

When the playhead reaches a labeled keyframe, it places all of the image layers in their correct
positions respective to the selected character in the landscape. A flag variable ensures that the
code is not repeated two times in a row.

Place the code to reposition the
landscape on each keyframe in
the **action script** layer.

4   Place this code in the `onClipEvent(load)` event handler of **nav**.

This function tests to see whether the associated person is centered onscreen. It determines this by comparing the `_x` property of `slider1` to a preselected value range. Setting the `flag` variable to `false` when moving the playhead prevents the frame script from moving the landscape while the navigation buttons are active.

```
function bookmarkTest(){
    if(_parent.slider6._x == 0){_root.flag = false; _root.gotoAndStop("reed")}
    if(_parent.slider5._x < -493 && _parent.slider5._x > -503){_root.flag =
➥false; _root.gotoAndStop("vondra")}
    if(_parent.slider4._x < -888 && _parent.slider4._x > -898){_root.flag =
➥false; _root.gotoAndStop("eck")}
    if(_parent.slider3._x < -1165 && _parent.slider3._x > -1175){_root.flag =
➥false; _root.gotoAndStop("afar")}
    if(_parent.slider6._x < -3230 && _parent.slider6._x > -3240){_root.flag =
➥false; _root.gotoAndStop("kimbell")}

}
```

The `bookmarkTest()` function constantly polls the image layers to determine when a character from the scene is centered onscreen. It then moves the playhead to that character's keyframe on the main timeline so that a bookmark can be set. Setting the `flag` variable to `false` prevents the keyframe's ActionScript from being executed.

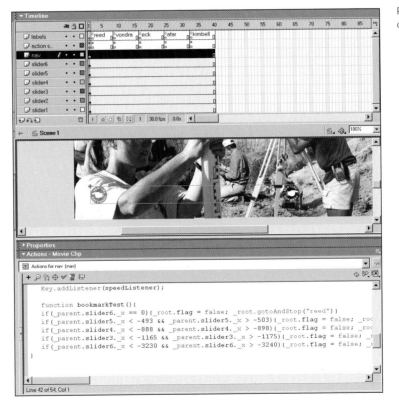

Place the bookmark testing code on **nav**.

5 Select File > Publish Settings. In the HTML tab, set the Template to Flash with Named Anchors. Select File > Publish.

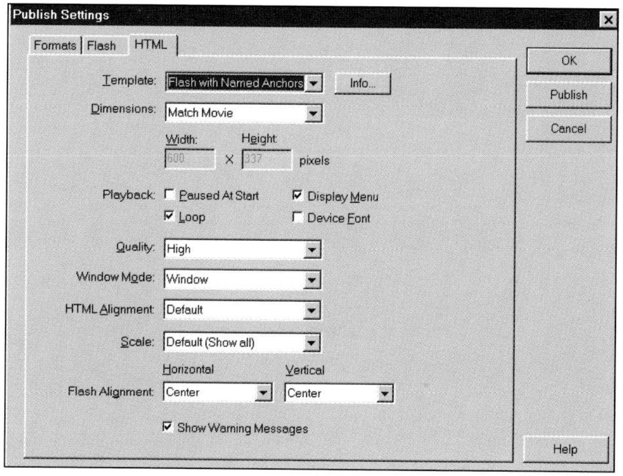

Change the publish settings to allow for bookmarking.

Publish Settings

| Formats | Flash | HTML |

Template: Flash with Named Anchors   Info...

Dimensions: Match Movie

Width: Height:
[600] X [337]   pixels

Playback: ☐ Paused At Start   ☑ Display Menu
          ☑ Loop   ☐ Device Font

Quality: High

Window Mode: Window

HTML Alignment: Default

Scale: Default (Show all)

              Horizontal   Vertical
Flash Alignment: Center   Center

☑ Show Warning Messages

OK
Publish
Cancel
Help

SUMMARY

With this simple technique, you've given the web site visitor a better window through which to view your creations. It is a window with both depth and life. Though it's not 3D in the usual sense of the word, it might just be hint enough to rekindle the simple awe we once held for nothing more than a moving landscape.

Flash's capability to communicate and talk to

JavaScript can be an extremely powerful tool.

A good example of this interaction is writing

cookies to customize and personalize your site

based on your users' needs and preferences.

Cookies are basically small bits of information

that are set on a user's system and that can

be retrieved at a later date. By integrating

Flash with cookies, you can add great features

to your site to offer more choices to your

visitors, such as storing their names, addresses,

choice of background color for the site,

favourite buttons, links, sounds, language,

bandwith details, and so on.

6

BOY NEXT WEEK

by Aria Danika

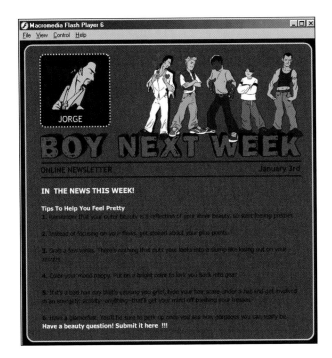

Difficulty Rating: ★★★★

Made with: Macromedia Flash MX

Final Size: 145KB

Modem Download Time: 27.6 seconds

Development Time: 3 hours

IT WORKS LIKE THIS

In this project, you will get Flash to send information to JavaScript, and JavaScript will set and get the cookies for a site called Boy Next Week that enables the user to select a particular theme. Each theme has its own style, background colour, and graphics. The user will be able to select a theme, meaning a combination of grouped elements such as background colour and images. The user's selection will then be stored in a cookie, and when the user visits the site again, the cookie will retrieve the selected theme.

Cookies are a general mechanism that server-side connections (such as CGI scripts) can use to both store and retrieve information on the client side of the connection. When a cookie arrives, your browser generally saves this information to your hard drive. When you return to that same site, some of the stored information will be sent back to the web server, along with your new request.

Flash can interact with popular web browser scripting environments such as JavaScript, and that opens many new possibilities for highly interactive and customized applications. When Flash receives the cookie information from JavaScript, it will use the variables to modify its movie. This project will also serve to demonstrate the similarities between ActionScript and JavaScript and how it's possible to extend your site with customizable features for your users without having to use complicated CGI scripting.

PREPARING TO WORK

Before starting, copy the **06_Boy_Next_Week** folder onto your hard disk, start Flash, and open the **boynextweek_start.fla** file. You'll start in the site's Homepage section, which currently has three layers. For a copy of the finished movie, you can open **boynextweek_final.fla**.

SETTING UP THE FLASH MOVIE

Let's start by setting up the Flash movie with all the graphic elements. At this stage, you need to decide which features you want to be customizable in the movie. This will enable you to determine just how many variables you need to store.

Each customizable feature (in this case, each theme) will be in its own scene. This helps organize the contents of the movie so that you know where everything is, and more importantly, it makes each section independent.

1   Add two more layers and name them **boy buttons** and **actions**.

2   Go to the **actions** layer. Add the **Stop** action to it.

3   Select the **boy buttons** layer and open the Library window. Drag these buttons and place them anywhere on the stage: casey button, jamie button, jorge button, stone button, and travis button.

4   Align the buttons as follows:

jorge   X = 241.5, Y = 30.8

casey   X = 299.9, Y = 32.1

travis   X = 364.4, Y = 29.8

jamie   X = 438.1, Y = 50.5

stone   X = 494.2, Y = 27

The Homepage section is done.

5   Select all five buttons and group them (Ctrl+G/ Cmd+G). Copy the group and paste it into the next scene (the Casey scene) on a new layer, as you did in Step 1. Align the group X = 241.5, Y = 27 and ungroup.

6   Repeat Step 5 for the remaining four scenes of the movie.

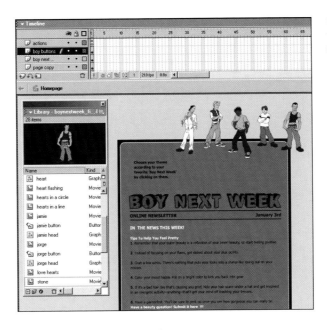

Drag and drop all five buttons onto the stage while in the Homepage section of the site.

Select a scene to edit by clicking on this drop-down menu. You have named the scenes after each boy's name: Casey, Jorge, Jamie, Travis, and Stone.

SCRIPTING THE MOVIE

With all the buttons added to all scenes, you can move on and start scripting the movie.

1   Go back to the Homepage section, select the jorge button on the stage, open the Actions panel, and add this code:

```
on (release) {
    gotoAndPlay("Jorge", 1);
    Setboy(1);
}
```

The code for the jorge button.

2   Similarly, add this code for the casey button:

```
on (release) {
    gotoAndPlay("Casey", 1);
    Setboy(2);
}
```

The code for the casey button.

3   Add this code for the travis button:

```
on (release) {
    gotoAndPlay("Travis", 1);
    Setboy(3);
}
```

The code for the travis button.

4   For the jamie button, add this code:

```
on (release) {
    gotoAndPlay("Jamie", 1);
    Setboy(4);
}
```

The code for the jamie button.

5 For the stone button, add this code:

```
on (release) {
    gotoAndPlay("Stone", 1);
    Setboy(5);
}
```

The code for the stone button.

Scripting the stone button.

6 Make sure that all the buttons in the remaining five scenes have the preceding scripts attached as well.

What you have done here is simply this: You attached an `on (release)` button event to each button that upon *release* loads the relevant scene (one of the five boys).

After the scene loads, you will call a user-defined function, `setboy`. We'll discuss how this function works in just a bit, but you should know that `setboy` will create a cookie that will be sent to the browser. This cookie will hold a value from 1-5, which will later be used to call up the right scene or theme.

The next step is to store the variable that will be used to call up the right theme and package it before the variable is sent to JavaScript. Numbering the variables will make things a lot easier later on. The Jorge scene becomes boy1, the Casey scene becomes boy2, and so on.

COMPLETING THE MOVIE

In this section, you will complete the movie by getting Flash to talk to JavaScript, which will store the variables you are sending. You will do so using the getURL() function.

1 Go to the Homepage scene and insert this code in the first frame of the Actions layer:

```
getURL("javascript:getCookie();");
boy=Number(boy);
function setboy(whatNum){
    boy=whatNum;
    getURL("javascript:setCookie();");
}
```

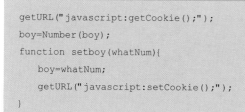

Assigning the getURL() action to keyframe 1.

The setboy function takes one parameter, a number, and is called when a user activates the mouse events on each of the boy buttons. The number is assigned to a variable called boy, and then a getURL() action calls a JavaScript function that will set a cookie on this variable.

The Flash movie is done. You can run it now and see how it works. The buttons work and load the various boy scenes. The variable is saved, and Flash then calls JavaScript both to check whether a cookie already exists and to set the cookie.

Note also, at this stage the JavaScript functions you are calling from the `getURL()` command don't exist yet, and if you test the movie now, it will not save any cookie information. If you test this movie from the authoring environment or open the .swf file directly in the player, the `getURL()` commands will cause browser windows to open for each of the JavaScript functions being called. You will build these JavaScript functions in the next section.

2 Publish your movie and open the .html.

BUILDING THE JAVASCRIPT FUNCTIONS

In this section, you will write the JavaScript functions necessary to communicate with the Flash movie so that they can accept the variables you are sending and write the cookie.

Note: Before you move on to the JavaScript functions `getCookie` and `setCookie`, review some of the basics about the JavaScript syntax:

In its simplest form, a cookie is just a name and a value, and it is set like this:

```
document.cookie = "NAME=VALUE"
```

A string is any series of characters (like "boy next week") as opposed to a number (like 9876). In JavaScript, all strings are string objects. To use the properties and methods of the string object, you need to use the following syntax:

```
stringName.propertyName
```

Or you could use the following:

```
stringName.methodName(parameters)
```

(Notice the similarities with ActionScript yet?)

In JavaScript, a string can be represented as follows:

```
var BoyNextWeek = "Jorge"
```

or

```
var BoyNextWeek = 'Jorge'
```

Here, the string `Jorge` is assigned to a variable named `BoyNextWeek`.

You can alternate between single and double quotation marks if you ever need to place one type of quotation mark within the string.

On both occassions, if we did the following:

```
document.write (BoyNextWeek)
```

It would return and display this on the screen:

```
Jorge
```

Finally, note that strings can be concatenated in JavaScript, and you can mix variables and literals using a plus (+) operator. For example:

```
var a = "Boy"
var b = "Jorge"
var c = a + " " + b + "!"
document.write (c)
```

This would give you the following:

```
Boy Jorge!
```

1 Open the .html file that you published earlier. With your text editor, start editing by inserting this script between the `</HEAD>` and `<BODY>` tags:

```
<SCRIPT LANGUAGE=JavaScript>
<!--
//
//this function calls the flash movie
//
function flashObj() {
if(navigator.appName == 'Netscape'){
return document.embeds[ 0]
} else{
return window[ 'flash']
        }
}
```

This is the function that calls the .swf file (the Flash movie) that is embedded in the .html page.

For this to work on Netscape, you have to do the following:

- Add this statement within the `<EMBED>` tag of your .html page:
  `swLiveConnect="true"`

- Type `id=flash` within the `<OBJECT>` tag.

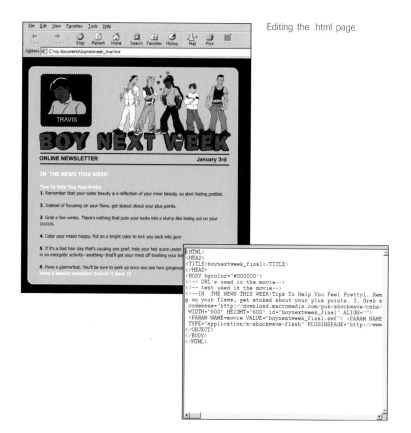

Editing the .html page.

2 Enter this code after the `flashObj()` function:

Here you need to be able to set cookies, but because there is no functionality in JavaScript that enables you to do this, you will have to script your own function.

This function sets a cookie, `name=value`, that expires after a certain period of time.

```
//
//this function sets the cookie which expires on the 13th of July 2010
//using the Date object and its methods
//
function setCookie(){
var mycookie = "boy="+flashObj().GetVariable('boy')+";";
var howlong = new Date("July 13, 2010");
howlong = howlong.toGMTString();
mycookie = mycookie+"expires="+howlong;
document.cookie = mycookie;
}
//end of function setCookie
```

```
<HTML>
<HEAD>
<TITLE>boynextweek_final</TITLE>
</HEAD>

<SCRIPT LANGUAGE=JavaScript>
<!--
//
//this function calls the flash movie
//
function flashObj() {
if(navigator.appName == 'Netscape'){
return document.embeds[0]
}else{
return window['flash']
    }
}

//
//this function sets the cookie which expires on the 13th of July 2010
//using the Date object and its methods
//
function setCookie(){
var mycookie = "boy="+flashObj().GetVariable('boy')+";";
var howlong = new Date("July 13, 2010");
howlong = howlong.toGMTString();
mycookie = mycookie+"expires="+date_string;
document.cookie = mycookie;
}
//end of function setCookie


//this is the getCookie function that restores the cookie
//
function getCookie(){
if(document.cookie == ' '){
//checks if the cookie property is empty
return;
}else{
//if not empty then sets a variable named 'boy'
flashObj().SetVariable('boy',unescape(getCookieValue('boy')));
    }
}
//end of getCookie function
```

Inserting the JavaScript functions.

3   Type in this script right after the `setCookie()` function:

In JavaScript, there is no built-in function to retrieve individual cookie values, so you need to build your own function. This function is called with a cookie name and returns the matching cookie value. The `unescape()` function is used to convert a string that has been escaped using the `escape()` function back into normal text. The `escape()` function changes non-ascii characters into ascii equivalents. For example, a blank `space()` converts into %20 when it is put through the `escape()` function. You can escape strings when you need to make sure that special characters are retained correctly, like when you need to store information as a cookie or when you're sending information over the URL.

```
//
//this is the getCookie function that restores the cookie
//
function getCookie(){
if(document.cookie == ' '){
//checks if the cookie property is empty
return;
} else{
//if not empty then sets a variable named 'boy'
flashObj().SetVariable('boy',unescape(getCookieValue('boy')));
    }
}
//end of getCookie function
```

The `getCookie` JavaScript function.

4 Add this code right after the `getCookie()` function:

What you have here is a function that accepts as a parameter the value of the variable you are passing.

Note: For the purpose of this exercise, you did not use a preloader because each section loads fairly quickly, but when you apply this on larger sites with much more content, sound, and graphics, you ought to consider building one. For Flash and JavaScript to communicate successfully, the entire movie must be downloaded, and all the variables in your Flash movie must be initialized.

You can build a preloader within your Flash movie as demonstrated in Project 3, "Preloading," or you can write a script using the JavaScript function `percentLoaded()` and insert it inside the JavaScript embedded in your .html page.

For example:

```
if (flashObj().PercentLoaded() = = 100){
myflashmovie_ready = = "true";
    }
```

In this code, `flashObj()` refers to the embedded .swf file.

```
//
//this function takes the value of the variable in the cookie
//
function getCookieValue(name){
var finalCookie = document.cookie;
//
var myfirstcook = finalCookie.indexOf(name);
//the index of function looks for the position of the character in the string
//if the result isnt -1 the character isnt in the string
if(myfirstcook != -1){
//our cookie boy=1
myfirstcook = name.length + 1;
var mylastcook = finalCookie.indexOf(';',myfirstcook);
if(mylastcook == -1){
mylastcook = finalCookie.length;
}
//returns the value of the variable
return finalCookie.substring(myfirstcook, mylastcook);
} else{
return false;
        }
}
//end
</SCRIPT>
```

The `getCookieValue` JavaScript function.

Summary

From this point, you could try to set more cookies for the movie by adding various sound clips and a section in which the user can enter his or her username, in effect customizing the movie further.

You should also consider—depending on how complex your movie gets and how many cookies you want to have—packaging your JavaScript functions as .js files.

If you have a much bigger and more complex site and have to embed your JavaScript in each .html file, packaging your scripts will make life a lot easier and will save lots of work. Each time you have to update an object or fix a bug, you won't have to update each .html file in which the object is located. Another advantage of this is that it enables you to separate your JavaScript code from your HTML. As a result, your .html files are smaller and easier to read and edit, and your JavaScript files are more manageable.

A .js file is a file that contains JavaScript code. It differs from an .html file in that it contains only JavaScript code and no <HTML>, <HEAD>, or <BODY> tags.

You include a .js file in your HTML documents using the <SCRIPT> tag, as follows:

```
<SCRIPT language="JavaScript" src="yourURL">
//
</SCRIPT>
```

You will find a .js file in the **boynextweek** folder on the accompanying CD-ROM, and it has the JavaScript functions you used here. Note that there are certain drawbacks to using JavaScript cookies. For example, some browsers either don't support them or let people turn them off. Listed here are some sites with further information on browser compatibility.

> **Note:** For reference and further reading, check out these sites:
>
> **http://www.webcoder.com/reference/2/**
> **http://developer.netscape.com/docs/manuals/**
> **http://www.builder.com**

Flash is an interactive medium used to create

compelling applications that engage the user.

Through the combination of buttons and movie

clips alone, you can add interactivity to your

site, enhance it with dynamic interfaces, and as

a result, offer a unique participatory experience.

SLIDING TRAY

by Aria Danika
with images by Sourface

Difficulty Rating: ★★★

Made With: Macromedia Flash MX

Final File Size: 35KB

Modem Download Time: 12 seconds

Development Time: 1 1/2 hours

IT WORKS LIKE THIS

With this sliding tray menu, the user can move more than one section at a time, enabling all sections to be visible.

The movie contains only two layers—the **Sections** layer and the **Handles** layer—as displayed in the main timeline of the .fla. You'll use ActionScript to drag the handles of the tray and each section.

This project covers the use of the `startDrag` and `startDrop` methods, the `attachSound` method, and `if` statements to demonstrate that although this interface utilizes some basic built-in functions, with the addition of a few lines of code, you can add logic to your application and make it smart.

You'll assign scripts to both objects and frames. The main tasks to be completed are setting up the various elements of the interface, declaring your variables, and scripting the Section Handler button and each **Section** movie clip.

PREPARING TO WORK

Before starting, copy the **07 Sliding Tray** folder onto your hard disk, start Flash, and open the initial **slidingtray_final.fla** file. Go ahead and view the completed tutorial in the authoring environment and run the movie. Choose View > Magnification > Show All. The magnified view enables you to see all the contents on the stage.

SETTING UP THE FLASH MOVIE

The sliding layered tray interface consists of four sections and three handles. **Section 1** is static and sits at the bottom. You want to be able to pick up any one of the other three sections and drag it across the X-axis.

When you pick up a section and start dragging it, you want to attach a sound clip to that action and similarly attach another sound for when you drop it. These sound clips give audio feedback to the user letting them know they are using the interface exactly as intended

If a section is being dragged, the others underneath it need to move as well.

1 Close **slidingtray_final.fla** and open **slidingtray_start.fla**.

2 Select the **Handles** layer. Open the Library and drag the **Section 2** movie clip onto the stage. Use the Properties panel to enter the coordinates X = 547.2 and Y = −0.2 to align the instance of this movie clip on the stage.

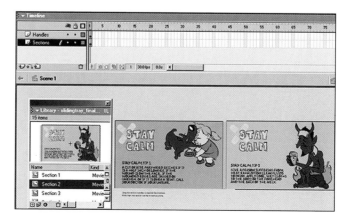

Place **Section 2** on the stage.

99

3   Do the same with the **Section 3** and **Section 4**
    movie clips. Align **Section 3** at X = 565.2, Y = –0.2.
    Align **Section 4** at X = 582.1 and Y = –0.2.

    Note that each movie clip has the Section Handle
    movie clip attached to it.

4   Name the instance of each movie clip: **Section 2**
    is Section2, **Section 3** is Section3, and **Section 4** is
    Section4.

The movie now has all four trays.

> **Note:** It's important to name the instances at
> this stage. If you forget to do this, at the end of this
> exercise the trays won't slide properly to the right
> and will slide underneath one another instead.

INITIALIZING THE MOVIE

Often, you will find that declaring variables, properties, and some functions before
your Flash movie begins to run is a useful technique. This process is called *initializing
the movie*. Here you will declare your variables in the **Section Handle** movie clip,
which you have attached to all three draggable sections.

1   Select the **Section Handle** movie clip from the
    Library. Open it in Edit mode.

    There are two layers. The **Button** layer has the
    invisible button you placed on the actual graphic.

2   Add a third layer and name it **ActionScript**. Add the
    following code to frame 1:

```
XOrigin = _parent._x;
YOrigin = _parent._y;
DragSpace = 545;
```

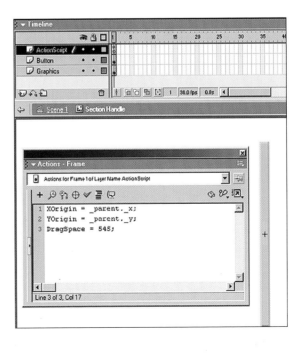

Initialize your variables
on the timeline of the
Section Handle
movie clip.

You have now declared the X and Y origin variables that store the values of the X and Y position of the movie clip and define the `DragSpace` that you want to take place. **Section 1** is 545 pixels wide, and you use this to define the space in which the movement can take place across the horizontal axis.

Stay in Edit mode; there is more to come.

SCRIPTING THE SECTION HANDLE MOVIE CLIP

It is now time to start scripting the movie clips, starting with the **Section Handle**. Here you will link two sounds from the Library by assigning linkage properties to each sound clip. You also will use the `startDrag` and `stopDrag` methods to make this movie clip draggable.

1 Select the **Latch Metal Click Verb** sound clip from the Library. Right-click/Ctrl-click to select **Linkage** and name it **Pickup**. Select the Export for ActionScript and Export in First Frame options.

2 Do the same with the **Latch Thud** sound in the Library. Set the name in the Linkage Properties dialog box to **Drop**.

Linkage properties for the sound clip **Latch Metal Click Verb**.

Note: Combining buttons and movie clips can be quite a strong technique. Embedding buttons in movie clips and vice versa enables you to create compelling and dynamic interfaces with endless possibilities. You can assign actions, for instance, to a frame, button, or movie clip that will control the movie clip (known as the controller) and then target the movie or movie clip that receives the action (known as the target movie clip).

3 Select the instance of the **Handle Button** on the stage. Open the Actions panel and add this code:

Scripts attached to buttons and movie clips execute when an event occurs. In this case, you scripted an invisible button to enable the **Section Handle** movie clip to react to mouse events. When the `press` event occurs, you want to start dragging the _parent movie clip in which the **Section Handle** movie clip is embedded. From the Library, you want to pick the sound clip you named **Pickup**.

For that, you created an instance of the `Sound` object using the constructor `new Sound` and named it **_parent.Pickup**. You then used the `attachSound` method to attach the sound specified and exported earlier.

You set the volume to 50 using one of the methods of the sound object.

Finally, in the last line, you called the `Sound` object named `Pickup` using `_parent.Pickup.start` to start playing.

Similarly, for the `release` event, you told it to stop playing when there is no dragging and to play the `Drop` sound instead. Again, you created a new instance of the `Sound` object and set the volume to 50 as before.

4 Run the movie at this stage. Test it and see what happens when you drag each section. It works fine, but there is still one problem: When you drag **Section 4**, it hides the other sections underneath it and makes it impossible to pick them up unless you drag **Section 4** back to its original position. Similar problems occur when you drag **Section 2** and **Section 3**.

```
on (press) {
    startDrag ("_parent", false, XOrigin - DragSpace, YOrigin, XOrigin, YOrigin);
    _parent.dragging = true;
    _parent.Pickup = new Sound ();
    _parent.Pickup.attachSound("Pickup");
    _parent.Pickup.setVolume(50);
    _parent.Pickup.start(0, 0);
}
on (release) {
    stopDrag();
    _parent.dragging = false;
    _parent.Drop = new Sound ();
    _parent.Drop.attachSound("Drop");
    _parent.Drop.setVolume(50);
    _parent.Drop.start(0, 0);
}
```

Scripting the Handle Button, which is embedded in the **Section Handle** movie clip.

Note: Use the default, 100, for full volume. You don't want to have a loud sound every time the user drags a section because this can be distracting. Feel free to change this if you prefer a different sound level.

SCRIPTING THE SECTIONS MOVIE CLIPS

What you want here is to be able to drag any **Section** at any time and slide it left and right. When any section has been moved to its farthest point left, it should not cover the handle of the previous section. If this happens, then you wouldn't be able to slide all of the sections back and forth all of the time.

For that you need to keep the **Section Handle** movie clip visible at all times. You'll need to script each draggable **Section** movie clip. Sections 2, 3, and 4 will use clip events that will calculate the _x property of each **Section** movie clip and compare them. Comparing the _x positions will let you decide when to stop a section movie clip from moving farther to the left and keep all of the section handles visible.

1   Go to the main movie and select the **Section 2** movie clip. Go to Edit mode.

2   Select the instance of the **Section Handle** movie clip, open the Actions panel, and add this code:

> What you have here is nested `if` statements. You first want to check whether the **Section 2** movie clip is being dragged.

3   If that condition is `true`, the next line of code is executed, and you move on to the second condition. This condition checks to see whether the _x property of the **Section 2** movie clip is greater than or equal to the _x property of the **Section 3** movie clip, minus the width of the **Section Handle** movie clip (in this case, 18 pixels). Then the _x property of the **Section 3** movie clip is equal to the _x property of the **Section 2** movie clip plus the width of the **Section Handle**. This ensures that the **Section Handle** movie clip (18×330) of **Section 2** is visible at all times.

> Similarly, for **Section 4**, if the **Section 2** movie clip is under **Section 4**, you add `2*this._width` (or 36 pixels) to ensure that **Section Handle** is visible at all times.

4   Back in the main movie, select the **Section 3** movie clip and go to Edit mode.

```
onClipEvent (enterFrame) {
    if (_root.Section2.dragging) {
        if (_root.Section2._x >= (_root.Section3._x - this._width)) {
            _root.Section3._x = _root.Section2._x + this._width;
        }
        if (_root.Section2._x >= (_root.Section4._x - (2*this._width))) {
            _root.Section4._x = _root.Section2._x + (2*this._width);
        }
    }
}
```

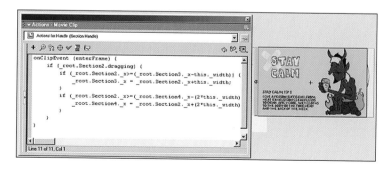

Assign a clip event to the **Section 2** movie clip.

5 Select the **Section Handle** movie clip and assign this code:

If the _x property of **Section 2** plus the width of the **Section Handle** is greater than or equal to the _x property of **Section 3** *and* the **Section 2** movie clip isn't being dragged, only then will the _x property of **Section 2** be equal to that of **Section 3** minus that width.

> **Note:** For more on the logical AND operator, check out the Reference panel from the authoring environment. It gives you additional information about the ActionScript you are entering. Simply select the action in the Actions toolbox or Script pane and click the Reference button.

6 Back in the main movie, select the **Section 4** movie clip on the stage and go to Edit mode.

7 Select the instance of the **Section Handle** movie clip nested in the **Section 4** movie clip and assign this code:

```
onClipEvent (enterFrame) {
    if (_root.Section3._x >= (_root.Section4._x - this._width)) {
        _root.Section4._x = _root.Section3._x + this._width;
    }
    if (((_root.Section2._x + this._width) >= _root.Section3._x) &&
    ➡ (_root.Section2.dragging != true)) {
        _root.Section2._x = _root.Section3._x - this._width;
    }
}
```

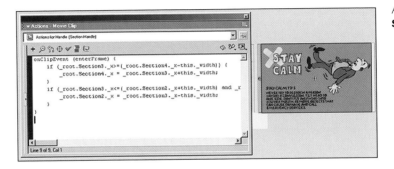

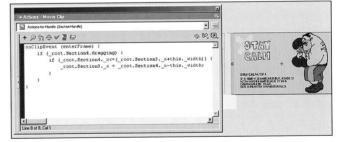

Assigning a clip event to the **Section 3** movie clip.

```
onClipEvent (enterFrame) {
    if (_root.Section4.dragging) {
        if ((_root.Section3._x + this._width) >= _root.Section4._x) {
            _root.Section3._x = _root.Section4._x - this._width;
        }
    }
}
```

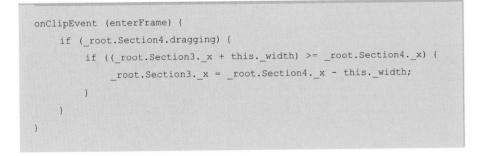

Assigning a clip event to the **Section 4** movie clip.

If the **Section 4** movie clip is being dragged, again, you ensure that the **Section Handle** of the section underneath it (**Section 3**) is visible at all times.

8 Run your movie and test it by dragging each section.
Note how it works now that you added a clip event
in each instance of Sections 2, 3 and 4.

SUMMARY

As you have seen, all the code is assigned to the **Section Handle** movie clip and
to its various instances on the stage. A movie clip is like a mini Flash movie with its
own properties, and you can build on that and extend it further to create a dynamic
interface like this sliding tray. You initialized your variables and embedded a button
that reacts to mouse movement at the very beginning so that if your variables change,
they can be easily edited if needed at a later date.

By using two key methods (startDrag and stopDrag), you were able to design
a simple yet interactive, engaging, and light interface that can be customized further
based on your needs and requirements. You could add more sections, and you could
experiment with vertical movement across the Y-axis rather than horizontal movement. You could add different sounds or have other movie clips loading when a
section is dragged. Whatever you do from here, have fun!

When considering the variety of visual

metaphors for describing sets of data,

invariably charts and graphs come to mind.

Unfortunately, with earlier versions of Flash,

you were somewhat limited by the extent to

which dynamic features could be incorporated

into your designs. However, with the introduc-

tion of several new features to Flash MX

(and improvements to a few existing features),

the barriers surrounding dynamic movies have

been substantially removed.

CHARTS AND GRAPHS

by Stephanie Novak and Eric Jordan

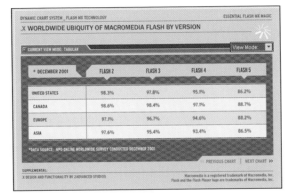

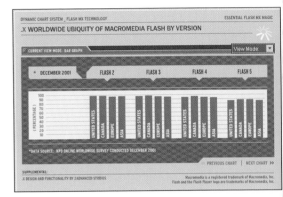

Difficulty Rating: ★★★★

Made With: Macromedia Flash MX

Final File Size: .swf = 286KB; .fla = 900KB

Modem Download Time: 56K = 39 seconds; DSL/cable/T-1 = 6 seconds

Development Time: Approximately 24 hours (3 regular workdays)

It Works Like This

In this project, you'll learn how to use the Dynamic Drawing API (a fancy term for Flash's new ActionScript drawing functions) and Flash's XML Object to create a functional movie that incorporates multiple dynamic capabilities. In all, you will learn the fundamentals to create a charting framework that enables you to do the following:

- Retrieve text and data from a data source (such as an .xml file)
- Perform accurate mathematical calculations to determine the size and bounds of visual components
- Build an interface that is technically capable of displaying calculated objects
- Use new ActionScript functions to draw graphic shapes on-the-fly while the movie is loading

Equipping yourself with the knowledge to create and deploy Flash movies in this fashion offers several key benefits. Most notably, you can virtually eliminate the frequent need to provide manual updates to your movies each time a set of data is changed. For example, say you are considering a "voting booth" feature that also provides users with the option to view the current results of the vote. Without the aid of dynamic functionality to retrieve and display the results, you would need to continually update and redeploy your movies. At best, you would be offering "near" real-time results. However, a properly constructed Flash movie that makes use of the functions described in this project provides true real-time results without the need for constant manual maintenance.

This project utilizes the adoption statistics data for the Flash Player, which is publicly available on Macromedia's web site at **www.macromedia.com/ software/player_census/flashplayer/**. For anyone involved with the creation and deployment of Flash–based solutions, this information is truly invaluable. The decisions surrounding which web technologies to leverage are often made without a solid understanding of browser capabilities. However, thanks to the good folks at Macromedia, you have a regularly updated resource of information showing the adoption rate of the Flash Player.

In consideration of the data set that has been selected, this charting project consists of a simple user interface from which two different chart types can be selected and viewed: tabular or bar graph. A tabular chart is much like an Excel spreadsheet in its presentation of raw data in standard table form. You are probably most familiar with a bar graph chart, which visually displays data in shaded rectangular regions, or bars. Because the Macromedia statistics are actually representative of three different studies (with each study being conducted on a different date), the data has been broken up into three separate charts that correspond to the date of the study. For navigation purposes, Previous Chart and Next Chart buttons were added to the lower-right of the interface, enabling users to quickly move from one study to the next.

Preparing to Work

Before starting, you'll need to copy the **08_Charts_Graphs** folder onto your hard disk, start Flash, and open the **Dynamic_Chart_Start.fla** file, which is the Flash file you will be working from. The completed Flash file is **Dynamic_Chart.fla**.

Designing the Shell Interface

With any new project, the daunting empty white stage provides arguably the most frightening moments (or even hours) of realization, in which decisions that determine the ultimate success or failure of a project must be made. Accordingly, it is important to follow a well-structured methodology that offers the best chance for success. The following describes the steps we went through.

To begin, we considered the overall task at hand, recognizing that we would need to build an easy-to-use interface with the lion's share of space allocated for our charts and graphs. In this case, the data set being used is conveniently based on percentages, with the maximum being 100. In other words, all of the data can easily be divided by 10. With this in mind, the area of our movie that is responsible for displaying the chart should be constructed in 100-pixel height increments. The following are the steps we took:

1   The overall size requirements for the movie have been set, a Frame Rate has been selected, and an appropriate background color has been chosen.

Here, the size is 671×444 pixels, the frame rate is 27fps, and the background color is #4F6273. At this point, the color scheme to be used throughout the movie has been determined.

2   Designed the shell of the interface—essentially, built the overall look and feel of the project. Placed text fields for labels and titles, drew frames and bounding boxes, introduced graphic eye-candy elements, and set the background in place.

We weren't too concerned with the actual chart itself just yet (although we set a placeholder shape for the chart area). The chart will ideally be placed inside a separate movie clip rather than directly on the main timeline. The shell of the interface is straightforward and will require few dynamic elements.

3   Thoroughly ran through the shell interface and converted each element to a symbol on its own layer, since we had a clear idea of our design in mind. Named each layer for reference purposes.

4   Introduced our opening sequence animations for the shell interface. Starting with frame 1, worked our way through animating each layer to our satisfaction. Here, we relied on our own creativity and style to guide us through the process. Opening animations are a process of trial and error. This would be a good time for you to review the completed Flash file for several examples of how opening sequence animations can be created and combined.

Note: To easily define colors for shapes and text used throughout the movie and to enforce consistency in the color scheme, all of the colors to be used have been selected from the Color Mixer panel and added as a swatch.

You should work through them until you are
completely satisfied with the motion and order of
events. For reference purposes, in the project's movie
the opening animation sequence can roughly be
defined as the animations occurring during playback
of the first 37 frames of the movie.

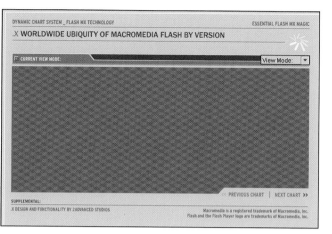

Designing the shell interface.

ADDING THE DYNAMIC COMPONENTS

With the design of the shell interface complete, we've created and added the essential
dynamic elements that control various functions of the chart. Two navigational buttons
(Next Chart and Previous Chart, each instances of the advancebuttons symbol) enable
the user to easily move between the various charts. A ComboBox component (one of
the new components in Flash MX) enables the user to select between the two chart
types: Tabular View and Bar Graph View. Finally, we created a chart movie clip called
ChartClip, which will be used to animate and display the XML data.

Now it's time for you to add some logic to the navigational buttons.

1 When viewing the first chart, you want the user to
be able to navigate to the second chart. In frame 38
of the **Next_Button** layer, select the NextChart
instance of the advancebuttons symbol. Add the
following ActionScript, using the Actions panel:

```
on (release)
{
    gotoAndPlay("chart2");
}
```

109

2 When viewing the second chart, you want the user to be able to navigate back to the first chart. In frame 52 of the **Prev_Button** layer, select the PreviousChart instance of the advancebuttons symbol. Add the following:

```
on (release)
{
    gotoAndPlay("chart1");
}
```

3 You also want the user to be able to navigate to the third chart. In frame 52 of the **Next_Button** layer, select the NextChart instance of the advancebuttons symbol. Add the following:

```
on (release)
{
    gotoAndPlay("chart3");
}
```

4 Finally, when viewing the third chart, you want the user to be able to navigate back to the second chart. In frame 66 of the **Prev_Button** layer, select the PreviousChart instance of the advancebuttons symbol. Add the following :

```
on (release)
{
    gotoAndPlay("chart2");
}
```

Next, configure the properties of the ComboBox. The displayed labels for the ComboBox have been previously set to display View Mode, Tabular, and BarGraph.

5 To set the corresponding Data values for the preceding labels, in frame 38 of the **ViewModeSelection** layer, select the ComboxBox component. In the Properties panel, double-click the values for data, or click once and then click on the magnifying glass, to bring up a pop-up panel. For value 1, enter **TabularMode**; for value 2, enter **BarGraphMode**. Leave value 0 blank.

6 To set the ChangeHandler, which specifies the ActionScript function to be called when the value of the ComboBox has been changed, select the ChangeHandler in the Properties panel. Enter **viewModeHandler**. You'll define the function later in the project.

7   With ActionScript, you also have the capability to customize the look and feel of the ComboBox component. For example, let's change the text color from the default color of black to blue. Since the ComboBox component is placed on the stage in frame 38 of the **ViewModeSelection** layer, add the following ActionScript, to frame 38 of the Actions layer, using the Actions panel:

```
chartmodebox.setStyleProperty("textColor", 0x4F6172);
```

Note: Optionally, you can customize components directly through the Library to ensure that all instances of a component inherit your changes. However, a full discussion of this process is beyond the scope of this project.

Finally, add three instances of the **ChartClip** to the main timeline for the three separate graphs.

8   For the first chart, highlight frames 38 to 51 of the **ChartClip1** layer. From the Library panel, drag an instance of the ChartClip symbol onto the stage. In the Properties panel, set the X and Y positions of the clip to 335.3 and 213.9, respectively. Then set the instance name to **ChartClip1**.

9   For the second chart, highlight frames 52 to 65 of the **ChartClip2** layer. From the Library panel, drag another instance of the ChartClip symbol onto the stage. In the Properties panel, set the X and Y positions of the clip to 335.3 and 213.9, respectively. Then set the instance name to **ChartClip2**.

10 For the third chart, highlight frames 66 to 80 of the **ChartClip3** layer. From the Library panel, drag one more instance of the ChartClip symbol onto the stage. In the Properties panel, set the X and Y positions of the clip to 335.3 and 213.9, respectively. Then set the instance name to **ChartClip3**.

ADDING ACTIONSCRIPT TO CONTROL THE COMBOBOX COMPONENT

Now that you have the overall interface and have properly placed your elements, the next step is to add some programming logic (ActionScript) to control the different view modes for the charts. You will begin this process by adding all of the ActionScript routines to control the ComboBox component. As previously stated, the ComboBox component is used to control the View mode of your project, switching between Tabular and Bar Graph modes.

1 You'll need a variable that holds the current View mode value. Initially, you'll want to set the view mode to TabularMode. In frame 1 of the **Actions** layer, add the following ActionScript at the top of the page, using the Actions panel:

```
viewMode = "TabularMode";
```

2 Another variable you'll need is one to hold the value of the current chart clip that's being viewed. In the frame where each instance of the three **ChartClip** movies are initially placed on the stage, you'll assign the instance name to the variable.

In frame 38 of the **Actions** layer, add the following for the first chart:

```
currentChart = ChartClip1;
```

In frame 52 of the **Actions** layer, add the following for the second chart:

```
currentChart = ChartClip2;
```

In frame 66 of the **Actions** layer, add the following for the third chart:

```
currentChart = ChartClip3;
```

3 Now you can define the `ChangeHandler` function for the ComboBox, which earlier you had set to `viewModeHandler`. In frame 1 of the **Actions** layer, add the following ActionScript to the bottom of the Actions Panel:

```
function viewModeHandler(component)
{
    // Don't process the "View Mode:" label
    if (component.getSelectedIndex() != 0)
    {
        // Save the selected View Mode
        viewMode = component.getSelectedItem().data;
        // Reset combo box to "View Mode:"
        component.setSelectedIndex(0);
        // Change the chart to display in the selected View Mode
        currentChart.gotoAndPlay(1);
    }
}
```

The function is automatically called each time a user selects a value in the ComboBox component. In short, if the View mode label is selected, the function ignores the selection, given that only Tabular and BarGraph are valid views. If a valid View mode is selected, the data value (TabularMode or BarGraphMode) is assigned to the `viewMode` variable. Then the current chart is redisplayed using the appropriate `viewMode` value.

Defining `ChangeHandler` for the ComboBox.

4   Finally, you're ready to make the view modes all
come together. Within the chart clip, you'll add
some ActionScript to display the correct view mode
of the chart, using the main timeline's `viewMode`
value, which you assigned in the preceding step.
Open the ChartClip symbol for editing and add the
following ActionScript to frame 1 of the **Actions**
layer, beneath the code that is already on the frame:

```
gotoAndPlay(_parent.viewMode);
```

This enables the **ChartClip** movie to determine after
it is launched whether it should be playing from the
TabularMode label or from the BarGraphMode label.

ADDING ACTIONSCRIPT TO IMPORT XML DATA

Although the amount of ActionScipt code actually required for the task to import
XML data from a file might seem somewhat cumbersome at first, the principles are
really quite easy to grasp with a little practice. The ActionScript for this section in
frame 1 of the main timeline has already been added, and for clarification, you will
now be given an explanation of the code.

Initially, a class (or object) was created to hold the data for each chart.

> **Note:** If you're unfamiliar with functions and constructors, the next set of code
> might be somewhat daunting. In short, a *function* is basically a group of programming
> statements that can be called to perform a series of tasks on a set of data. In Flash
> MX, a *constructor* (or class) gives you the ability to create custom attributes for
> an object.
>
> For example, assume you have a class called FlashGuy. Some of the attributes
> you could give a FlashGuy object might include height, weight, and age. After you
> create an instance of the FlashGuy class, perhaps calling your instance Bill or Ted,
> you would then have access to the new attributes: Bill.Height, Ted.Weight, Bill.Age,
> and so on. Confused yet? In reality, these concepts are not simple enough to grasp
> in a short note. However, you should be aware that functions and constructors
> can go a long way toward simplifying your code and reducing the burden of
> complex maintenance.

The class is defined by the following function, along with approximately 26 different attributes that are initialized and later accessed.

```
function ChartData()
{
    this.monthyear = "";
    this.datasource = "";
    this.versionA = "";
    this.versionB = "";
    this.versionC = "";
    this.versionD = "";
    this.area1 = "";
    this.area2 = "";
    this.area3 = "";
    this.area4 = "";
    this.area1_versionA = "";
    this.area2_versionA = "";
    this.area3_versionA = "";
    this.area4_versionA = "";
    this.area1_versionB = "";
    this.area2_versionB = "";
    this.area3_versionB = "";
    this.area4_versionB = "";
    this.area1_versionC = "";
    this.area2_versionC = "";
    this.area3_versionC = "";
    this.area4_versionC = "";
    this.area1_versionD = "";
    this.area2_versionD = "";
    this.area3_versionD = "";
    this.area4_versionD = "";
}
```

Immediately following the class definition for
ChartData, a class method was defined that will be
used to format various data attributes after they have
been read in from the .xml file. This ensures that all
data is presented consistently. It should be noted that it is
traditionally appropriate to place a method right next to a
corresponding class function to enhance readability.

```
ChartData.prototype.formatData = function()
{
    this.monthyear = this.monthyear.toUpperCase();
    if (this.datasource != "")
        this.datasource = this.datasource.toUpperCase() + " CONDUCTED " + this.monthyear;
    this.area1 = this.area1.toUpperCase();
    this.area2 = this.area2.toUpperCase();
    this.area3 = this.area3.toUpperCase();
    this.area4 = this.area4.toUpperCase();
    this.versionA = this.versionA.toUpperCase();
    this.versionB = this.versionB.toUpperCase();
    this.versionC = this.versionC.toUpperCase();
    this.versionD = this.versionD.toUpperCase();
}
```

Now that the ChartData class and its relevant methods
have been defined, three instances of the object were
subsequently created and placed after the default setting
of the View Mode. In essence, each instance will be
used to represent the complete data set for each of the
three charts. The following code instantiates the three
class objects:

```
chart1Data = new ChartData();
chart2Data = new ChartData();
chart3Data = new ChartData();
```

Having created the necessary instances of the `ChartData` class, you're now ready to read in the data from the external .xml file. For reference, a single data record in the .xml file is presented in the following code. The complete .xml file can be viewed in the file **chartData.xml**.

```xml
<charts>
    <chart monthyear="December 2001" datasource="NPD Online Worldwide Survey">
        <areas>
            <area1>United States</area1>
            <area2>Canada</area2>
            <area3>Europe</area3>
            <area4>Asia</area4>
        </areas>
        <versions>
            <versionA>Flash 2</versionA>
            <versionB>Flash 3</versionB>
            <versionC>Flash 4</versionC>
            <versionD>Flash 5</versionD>
        </versions>
        <percentages>
            <area1_versionA>98.3</area1_versionA>
            <area1_versionB>97.8</area1_versionB>
            <area1_versionC>95.1</area1_versionC>
            <area1_versionD>86.2</area1_versionD>
            <area2_versionA>98.6</area2_versionA>
            <area2_versionB>98.4</area2_versionB>
            <area2_versionC>97.1</area2_versionC>
            <area2_versionD>88.7</area2_versionD>
            <area3_versionA>97.1</area3_versionA>
            <area3_versionB>96.7</area3_versionB>
            <area3_versionC>94.6</area3_versionC>
            <area3_versionD>88.2</area3_versionD>
            <area4_versionA>97.6</area4_versionA>
            <area4_versionB>95.4</area4_versionB>
            <area4_versionC>93.4</area4_versionC>
            <area4_versionD>86.5</area4_versionD>
        </percentages>
    </chart>
</charts>
```

At first glance, it is really quite easy to understand the formatting and structure given how closely an XML record resembles traditional HTML tags. At the time your movie loads (or at any other time you see fit), it will only take a single line of code in the Flash document to start the process of running the various read and parse functions for the XML data file, which has been defined as follows:

```
getChartData();
```

Now you're ready to actually define the function, back in the actions on frame 1. (Note that you can actually call a function before it has been defined.) The function is coded as follows:

```
function getChartData()
{
    xmlData = new XML();
    xmlData.ignoreWhite = 1;
    xmlData.load("chartData.xml");
    xmlData.onLoad = parseData;
}
```

This function tells Flash first to create an XML Object reference in memory and then to ignore any whitespace it might encounter while reading the XML data file. This is followed by a statement to actually load the file titled **chartData.xml**. Finally, it executes the parseData function after the load process has been completed.

XML parsing is a technical term to describe the task of pulling each element of data out of an XML data file, processing the data, and then placing the data into variables (or, in this case, the instances of your class objects previously defined). To accomplish this task, the following function is defined:

```
function parseData()
{
    chartCount = 0;    // Chart count
    chartNodes = new Array();
    chartNodes = xmlData.firstChild.childNodes;
    // Process each chart
    for (i = 0; i < chartNodes.length; i++)
    {
        if (chartNodes[ i] .nodeName != null)
        {
            chartCount++;    // Increment chart count
            chartNode = chartNodes[ i] ;    // chart node
            // Get the month/year and datasource
            set("chart" + chartCount + "Data.monthyear",
            ➥chartNode.attributes.monthyear);
            set("chart" + chartCount + "Data.datasource",
            ➥chartNode.attributes.datasource);
            children = new Array();
            children = chartNode.childNodes;
            // Process areas, version, and percentages
            for (j = 0; j < children.length; j++)
            {
                if (children[ j] .nodeName != null)
                {
                    // Process the node and store the data
                    processNode(eval("chart" + chartCount + "Data"),
                    ➥children[ j] );
                }
            }
        }
    }
    // Format the data
    chart1Data.formatData();
    chart2Data.formatData();
    chart3Data.formatData();
}
```

Running through the code, the initialization of the `chartCount` variable serves as an index to indicate which `chartXData` is currently being parsed (`chart1Data`, `chart2Data`, or `chart3Data`). The code then gets all the `childNodes`, which are the nodes for each chart. (*Nodes* is another term for XML tags/elements, such as charts, areas, versions, and percentages.) For each chart node, its child nodes are then processed and stored. After the data for all the charts has been read in and stored, the data is formatted using the `formatData()` object method that was previously defined while creating the class.

The remaining functions in this frame were defined to support the preceding function. The first function listed utilizes the parameters (chart, node) that are passed from the `parseData()` function to determine which node type is being processed and to call the appropriate functions to actually handle the processing and assigning of data to the passed-in chart. The `switch` statement was utilized to easily handle the logic.

Note: The `switch` statement is a much cleaner way of handling multiple `If...Else If` statements. The `switch` statement evaluates a variable and calls the appropriate `case` statement, depending on the value of the variable. If the value of the variable doesn't match any of the specified `case` statements, the default `case` is called. Once a `case` statement has been matched, the corresponding statements following the `case` statement are executed.

```
function processNode(chart, node)
{
    switch(node.nodeName)
    {
        case "areas":        processAreas(chart, node);
                             break;
        case "versions":     processVersions(chart, node);
                             break;
        case "percentages":  processPercentages(chart, node);
                             break;
        default:             break;
    }
}
```

Next, the following three functions referenced from the previous function were defined. The first function is responsible for processing and assigning the data associated with geographic regions (that is, the United States, Asia, and so on). All the area nodes are retrieved and evaluated. They are then assigned appropriately according to which area is being processed.

```
function processAreas(chart, node)
{
    areas = new Array();
    areas = node.childNodes;
    for (n = 0; n < areas.length; n++)
    {
        if (areas[n].nodeName == null)
            continue;

        value = areas[n].firstChild.nodeValue;
        switch(areas[n].nodeName)
        {
            case "area1": chart.area1 = value;
                        break;
            case "area2": chart.area2 = value;
                        break;
            case "area3": chart.area3 = value;
                        break;
            case "area4": chart.area4 = value;
                        break;
            default:      break;
        }
    }
}
```

The second function is responsible for processing and assigning data associated with the various versions of the Flash Player (that is, Flash 4, Flash 5, and so on). All the version nodes are retrieved and evaluated. They are then assigned appropriately according to which version is being processed.

```
function processVersions(chart, node)
{
    versions = new Array();
    versions = node.childNodes;
    for (n = 0; n < versions.length; n++)
    {
        if (versions[n].nodeName == null)
            continue;

        value = versions[n].firstChild.nodeValue;
        switch(versions[n].nodeName)
        {
            case "versionA": chart.versionA = value;
                             break;
            case "versionB": chart.versionB = value;
                             break;
            case "versionC": chart.versionC = value;
                             break;
            case "versionD": chart.versionD = value;
                             break;
            default:         break;
        }
    }
}
```

The last function is responsible for handling and assigning the raw data relative to an area and a version. All the percentage nodes are retrieved and evaluated. They are then assigned appropriately according to which area and version are being processed.

```
function processPercentages(chart, node)
{
    percentages = new Array();
    percentages = node.childNodes;
    for (n = 0; n < percentages.length; n++)
    {
        if (percentages[n].nodeName == null)
            continue;

        value = percentages[n].firstChild.nodeValue;
        switch(percentages[n].nodeName)
        {
            case "area1_versionA":
                        chart.area1_versionA = value;
                        break;
```

```
                case "area1_versionB":
                        chart.area1_versionB = value;
                        break;
                case "area1_versionC":
                        chart.area1_versionC = value;
                        break;
                case "area1_versionD":
                        chart.area1_versionD = value;
                        break;
                case "area2_versionA":
                        chart.area2_versionA = value;
                        break;
                case "area2_versionB":
                        chart.area2_versionB = value;
                        break;
                case "area2_versionC":
                        chart.area2_versionC = value;
                        break;
                case "area2_versionD":
                        chart.area2_versionD = value;
                        break;
                case "area3_versionA":
                        chart.area3_versionA = value;
                        break;
                case "area3_versionB":
                        chart.area3_versionB = value;
                        break;
                case "area3_versionC":
                        chart.area3_versionC = value;
                        break;
                case "area3_versionD":
                        chart.area3_versionD = value;
                        break;
                case "area4_versionA":
                        chart.area4_versionA = value;
                        break;
                case "area4_versionB":
                        chart.area4_versionB = value;
                        break;
                case "area4_versionC":
                        chart.area4_versionC = value;
                        break;
                case "area4_versionD":
                        chart.area4_versionD = value;
                        break;
                default:    break;
        }
    }
}
```

ADDING ACTIONSCRIPT TO ASSIGN THE DATA

Now that all of the ActionScript is in place to read and parse the data from an .xml file (specifically **chartData.xml**) into the appropriate instances of the chartData class object, you are ready to assign or pass the data to each **ChartClip** movie instance you added during the design portion of this project. On the load of each instance of the **ChartClip** movie, you want to assign the data for it with the appropriate instance of the chartData class object read in from the previous section.

1. Beginning on the main timeline of your movie, in frame 38 of the **ChartClip1** layer, select the **ChartClip** movie clip instance, **ChartClip1**, positioned on the stage. Open your Actions panel, and you should be successfully in position to edit your movie clip actions. For this instance, add the following ActionScript:

```
onClipEvent (load) {
    chartData = _root.chart1Data;
}
```

2. In frame 52 of the **ChartClip2** layer, select the **ChartClip** instance, **ChartClip2**, and add the following ActionScript:

```
onClipEvent(load) {
    chartData = _root.chart2Data;
}
```

3. In frame 66 of the **ChartClip3** layer, select the **ChartClip** instance, **ChartClip3**, and add the following ActionScript:

```
onClipEvent(load) {
    chartData = _root.chart3Data;
}
```

Return now to the **ChartClip** movie clip for editing. On frame 1 of the **Actions** layer, the following ActionScript was inserted for variable assignments. The variables correspond to the dynamic text fields displayed in the chart.

```
monthyear = chartData.monthyear;
datasource = chartData.datasource;
versionA = chartData.versionA;
versionB = chartData.versionB;
versionC = chartData.versionC;
versionD = chartData.versionD;
area1 = chartData.area1;
area2 = chartData.area2;
area3 = chartData.area3;
area4 = chartData.area4;
```

In this movie clip, you'll also see 16 instances of the **Percentage_Field_Clip** movie clip, which is used to display the percentage in the Tabular view mode. On the load event for each instance of the **Percentage_Field_Clip** movie, you'll see the following similar ActionScript, which assigns the formatted percentage to the dynamic percentage text field within the movie.

```
onClipEvent (load) {
        percentage = _root.formatPercentage (_parent.chartData.area1_versionA);
}
```

Finally, as you might have noticed in the previous step, a new function was referenced. The `formatPercentage()` function is responsible for evaluating a number to add a percentage sign (%)—or if there is no data available, to return the value as is. The following code can be found in frame 1 of the main timeline **Actions** layer, following the chartData prototype and objects:

```
function formatPercentage(amount) {
    if (amount != "")
        return(amount + "%");
    else
        return(amount);
}
```

ADDING DYNAMIC DRAWING API ACTIONSCRIPT

You are almost done! There is just one more task to perform in ActionScript before you are on your way to an endless pursuit of dynamic charting. At this point, the TabularMode chart is complete and should run without error. However, your BarGraphMode is unfortunately missing its bars. Thus enters the Dynamic Drawing API, a new feature to Flash MX, consisting of several new functions that enable you to take programmatic control over shapes, lines, colors, fills, and more—in essence, the capability to draw right from ActionScript.

You've previously added the calls to draw the 16 bars, assuming data exists for these bars. To see the following ActionScript, open the **ChartClip** movie clip for editing, select frame 46 (which should be the first frame of the BarGraphMode label) of the **Actions** layer, and view the Actions panel.

```
depth = 0;

if ((chartData.area1_versionA != "") && ((new Number(chartData.area1_versionA)).valueOf() > 0))
{
    createEmptyMovieClip("Area1VersionA", ++depth);
    drawBar(Area1VersionA, 1, 1, chartData.area1_versionA, chartData.area1);
}
if ((chartData.area2_versionA != "") && ((new Number(chartData.area2_versionA)).valueOf() > 0))
{
    createEmptyMovieClip("Area2VersionA", ++depth);
    drawBar(Area2VersionA, 1, 2, chartData.area2_versionA, chartData.area2);
}
if ((chartData.area3_versionA != "") && ((new Number(chartData.area3_versionA)).valueOf() > 0))
{
    createEmptyMovieClip("Area3VersionA", ++depth);
    drawBar(Area3VersionA, 1, 3, chartData.area3_versionA, chartData.area3);
}
if ((chartData.area4_versionA != "") && ((new Number(chartData.area4_versionA)).valueOf() > 0))
{
    createEmptyMovieClip("Area4VersionA", ++depth);
    drawBar(Area4VersionA, 1, 4, chartData.area4_versionA, chartData.area4);
}
if ((chartData.area1_versionB != "") && ((new Number(chartData.area1_versionB)).valueOf() > 0))
{
```

```
    createEmptyMovieClip("Area1VersionB", ++depth);
    drawBar(Area1VersionB, 2, 1, chartData.area1_versionB, chartData.area1);
}
if ((chartData.area2_versionB != "") && ((new Number(chartData.area2_versionB)).valueOf() > 0))
{
    createEmptyMovieClip("Area2VersionB", ++depth);
    drawBar(Area2VersionB, 2, 2, chartData.area2_versionB, chartData.area2);
}
if ((chartData.area3_versionB != "") && ((new Number(chartData.area3_versionB)).valueOf() > 0))
{
    createEmptyMovieClip("Area3VersionB", ++depth);
    drawBar(Area3VersionB, 2, 3, chartData.area3_versionB, chartData.area3);
}
if ((chartData.area4_versionB != "") && ((new Number(chartData.area4_versionB)).valueOf() > 0))
{

    createEmptyMovieClip("Area4VersionB", ++depth);
    drawBar(Area4VersionB, 2, 4, chartData.area4_versionB, chartData.area4);
}
if ((chartData.area1_versionC != "") && ((new Number(chartData.area1_versionC)).valueOf() > 0))
{
    createEmptyMovieClip("Area1VersionC", ++depth);
    drawBar(Area1VersionC, 3, 1, chartData.area1_versionC, chartData.area1);
}
if ((chartData.area2_versionC != "") && ((new Number(chartData.area2_versionC)).valueOf() > 0))
{
    createEmptyMovieClip("Area2VersionC", ++depth);
    drawBar(Area2VersionC, 3, 2, chartData.area2_versionC, chartData.area2);
}
if ((chartData.area3_versionC != "") && ((new Number(chartData.area3_versionC)).valueOf() > 0))
{
    createEmptyMovieClip("Area3VersionC", ++depth);
    drawBar(Area3VersionC, 3, 3, chartData.area3_versionC, chartData.area3);
}
if ((chartData.area4_versionC != "") && ((new Number(chartData.area4_versionC)).valueOf() > 0))
{
    createEmptyMovieClip("Area4VersionC", ++depth);
    drawBar(Area4VersionC, 3, 4, chartData.area4_versionC, chartData.area4);
}
```

continues

127

continued

```
if ((chartData.area1_versionD != "") && ((new Number(chartData.area1_versionD)).valueOf() > 0))
{
    createEmptyMovieClip("Area1VersionD", ++depth);
    drawBar(Area1VersionD, 4, 1, chartData.area1_versionD, chartData.area1);
}
if ((chartData.area2_versionD != "") && ((new Number(chartData.area2_versionD)).valueOf() > 0))
{
    createEmptyMovieClip("Area2VersionD", ++depth);
    drawBar(Area2VersionD, 4, 2, chartData.area2_versionD, chartData.area2);
}
if ((chartData.area3_versionD != "") && ((new Number(chartData.area3_versionD)).valueOf() > 0))
{
    createEmptyMovieClip("Area3VersionD", ++depth);
    drawBar(Area3VersionD, 4, 3, chartData.area3_versionD, chartData.area3);
}
if ((chartData.area4_versionD != "") && ((new Number(chartData.area4_versionD)).valueOf() > 0))
{
    createEmptyMovieClip("Area4VersionD", ++depth);
    drawBar(Area4VersionD, 4, 4, chartData.area4_versionD, chartData.area4);
}
```

Essentially, this lengthy routine is responsible for traversing through every combination of area and version data to see if data actually exists. This is particularly important given the absence of one line of data in the third chart. If data is present, the ActionScript will then create an empty movie clip and place an instance of that empty movie clip onto the stage. The purpose of the movie clip is to provide a container for the Drawing API to do its magic. Following the successful creation of an empty movie clip, the drawBar() function is called to execute the underlying calculations and drawing routines. One important consideration to keep in mind at this point is that each newly created movie clip must be placed at its own depth. Therefore, at the start of the routine, depth is initialized to 0 and is incremented each time an empty movie clip is created.

Now it is necessary to define the drawBar() function, which is responsible for handling all Drawing API activities and calculations.

1　The parameters passed into the function are the movie clip in which to draw the bar, the number of the set of bars in which this bar resides, the number within the set of bars that is this bar's number, the percentage data, and the label that the bar will display. Therefore, in frame 46 of the **Actions** layer of the **ChartClip** movie, append the following initial definition for the function in the Actions panel below the existing code:

```
function drawBar(clip, groupNum, barNum, percentage, label) {

}
```

2　To initialize the variables used within the function, insert the following ActionScript within the function:

The initX and initY values are the X and Y values for the first bar. Each X and Y for the subsequent bars will be based on these values, depending on their position. barWidth is the width of each bar in pixels. barSpace is the space between each bar. groupSpace is the space between each group/set of bars. numPerGroup is the number of bars per group/set. The remaining variables determine the attributes of the line and fill for the drawing of the bar.

```
// Initialize variables
initX = -142;
initY = 95;
barWidth = 16;
barSpace = 7;
groupSpace = 19;
numPerGroup = 4;
lineColor = 0x5E7182;
fillColor = 0x5E7182;
lineAlpha = 100;
fillAlpha = 100;
lineWidth = 1;
```

3　Next you will position the bar's movie clip on the screen, utilizing which bar you are drawing within the group, the bar width, and the bar and group spacing. Following the preceding code and still within the function, add the following ActionScript:

```
// Position the movie clip containing the bar
clip._x = initX
        + ((groupNum - 1) * groupSpace)
        + ((((groupNum - 1) * numPerGroup) + barNum - 1) * (barWidth +
        ➥barSpace));
clip._y = initY;
```

4   Now it's time to utilize the Drawing API to draw the actual bar. Add the following ActionScript after the preceding code inside the function:

First you set a start for X and Y within the new movie clip to 0,0. To set the fill attributes and the line style, use the `beginFill()` and the `lineStyle()` functions, respectively. To begin drawing the bar, set the initial starting point to the bottom-left corner of the bar, using the `moveTo()` function. Then use the `lineTo()` function to draw a line to the top-left corner of the bar, and again to draw the top-right corner and the bottom-right corner. To complete the bar, use the function call to go back to the initial starting point. Then call the `endFill()` function to stop filling the bar.

5   Lastly, you need to label the bar with the area. Do this by creating and attaching the **BarLabelClip** movie clip and setting the dynamic area text field to the area label. Add the following ActionScript after the preceding code:

```
// Attach bar label
clip.attachMovie("BarLabelClip",
➥"areaName", 0);
clip.areaName._x = startX + 1;
clip.areaName._y = startY;
clip.areaName.area = label;
```

```
// Draw the bar
startX = 0;
startY = 0;
with (clip) {
    _alpha = 0;
    beginFill(fillColor, fillAlpha);
    lineStyle(lineWidth, lineColor, lineAlpha);
    moveTo(startX, startY + 1);        // Start 1 pixel below to fix a bug where
                                       // a white pixel is at the starting point
    lineTo(startX, startY - percentage);
    lineTo(startX + barWidth, startY - percentage);
    lineTo(startX + barWidth, startY);
    lineTo(startX, startY);
    endFill();
}
```

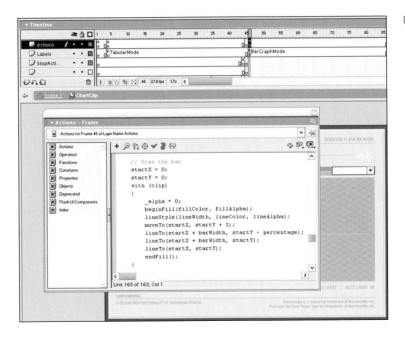

Drawing the bar.

The complete drawBar() function should look as follows:

```
function drawBar(clip, groupNum, barNum, percentage, label)
{
    // Initialize variables
    initX = -142;
    initY = 95;
    barWidth = 16;
    barSpace = 7;
    groupSpace = 19;
    numPerGroup = 4;
    lineColor = 0x5E7182;
    fillColor = 0x5E7182;
    lineAlpha = 100;
    fillAlpha = 100;
    lineWidth = 1;

    // Position the movie clip containing the bar
    clip._x = initX
        + ((groupNum - 1) * groupSpace)
        + ((((groupNum - 1) * numPerGroup) + barNum - 1) * (barWidth +
        ➥barSpace));
    clip._y = initY;

    // Draw the bar
    startX = 0;
    startY = 0;
    with (clip)
    {
        _alpha = 0;
        beginFill(fillColor, fillAlpha);
        lineStyle(lineWidth, lineColor, lineAlpha);
        moveTo(startX, startY + 1);        // Start 1 pixel below to fix
        ➥a bug where
// a white pixel is at the starting point
        lineTo(startX, startY - percentage);
        lineTo(startX + barWidth, startY - percentage);
        lineTo(startX + barWidth, startY);
        lineTo(startX, startY);
        endFill();
    }

    // Attach bar label
    clip.attachMovie("BarLabelClip", "areaName", 0);
    clip.areaName._x = startX - 1;
    clip.areaName._y = startY;
    clip.areaName.area = label;
}
```

Now that all the bars have been drawn, attached, and displayed, there is still one important step that remains: garbage collection. In the event that a user selects the TabularMode view, the presence of these dynamic movie clips on stage will adversely affect the Tabular view. Therefore, the following code was added to frame 4 of the **Actions** layer in the **ChartClip** movie clip:

```
if (Area1VersionA)
    removeMovieClip(Area1VersionA);
if (Area2VersionA)
    removeMovieClip(Area2VersionA);
if (Area3VersionA)
    removeMovieClip(Area3VersionA);
if (Area4VersionA)
    removeMovieClip(Area4VersionA);
if (Area1VersionB)
    removeMovieClip(Area1VersionB);
if (Area2VersionB)
    removeMovieClip(Area2VersionB);
if (Area3VersionB)
    removeMovieClip(Area3VersionB);
if (Area4VersionB)
    removeMovieClip(Area4VersionB);
if (Area1VersionC)
    removeMovieClip(Area1VersionC);
if (Area2VersionC)
    removeMovieClip(Area2VersionC);
if (Area3VersionC)
    removeMovieClip(Area3VersionC);
if (Area4VersionC)
    removeMovieClip(Area4VersionC);
if (Area1VersionD)
    removeMovieClip(Area1VersionD);
if (Area2VersionD)
    removeMovieClip(Area2VersionD);
if (Area3VersionD)
    removeMovieClip(Area3VersionD);
if (Area4VersionD)
    removeMovieClip(Area4VersionD);
```

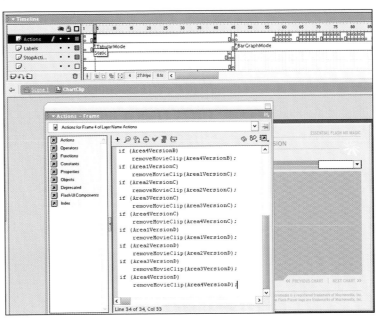

Preparing for selection of TabularMode view.

Summary

Now that was a mouthful. In this project, you touched on several Flash MX concepts, some new and some old. More importantly, you hopefully gained some insight into the complexities of bringing a complete project from conception to delivery. This project was specially designed to show you how several features of Flash MX can be woven together to deliver visually pleasing solutions that are rich with motion and loaded with functionality. As you continue to enhance your skills with Flash MX, be sure to pay particular attention to the concepts you have seen here. It is just as important to create aesthetically pleasing animation sequences as it is to build bug-free and complex functionality.

Over the past few years, MP3s have become quite popular. Many web sites and file-sharing programs have gotten these compressed audio files to tons of people's computers. MP3 files are great for downloading to your local drive and listening to them with one of the many MP3 players available, but many sites want to play their music on the Internet so that the visitor doesn't have to download the files.

Flash MX introduces a new concept that enables developers to present users with an MP3 file that can be played directly from a web site. This new feature enables you to directly load MP3 files into the Flash Player via ActionScript. This makes it easy for you to create one interface to control an unlimited number of audio files while making small modifications to load the external files.

AUDIO AND BITMAP

by Jim Caldwell

Difficulty Rating: ★★

Made With:

    Graphics created using Adobe Photoshop, Swift 3D V2

    Audio processed using Sound Forge

    Stock sourced from PhotoDisc.com

Final File Size: 60KB

Modem Download Time: 10 seconds

Development Time: 10 hours

Preparing to Work

Before starting, copy the **09_Audio_and_Bitmap** folder onto your hard disk, start Flash, and open the **mp3_player_01.fla** file.

Building the MP3 Player

When building a new project, it's usually easier to start with the core components. For this project, starting with the basic functionality of a Flash MP3 player will help keep everything built in modular components. This is beneficial because you can later use portions of code or layouts in other projects to save time.

1   With the file **mp3_player_01.fla** open, use the Property Inspector to set the stage dimensions to 500×200 pixels and the frame rate to 20fps.

   This sets the stage dimensions large enough to hold the MP3 interface built for this project. If you prefer, you can create your own Flash file instead of starting with the one provided on the accompanying CD-ROM.

Creating the action_clip Movie Clip

Event procedures enable you to write code directly on a movie clip, thereby enabling you to confine your code to one movie clip. Combining your code in one common place makes it easier to debug and decipher, especially when sharing your work files with other developers. In this section, you will add an event procedure to a movie clip to contain the bulk of the code used for this project.

1   Create a new, blank movie clip (Ctrl+F8/Cmd+F8), name it **invis_clip** (leaving all other settings at the default), and click OK.

   This brings you to the new movie clip's timeline. There is no need to add any elements to this movie clip because it will hold only the actions for the MP3 player.

Note: The frame rate used in Flash movies is probably one of the most arguable aspects of Flash. Many people feel that the default 12fps is sufficient for most web projects, but I rarely build anything at anything less than 20fps. It just seems to provide the smoothest flowing animations for most of my projects. Others use frame rates in excess of 100fps. Such high settings enable the Flash movie to display blistering effects that seem impossible with lower settings. Just for comparison, standard television using NTSC format is displayed at approximately 30fps.

2   Back on the main timeline, rename the default first
    layer to **action clips**. This makes it easy to locate
    action_clip. Any other movie clips that contain
    actions can also be placed onto this layer.

3   Open the Flash Library (Ctrl+L/Cmd+L). Locate the
    new movie clip you just created and drag an instance
    onto the stage.

4   With the movie clip selected, open the Property
    Inspector and add **action_clip** as the instance name.

    This enables the movie clip to be accessed by other
    elements within the Flash movie via ActionScript.

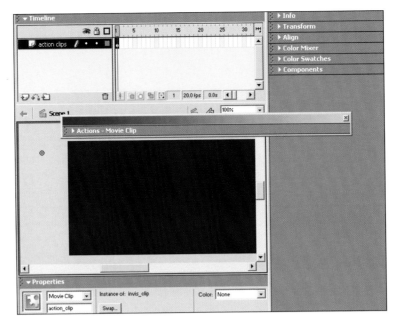

Adding the **action clips** layer.

ADDING A SONG LIST

The first thing that needs to be made is a list of songs that will be used with the Flash
MP3 player. Basically, you need to create an array that will contain the song titles you
would like to play within your Flash MP3 player.

1   Select the instance of the **invis_clip** movie clip, open
    the Actions panel, and add this code:

    Because there is no reason to build the array more
    than once, use the onClipEvent event handler with
    an argument of load for the array.

Load event procedure.

```
onClipEvent (load) {

}
```

> **Note:** If you are using the Expert mode of the
> Actions panel, you can just manually type in all of your
> ActionScript code. Otherwise, you'll have to use the
> pull-down menu to access the ActionScript elements
> used in this project.

2 Inside of the `onClipEvent` create a new array called `songList`. Then create a list of MP3s to be used, each enclosed in quotes and separated by a comma.

Using simple names such as `songList` helps keep your coding organized and lessens the chance of errors. By stacking the list, you can quickly browse through it later.

```
songList = new Array(
"onlyadream.mp3",
"yourman.mp3",
"anonymous.mp3",
"talkingaboutme.mp3"
);
```

Complete `songList` array.

Note: Be sure to always close the parentheses and add the semicolon after the array. Using arrays will greatly cut down on the amount of code you need to maintain compared to using local variables.

CREATING THE PLAYSONG FUNCTION

After your play list has been created, you need to make a set of functions to load and play the files. Start by building the `playSong` function. This function will create the sound object; check for existing sounds and load the MP3.

1 Create a new function named `playSong` within the `onLoad` event procedure. This code will only need to run once because it will not run again until the function is called elsewhere.

When calling functions, you just have to add the name of the function followed with an opening and closing parenthesis: `playSong()`. You can pass variables within the functions when needed.

```
function playSong() {
}
```

Construcing the `playSong` function.

2 Create a new variable called `playing` before the `playSong` function with the other variables. Set the initial value to `false`.

All of the actions within `playSong` must be wrapped within an `if` statement so that they run only when another song isn't already playing.

```
playing  = false;
```

Set the `playing` variable to `false`.

137

3 Within the `playSong` function, add the `if` statement and set the `playing` variable to `true`.

```
if (playing == false) {

    playing = true;

}
```

Completed `if` statement.

4 Create a new sound object within the previously created `if` statement. Set `s` as the name but do not set a target for the constructor.

```
s = new Sound();
```

Create the new sound object.

While still working within the previously created `if` statement, use the sound constructor to create a new sound object. This enables you to control the loaded MP3 files. You'll need to set a target to load the music files if you plan on having more than one sound playing at once.

Next you need to load an external MP3 file from the `songList` created earlier.

5 Create another variable called `i` outside of the `playSong` function but still within the `onLoad` event procedure. Set the initial value to `0`. Placement is not important because the code will work either way, but usually it's best to declare all variables at the top of a set of actions or an event procedure. Following this unwritten rule, declare the `i` variable at the beginning of the `onLoad` event procedure.

```
i = 0;
```

Set the `i` variable equal to 0.

It's important to set the variable to 0 because it will be selecting the first song of the array. All array elements label their first entry as 0 and increase from there. Therefore, to access the third song from the songList array, you'd use songList[2].

6   Back inside the playSong function, add a loadSound action to load an external MP3 file after the new sound object.

> **Macromedia Flash MX:** You can now load external MP3 files via ActionScript. Using the loadSong command, MP3 files are loaded into the Macromedia Flash movie and are treated as sounds that were imported directly into the Flash authoring environment.

Access the sound object by preceding the loadSound method with s. Be sure to note the dot (.) that separates the variable name from the method. The loadSound method has two arguments, the first being the URL of the sound to load. You want to access the songList array using i as the array access operator within the brackets. The second argument of loadSound determines whether to stream the sound; here it's set to true.

```
s.loadSound(songList[ i], true);
```

Completed loadSound command, pulling song from array.

7 Finally, add a `stop()` action for the sound object as the first action within the `if` statement.

This ensures that the song currently playing stops when another song is loaded.

Completed `playSong` function.

```
function playSong() {
stop();
if (playing == "false") {
    s.stop();
    s = new Sound();
    s.loadSound( songList[ i], true);
    playing = "true";
}
}
```

CREATING THE STOPSONG FUNCTION

The `stopSong` function is much easier to create because it only contains two actions.
This function is used to stop a currently playing song by using the `stop()` command.
If you can load a sound, it follows that you should be able to unload a sound, right?
But that's not the case. You cannot unload a sound.

1 Working within the `onLoad` event procedure, create a new function called `stopSong` after the `playSong` function.

The first action to take place when the function is called is to stop any sound that might have already been loaded using the `playSong` function.

Constructing the `stopSong` function.

```
function stopSong() {
}
```

2 Use the `stop` command to stop the sounds.

The `stop` sound command.

```
s.stop();
```

3 Set the `playing` variable to `false` so that the `playSong` function can fully execute.

Set the `playing` variable to `false`.

```
playing = false;
```

CREATING THE NEXTSONG AND PREVSONG FUNCTIONS

The preceding two functions are basically all you need to successfully load, play, and stop songs, but that isn't much interactivity for an MP3 player, is it? To further the interaction, you'll create functions to play the next and previous songs.

Both functions are built with the same concept and structure. An `if` statement determines which song is currently selected, and the next or previous song is then selected from the `songList` array.

1. While still working within the `onLoad` event procedure, create two new functions named `nextSong` and `prevSong` after the `stopSong` function.

```
function nextSong() {

}
function prevSong() {

}
```

Constructing the `nextSong` and `prevSong` functions.

2. Inside the `nextSong` function, add an `if...else` statement.

   The `if` logic determines whether the `i` variable is less than the length of the `songList` array minus 1. You have to subtract 1 from the length because the array index always starts with 0.

   If the condition in the `if` statement is met, the `i` variable increases by 1 by using the ++ operand. This will select the next song from the `songList` array. If the condition is not met, set the `i` variable to 0 so that it rotates back to the first song in the array.

```
if (i < (songList.length - 1)) {
    i++;
} else {
    i = 0;
}
```

The `if...else` statement to decipher next song in array.

3 Following the `if` statement but while still in the `nextSong` function, set the `playing` variable to `false` so that the `playSong` function will fully execute. Call the `playSong` function.

```
playing = false;
playSong();
```

Set the playing variable to `false` and call the `playSong` function.

Completed `nextSong` function.

The `prevSong` function works basically the opposite of the `nextSong` function.

4 Create an `if...else` statement inside the `prevSong` function.

This time, check to see if the `i` variable is greater than 0. If this condition is met, reduce the `i` variable by 1 by using the – operand. If the condition isn't met, set the `i` variable to the length of the `songList` array minus 1. This selects the last song of the array if the `prevSong` function is called while the first song of the array is playing.

```
if (i > 0) {
    i--;
} else {
    i = songList.length - 1;
}
```

The `if...else` statement to decipher the previous song in the array.

5 Set the `playing` variable to `false` and call the `playSong` function.

```
playing = false;
playSong();
```

Set the `playing` variable to `false` and call the `playSong` function.

This is just the same as the `nextSong` function.

Completed `prevSong` function.

CALLING THE SONG FUNCTIONS

Before starting the steps in this section, you'll need to create a new layer and name it **face**. This will be the layer that all of the buttons will reside on. Drag an instance of the Stop button onto the stage. You need to call the stopSong function when this button is clicked. You'll find that it's much easier to code using functions. The only thing you have to do is write three simple lines of code for each button.

Note: Many people ask, "Why not use press as the event for most buttons?" Either way is fine, but most operating systems and applications do not perform an action until you release your mouse after clicking it. It's a good idea to simulate the operating system's functionality as much as possible so that the buttons feel more natural.

1 Create a mouse event in the Action window attached to the stop button so that the user can click the button.

   Use release as the argument so that the actions within will execute when the user releases the mouse while over the button and after clicking.

```
on (release) {

}
```

Constructing an on (release) mouse event.

2 Within the mouse event, add this code:

   This action calls the stopSong function. Use the dot syntax to target the action found on the **action_clip** movie clip.

```
action_clip.stopSong();
```

Calling the stopSong function.

3 Repeat the introductory paragraphs as well as Steps 1 and 2 for each of the other buttons so that each button calls the appropriate function.

   Play button
   ```
action_clip.playSong();
```

   Previous button
   ```
action_clip.prevSong();
```

   Next button
   ```
action_clip.nextSong();
```

VOLUME CONTROL ACTIONS

Now that you can load and play songs, you should be able to crank it up if you want, right? In this section, you'll add an `if` statement within the `enterFrame` event procedure. This will constantly check to see if the volume buttons are pressed and will change the volume of the song. It is important to add it into the `enterFrame` event procedure so that you can make a button that can be pressed and held to continually increase or decrease the volume.

1   Declare a variable to use to establish the volume level within the `onLoad` event procedure. As previously mentioned, you should keep all of your variables together for ease of maintenance. Select the **invis_clip** movie clip and open the Actions panel. Below the previously set variables, create a new variable `vol` set to 52.

The rest of the code for the volume control has to run continuously to work properly; therefore, the code will not run properly within the `Load` event procedure.

```
vol=52;
```

Set the `vol` variable equal to 52.

2   Create a new event handler after the existing code with `enterFrame` as the argument.

All of the code nested within this event procedure will run once every time a frame is displayed. At 20 frames per second, the code runs 20 times per second. Using this code, the user will be able to press and hold the Up or Down buttons to continuously increase or decrease the volume.

```
onClipEvent (enterFrame) {

}
```

Constructing the `enterFrame` event procedure.

3   Create an `if...else if` statement within the `onClipEvent` handler to check to see whether the visitor is pressing the Up or Down volume buttons. (Code will have to be applied to them in the next section.)

```
if (volChange == "up" & vol < 100) {

}
```

The `if` statement to determine the value of the `volChange` and `vol` variables.

In the `if` statement, check to see if the `volChange` variable is equal to the value of `up` and if the value of the `vol` variable is less than 100.

4 If the conditions are met, set the `vol` variable equal to the `vol` variable plus 4 within the `if` statement. Use the addition assignment operand to set the `vol` variable equal to itself plus 4.

```
vol += 4;
```

Increase the `vol` variable by 4.

Note: You can also write the code as `vol = vol + 4;`. It will work just the same.

5 If the conditions aren't met, check to see if the `volChange` variable is equal to `down` and the `vol` variable is greater than 0. Add this code below the `if` statement:

```
else if (volChange == "down" & vol > 0) {

}
```

Determine the value of the `volChange` and `vol` variables.

6 If the conditions are met, set the `vol` variable equal to the `vol` variable minus 4 within the `if` statement. Use the subtraction assignment operand to set `vol` equal to itself minus 4.

```
vol -= 4;
```

Decrease the `vol` variable by 4.

Note: You can also write the code as `vol = vol - 4;`. It will work just the same.

7 Following the previous `if...else` statement, set the volume of the sound object named `s` equal to the `vol` variable. Use the `setVolume` method of the sound object with `vol` as the argument.

```
if (playing == true) {
    s.setVolume(vol);

}
```

The `if` statement to determine the value of the `playing` variable, and setting sound object volume equal to `vol` variable.

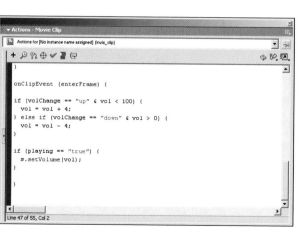

Completed volume control actions.

VOLUME BUTTON ACTIONS

To complete the project, drag the volume control buttons (volume_up and volume_down) onto the **face** layer from the Flash Library, and add the actions to the volume buttons.

1 Create a button event handler with `press` as the argument on the + button.

   When the user presses the Up button, the volume should increase until the button is released. While the button is held, set the `volChange` variable to `up`.

```
on (press) {
    action_clip.volChange = "up";
}
```

Mouse event setting the `volChange` variable to up.

2 Create another button event handler with `release` and `releaseOutside` as the arguments on the + button.

   When the mouse button is released, set the `volChange` variable to `null`. This breaks the looping `if` statement on the **action_clip** movie clip.

   The Down button uses the same type of logic.

```
on (release, releaseOutside) {
    action_clip.volChange = null;
}
```

Mouse event setting `volChange` to `null`.

3 Create a button event handler with `press` as the argument on the - button.

   When the user presses the Down button, the volume should decrease until the button is released. While the button is held, set the `volChange` variable to `down`.

```
on (press) {
    action_clip.volChange = "down";
}
```

Mouse event setting `volChange` to `down`.

4 Create another button event handler with `release` and `releaseOutside` as the arguments on the - button.

   When the mouse button is released, set the `volChange` variable to `null`. This breaks the looping `if` statement on the **action_clip** movie clip.

```
on (release, releaseOutside) {
    action_clip.volChange = null;
}
```

Mouse event setting `volChange` to `null`.

Summary

In this project, you probably learned a few new features of Flash MX and discovered how you could use them to enhance your projects. The sound object has many advantages over the standard way of importing the sounds into Flash, and it should be used if at all possible.

Loading the sounds from external MP3 files will be very useful if you plan to use the same sounds in many Flash movies, such as a theme song for Flash movies on a web site.

How to Improve

Although this MP3 player is fully functional, other elements can easily be added to enhance its overall look and functionality.

Open the file **mp3_player_02.fla**. You will see the elements I added for further functionality.

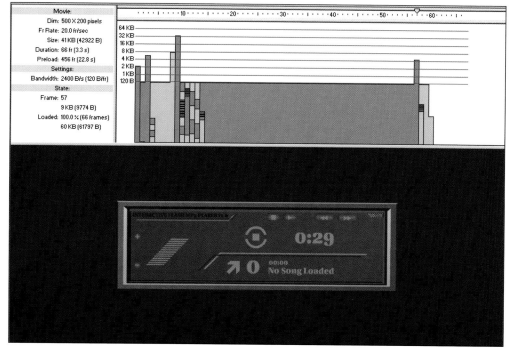

The final interface.

The web is about interaction, and what better way to interact than by sending a colorful, personalized greeting card to a friend? The combination of Flash's quick-downloading vector animations and its powerful new timeline-independent scripting tools makes the process of sending and receiving information to and from a server-side script easier than ever.

10

ECARDS

by Helen Triolo

Difficulty Rating: ★★★★

Made With: Macromedia Flash MX, Adobe Photoshop, Homesite or other HTML editor

Final File Size: cardsender.swf (60k), 3 card files (60k each), and 3 ASP files (around 1k each)

Modem Download Time: 10 seconds for the initial .fla, plus 10 seconds for each card when it's previewed

Development Time: 1-2 days

IT WORKS LIKE THIS

In this project, you'll create a greeting card site using some sample Flash and ASP content I've created. You'll use a template file and built-in components to make your job easier. You will learn how to create vector-animated cards from a Flash MX template, display thumbnails of the eCards, and allow visitors to view, select, and email a card with a personalized message!

I've also built this project to be able to communicate with a database that is used to save eCard information and then retrieve it when the eCard recipient is ready to view the card.

Users entering the eGreeting site will see a selection of thumbnail graphics, each with its own View and Send buttons. Choosing View pops up a preview of the selected card with its own animation, message fields, and Close button. When the Close button is clicked, the card preview is closed and the main screen reappears.

Choosing Send takes the user to a screen where sender and recipient information can be entered. Clicking the Send button on that screen causes a record to be written to the database with the current card information, and it sends an email message to the recipient with a link to view the card. Finally, the user is sent to a response page where a message indicates whether the card was successfully emailed.

> **Note:** Although I used ASP for the backend coding and a Microsoft Access database, you can effectively substitute the server-side script of your choice: JSP, Perl, PHP, ColdFusion, or another, along with any ODBC-compliant database.

The eGreeting site uses multiple Flash movies to build this effect:

- A template movie used to build stock greeting card movies
- Three premade greeting card movies
- A movie that provides the user interface and processes database and email communication

This project is broken down into several smaller tasks:

- Using a predefined eCard template to create additional customized card movies
- Customizing the Flash Component scrollbar
- Defining the structure of the database
- Enabling the Flash movie to communicate with server scripts via the `LoadVars` object
- Testing Flash–ASP communication and the email program

PREPARING TO WORK

To use this project as is, you'll need to be running Microsoft Internet Information Server (IIS) or PWS under Windows, have Microsoft Access installed, and store the files on the accompanying CD-ROM in a subdirectory of your Inetpub/wwwroot directory. Alternatively, you can use any other scripting and database combination (such as PHP and MySQL), but you will need to translate the functionality of the ASP scripts in this project into the scripting language of your choice.

You'll also need to have a program that sends mail and enables you to specify the email's sender, recipient, and message. This project uses ASPMail, but you can use whatever mail program is available on your server. This might require substituting **sendit.asp** with a script that can communicate with your alternative mail server.

1   Copy all files in the **10_Flash_eCards** folder to a directory under Inetpub/wwwroot. Check your IIS or PWS settings if you are not sure.

2   Set up a DSN connection for **greetings.mdb**, the Access database you just copied into a directory under your webroot. If you are using Windows 2000, navigate to Control Panel > Administrative Tools Folder > ODBC Settings. The DSN name used in the script files is greetingsDSN.

With the accompanying CD-ROM files copied to the webroot and the data source connection set up, you've completed the prep work. Next you will examine the template used to create the individual greeting cards already in the project—**card01.fla** and **card02.fla**— and you will make a new greeting card for the project.

WORKING WITH THE CARD TEMPLATE

Each greeting card is a separate .swf in this system. The cards are individually loaded into a user interface movie when the end user picks one from a selection screen. Because each greeting card movie uses the same format and conforms to the same rules, you use a template movie to build the new cards and then File > Save As for each new greeting card.

Macromedia Flash MX: After you have created a Flash movie that contains the basic structure (graphic content and/or code) you need, you can save it as a template by using File > Save As Template.

1 Open **cardtemplate.fla**. Select the empty movie clip in the upper-left corner of the stage and open the Actions panel.

The cards made from this template will be accessed through two different environments. When an end user is customizing an eCard, the eCard movies are loaded into the user interface movie, but when a recipient collects the card to view, it's loaded directly into a table cell via HTML tags. As a result, the eCard itself must control the loading of its own contents, delaying visibility until all elements have been loaded.

I have done this by making the first frame of all greeting card movies empty of visible content, containing only a movie clip with ActionScript that checks the progress of the loading process. Only when everything has loaded is the greeting card allowed to play.

```
onClipEvent(enterFrame) {
    if (_parent.getBytesLoaded()>1 && _parent.getBytesLoaded() >=
    ➡ _parent.getBytesTotal()) {
        if (!_root.fromBrowser) {
            _parent._x = 14;
            _parent._y = 14;
        }
    _parent.play();
```

Code on a blank movie clip in frame 1 of the card template detects when the card has been loaded, positions the card correctly if it is being previewed, and displays the content with the play() command.

2 Select the first frame of the **actions** layer and look at
the ActionScript.

Planning the structure of the cards so that they can
be used in multiple situations (the initial preview, a
preview with data, and the viewing by final recipient)
requires thinking ahead. For this example, I decided
that previewed cards would be loaded into level1 (so
that they would overlay the base movie in level0). I
also knew that the recipient of the card will be viewing it from HTML tags in a browser, so I decided to
indicate that to the card movie by passing a variable
fromBrowser (set to 1) from the HTML tags.

With that information in mind, you put code in
frame 1 of the card movie to determine where
the card is being called from and to set variables
accordingly.

Code in frame 1 checks to see from where the card is
being called. If it is called from the browser directly
(which means a recipient is viewing the card) or if it
is being previewed with data entered by an end user,
the message variable will already have a value. If not,
the end user is initially viewing the card, and you
should supply a "dummy message" to put in the card.

If the user has already entered information about the
recipient, sender, and message and is now previewing
the card with that information, you will read that
information from the form in level0. (The card itself
will have been loaded into level1.)

There is one more block of ActionScript in frame 2 of the
cardtemplate.fla movie. You will review its purpose in
just a bit. First, you will actually use this template to make
a new greeting card.

```
if (fromBrowser == null && _level0.preview != 1) {
    message = "Jack, \tThanks so much to you and Jane for looking after the boys
for us last weekend. Hope you have a great time camping! \t- Al";
} else {
    // if user is previewing with data, use data from form
    if (_level0.preview == 1) {
        message = _level0.message;
        fromName = _level0.fromName;
    }
    bottomMsg = "This card was sent to you from " + fromName;
}
stop();
```

Variables used in the card movie are set based on how the movie is called.

Note: Not only can you quickly set the visibility or lock status of multiple
layers via their folder, but also saving layers in folders enables you to collapse
the folder when not working on its layers, making more stage space available
to see the content you are working on.

3   With **cardtemplate.fla** still open, open
    dropanimation.fla. Select all content by clicking on
    frame 1 in the top layer and dragging the mouse over
    all layers and all frames up through frame 52. With all
    frames highlighted, choose Edit > Copy Frames.

4   Choose Window > **cardtemplate.fla**. Click on
    the **unique anim** layer folder and use the menu
    option Insert > Layer or the Add Layer icon to add
    a new layer.

    A new layer appears above the **unique anim**
    layer folder.

5   Click on frame 2 of the new layer and select
    Edit > Paste Frames. The four layers from
    dropanimation.fla will replace the new layer.
    These are **ripple2**, **ripple1**, **drip**, and **background**.
    Select the layers and drag them into the **unique
    anim** folder. Finally, click the arrow to the left
    of the **unique anim** folder icon to display the layers
    within it.

    The **dropanimation.fla** file contains a background
    image and three movie clips that make up a drop of
    water rolling down a leaf into rippling water below.
    You copied these frames into **cardtemplate.fla** as
    the first step of turning the scenic interlude into a
    greeting card.

There are still some slight modifications you need to
finish. The animation did not paste neatly in the square
laid out by the border, and you'll want to customize the
scrollbar colors to better complement the new animation.

6   Click the padlock icon at the top to lock all layers.
    Click in the lock column of the **unique anim** folder
    to unlock all layers in the folder.

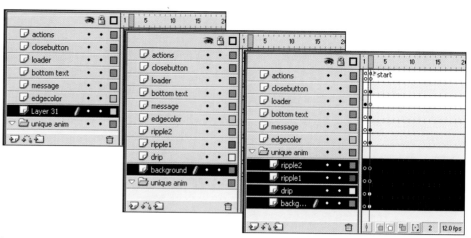

Layer folders enable you to organize layers by content and to use
screen space more efficiently.

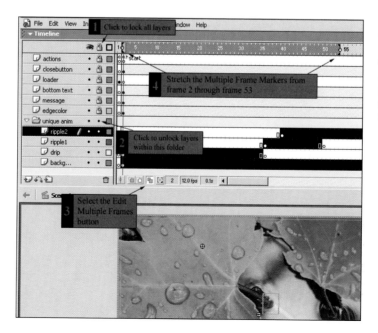

The Edit Multiple Frames button,
together with the multiple frame
markers, enables you to move
the contents of multiple frames
in multiple layers at once. The
move is carried on all selected
objects. (They must be in
unlocked layers to be selected.)

7 Click the Edit Multiple Frames button below the layers. Drag the multiple frame markers in the top timeline to cover frames 2 through 53. Click Edit > Select All.

Now you should have the background, the water drop, and two **ripple** movie clips selected.

8 Press the right-arrow key 10 times and the down-arrow key 10 times to move all the new content to its correct position within the card template.

9 Turn off Edit Multiple Frames by clicking the button again.

10 Save the new file as **card03.fla**. Select Control > Test Movie to make sure the content and animation look correct.

APPLYING THE SCROLLBAR

In previous versions of Flash, you had to program a scrollbar manually if you wanted a scrolling text field. Flash MX makes that enhancement much easier. You'll walk through the steps for using the built-in scrollbar component and customize its color scheme to match the movie.

The scrollbar is a specialized movie clip that is associated with an instance of a text field. For the association to work, the text field must have an instance name. Other than this, all you have to do is drag an instance of the scrollbar from the Components panel onto the text field, and you've got a scrolling text box.

1 In **card03.fla** that you just created, select Window > Components to open the Components panel if it is not already open. Unlock the **message** layer and select the text field.

2 In the Property inspector, assign it an instance name of mcMessage and a Var value of message.

As previously mentioned, the text field must have an instance name for a scrollbar to be associated with it. Additionally, you need to give it a variable name

Add a scrollbar to your text field by simply giving the text field an instance name (in the Property inspector) and then dragging the scrollbar component into the text field from the Components panel.

(message) so that a value can be assigned to the message in frame 1 before the text field itself even exists.

3   With the **message** layer still selected, drag the scrollbar component from the Components panel and drop it on the text field.

It is easiest if you don't attempt to line up the edge of the component with the edge of the field. The two will align automatically if you drop the component in the middle of the target text field.

Check the Property inspector. You will see that the scrollbar component has a `Target TextField` property that has been set to `mcMessage`. The component and text field have been associated.

4   In the Property inspector, enter `mcScroll` as the instance name of the scrollbar.

5   Click frame 2 of the **actions** layer and open the Actions panel if it is not already open.

Now let's test the scrollbar. Frame 1 of the **actions** layer has the default message text that will be used in the text field. First you should modify the text so that it is long enough to cause the text field to scroll.

6   Select frame 1 of the **actions** layer in **card03.fla** and open the Actions panel. Locate this line:

```
message = "Jack, \tThanks so much to you
and Jane for looking after the boys for
us last weekend. Hope you have a great
time camping! \t- Al
```

Frame 2 contains four sections of code, each beginning with a comment line:

- The first section checks to see if the card was opened from outside the movie (that is, by the recipient) by looking at the `fromBrowser` variable. If so, the Close button is not needed and is set to invisible.

- The second section sets the text property of the text field to the value of the variable `message`. This is necessary to make the scrollbar work with the text field.

- The third section creates an object that will define the colors used to customize the scrollbar. The line that defines the colors is commented out for now; you'll be setting that later in this section.

- The final section of code in frame 2 hides the scrollbar if scrolling is not needed with this code. The `maxscroll` property of a text field is equal to the number of lines in the field when the whole message is placed in it, minus the maximum number of lines the field can display at its given height, plus 1. It can only be accessed in the frame following the one in which the value of the field is set. Here you use it to "turn off" the scrollbar when it is not needed by making it invisible.

7 Add another sentence in the middle of the message variable and test the movie.

A gray scrollbar should appear and should allow scrolling through the message.

8 Remove the extra sentence from the text field assignment and retest the movie.

The scrollbar should no longer be visible.

The scrollbar will blend in with your greeting card even better if you customize its colors. You can use one of the scrollbar's scriptable methods, `setStyleProperty()`, to do this.

CUSTOMIZING THE SCROLLBAR

In this example, you'll create a `scrollColors` object whose properties define the colors to be used. That way, you can keep all of the scrollbar colors in one place (in the `scrollColors` object), and your assignment statements can remain the same in every card.

To choose your scrollbar colors:

1 Open the Color Mixer (Window > Color Mixer).

2 Click on a dark green area of the card using the Eyedropper tool. The Color Mixer will change to reflect your choice, showing the color, its hexdecimal value, and shades of color that match it.

3 Record the hexadecimal value of the color you selected in the last step. You'll use it to set the darkest property of the **scrollColors** object, which is in frame 2 of the **actions** layer. Replace the pound sign with 0x (as in 0x9f9600).

```
scrollColors = { lightest:0xa9a700, medium:0xb4ac00,
➥darker:0x9f9600, darkest:0x8b7600};
trace(scrollColors.lightest.toString(16));   // test
mcScroll.setStyleProperty("arrow", scrollColors.darker);
mcScroll.setStyleProperty("face", scrollColors.lightest);
mcScroll.setStyleProperty("shadow", scrollColors.darker);
mcScroll.setStyleProperty("darkshadow", scrollColors.darkest);
mcScroll.setStyleProperty("highlight", scrollColors.lightest);
mcScroll.setStyleProperty("highlight3d", scrollColors.medium);
mcScroll.setStyleProperty("scrollTrack", scrollColors.darker);
```

Define the `scrollColors` object to contain values that will be applied to the style properties of the scrollbar.

4 To assign the three remaining colors for darker, medium, and lightest, either use the Eyedropper tool again and repeat steps 1 through 3, or click on the sliding color bar in the Color Mixer and record the hexadecimal values you select.

5 Click frame 2 of the **actions** layer and open the Actions panel if it is not already open. Remove the comment marks (//) from the beginning of line 9 (the line in which scrollColors are assigned). Substitute the values you recorded in the previous step into this assignment statement.

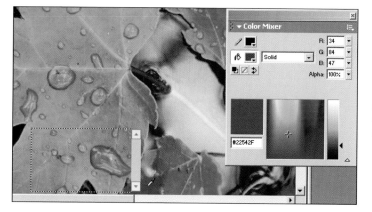

Macromedia Flash's built-in components can be assigned custom colors either individually or globally. Using the Fill tool's eyedropper with the Color Mixer enables you to grab the hex value of any color easily and to find a range of related values (shown in the far right of the Color Mixer).

After you've filled all of the scrollColors properties with your selected values, test the card to make sure it works. Save it and, if you like, compare it with **card03final.fla** on the accompanying CD-ROM. The files should be the same, except for the colors you selected for the scrollColors object.

The eGreeting Interface

By now, you have thoroughly explored the **cardtemplate.fla** file and know how to use it to build eCards. The next step is to take a look at the movie that will be the user interface, where the eCard users will pick a card and personalize its message and recipient.

cardSender.fla is the main movie of eGreetings. In its contents is an ActionScript object that sends eCard data through a server-side script into a database and also receives data sent back from the server-side script. It is here that the project begins to tie the eCard movies with user-defined data and backend server connections.

Take a few moments to examine the layout of **cardsender.fla**, referring to this figure. You will look closer at the ActionScript contained in its frames after you've come to understand the role that the Access database will play.

The contents and code in each of the three sections of **cardsender.fla** are shown here. Use this as a reference as you examine the contents of the file.

Structure of cardsender.fla

view frame	*send* frame	*respond* frame
purpose: allow visitor to view card content, select one to send	**purpose:** gather information from visitor, pass to ASP to write to database	**purpose:** show visitor results of mail attempt
content: view button: opens card swf in level 1 send button: goes to send frame	**content:** form fields preview button: opens card swf in level 1 w/form info send button: creates lvo LoadVars object, calls writetodb.asp, which sends its output to function formResponse, defined in *view* frame back button: goes to *view* frame textfield: to show error message if required fields not filled in	**content:** textfield which shows whether mail sent successfully back button: goes to view frame
code: • define functions to be used on return from ASP scripts: formResponse: display error message if needed, or call sendit.asp, which mails a message to the recipient and returns data to mailResponse mailResponse: go to *respond* frame	**code:** • display small picture (aesthetics only; main code for this frame is on send button)	**code:** • fill in textfield • display small picture

In **cardsender.fla**, the View and Send buttons in frame 1 are button movie clips. To define the actions that will be carried out when the button is pressed, you define a function that will be used as an event handler for the button and assign that function to the button's onRelease property. This is the code that appears in frame 1 of the **actions** layer in the viewButtonMC symbol:

```
function viewit() {
    // load selected card
    root.cardID = this._name.substr(4,2);
    loadMovieNum("card" + _root.cardID + ".swf",1);
}

this.onRelease = viewit;
stop();
```

Putting code inside a button movie clip allows that same code to be used for all instances of the button movie clip, something that could not be done with buttons previously.

By giving the button movie clips appropriate names (View01, View02, and View03 in this example), you can use the same code in each clip to get the ID of the card associated with the button from a substring of the button's name, set variable cardID accordingly, and then open the corresponding card movie in level1. Other frames in the button movie clip are used to specify the button's over and down states. A stop(); must be added in frame 1 to keep those frames from being executed when the button is not being moused over.

cardsender.fla also contains standard buttons (the Preview, Send, and Back buttons in the send frame). Because the code is different on each of these buttons, you use a standard button with code placed on the button rather than within it. On the Preview button in the frame labeled send, for example, you'll see this code:

```
on (release) {
    preview = 1;
    loadMovieNum("card" + _root.cardID + ".swf",1);
}
```

If a button is used instead of a button movie clip, code must be placed within an on (<event>) handler, in the button's Object Actions.

This enables the user to preview the card specified by variable cardID with any information the user has entered on the form included.

DEFINING THE STRUCTURE OF THE DATABASE

In this example, I used a Microsoft Access database with the structure shown here. MySQL or any other database suitable for web applications could be used instead. If you have Access installed, open **greetings.mdb**. Click Design, and you should see the same structure as pictured.

Only one database table is needed for this project, `cardInfo`. Each eCard is stored in the table as a single record. Each record in `cardInfo` contains a unique `msgID` field. The `msgID` is set up as an AutoNumber data type, which guarantees a unique `msgID` value for each new record you insert. Having a unique value makes it possible for you to find any given card and pull all of its information to display when a recipient wants to view it.

All other fields in the table are text fields. The remaining fields store the recipient's name and email address and the sender's name and email address. Retaining sender information makes it possible for the recipient to reply, perhaps to thank the sender for his or her thoughtful message.

The structure of the Access table used to store card information.

USING THE LOADVARS OBJECT TO SEND DATA

Now that you have an idea of what data is expected in the database, how do you get it there from the Flash movie? You can use the `LoadVars` object, new to Flash MX, to accomplish all of your data transfers.

1 If you haven't already, open **cardsender.fla**. Click on the frame labeled **send**, which is where information is collected and sent to an ASP page to be written to the database.

2 Select the Send button and open the Actions panel. In addition to some error–checking code, which will be discussed in a bit, you'll see the code shown in the figure.

This creates a new `LoadVars` object, whose function is to pass data to and receive data from your ASP scripts. Variables to be passed to the script are passed as properties of the object (`toName`, `toEmail`, `fromName`, `fromEmail`, `message`, and `cardID`).

> **Note:** You'll notice that the same names are used for variables, lvo properties, and Access field names. This was done for consistency but is not necessary. The variable names passed to ASP will be whatever property names are assigned to lvo, and they might be stored in the database with completely different field names if desired.

After the `LoadVars` object lvo has been created, it can be used for multiple transfers of data. Refer to the figure to see which parts of cardsender fill in which properties of lvo and which properties are set by the ASP scripts.

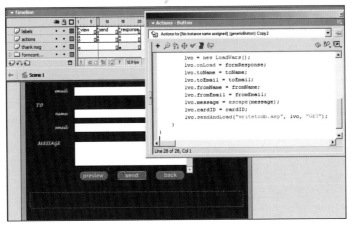

Creating a new `LoadVars` object.

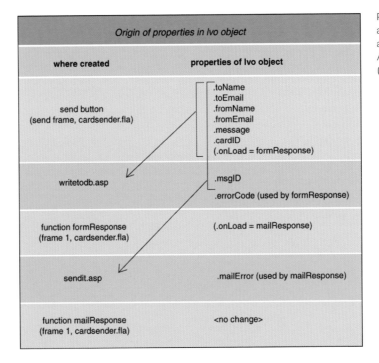

Properties of the `LoadVars` object, lvo, are used to pass variable values back and forth between the Flash movie and ASP scripts. Arrows indicate properties (variables) being passed to ASP scripts.

Because the variables passed to and from the `LoadVars` object are just properties of the object, they remain in place until deleted. This means that once they have been set as properties (as in the previous code), they can be sent to any number of ASP scripts simply by using any of the following data-transfer methods available with the `LoadVars` object (here called lvo):

- `send`. Properties of lvo are sent to ASP (or another server-side script) as variables via either HTTP GET or HTTP POST, as specified in the `send` parameters.

- `sendAndLoad`. Properties of lvo are sent to ASP and variables are sent from ASP (via `response.write` statements or other server-side print statements) and are received as additional properties of lvo.

- `load`. Variables sent from ASP (via `response.write`) are received as properties of lvo.

In the final version of the movie, you use the `sendAndLoad` method to transfer data, as shown in this data-flow diagram. When debugging a program, however, you always start with a simple `send` (with all `response.write` going to the browser window instead of back to Flash) to make sure variables are being received by the ASP script as you expect.

For any application in which Flash and the server are sending data back and forth, it's a good idea to dump the data being sent to a browser window to see if it's being sent correctly before trying to do anything with it in your server-side script.

1   Using Homesite or another editor, open **writetodb.asp**, the file that writes a card record to the database and sends back the `msgID` associated with that card.

Displaying the content of your query with variables passed from Macromedia Flash in the browser window.

2 Save it as **testwritetodb.asp**. Delete all lines except lines 5 through 7, and uncomment line 7. You should end up with the code as shown at right:

3 Save **testwritetodb.asp**.

This causes your insert string to be written to the browser. You'll need to change cardsender temporarily to call this file.

```
<%

   insertStr = "INSERT INTO cardInfo (fromName, fromEmail, toName,
toEmail, message, cardID) VALUES ('" & request.querystring("fromName") &
"', '"  & request.querystring("fromEmail") & "', '"  &
request.querystring("toName") & "', '"  & request.querystring("toEmail")
& "', '" & request.querystring("message") & "', '"  &
request.querystring("cardID") & "')"


   response.Write insertStr

%>
```

Sending your query to the browser before using it enables you to first make sure your variables are being passed correctly from Flash to the ASP file.

4 Open **cardsender.fla**. Click frame 2, select the Send button, and open the Actions panel. Change the line `lvo.sendAndLoad("writetodb.asp", lvo, "GET");` to the code shown:

```
lvo.send("testwritetodb.asp", lvo, "GET");
```

5 Save the movie as **testcardsender.fla** and publish it to produce testcardsender.swf and testcardsender.html. Open the .html file in a browser, with the URL **http://localhost/ <directory-within-wwwroot>/ testcardsender.html**. Click Send on the opening page, fill out the form, and click Send on the form page.

You should see a new browser window open with a query that includes the values you typed in and sent to the ASP.

Displaying the return string in the browser.

After you're sure the variables are being sent correctly (either via GET/request.querystring as used here or via POST/request.form), it's a good idea to make sure the variables are also being returned as you expect. You can do this by displaying your output string to the browser, using the send command (which sends data only one way—out of Flash). When the correct output string is displayed in the browser, you can then use the more powerful sendAndLoad, which returns the data "invisibly" to Flash.

6 To make this test, change the line in Step 3 to:

7 Save and publish **testcardsender.fla**. If you open **testcardsender.html** in the browser, as above, you should see a new window open with output, as well as a new entry in cardInfo in **greetings.mdb**.

If not, you'll need to fix whatever is causing the problem. This could be an incorrect DSN entry, the location of the .mdb file, or the properties of the .mdb file. A common problem, for example, is failing to check Write Allowed in the Everyone setting of the .mdb file's properties. This produces an error message stating that "Operation must use an updateable query."

In this project, you check for errors (blank required fields) from within the code on the Send button in the frame labeled send before sending any data to ASP. More complex error checking (such as string manipulations that involve checking for a valid email address) might be better handled on the server side, with an appropriate code being sent back to Flash to indicate any errors.

```
lvo.send("writetodb.asp", lvo, "GET");
```

Sending the ASP output to the browser, using the send method, enables you to ensure that the return string is being generated correctly in the ASP file. You can then substitute sendAndLoad to have the output returned to Macromedia Flash.

```
fieldError = 0;
requiredFields = ["fromName", "fromEmail", "toEmail"];
for (i=0; i<requiredFields.length; i++) {
    if (this[ requiredFields[ i]] == "" ||
        this[ requiredFields[ i]] == null) {
        fieldError++;
    }
}
```

Code on the Send button (in the send frame) enables you to make sure entries have been made for sender name and email and recipient email before attempting to send.

163

ERROR CHECKING

Notice that before the Send button performs a `sendAndLoad`, there is a section of code that checks to make sure all required fields have been filled in. This is done before attempting to send data to the server-side script so that any obvious problems with the data can be corrected before the script is (needlessly) called. If, however, there is a great deal of error checking to be done or if it involves complex string manipulations, it might be more efficiently handled by the server-side script instead of bogging down the client's machine. In that case, one would simply send the data, let the server-side script thoroughly check it, and have it send back error codes indicating any problems, which the Flash movie would deal with accordingly.

SETTING UP AND TESTING THE EMAIL PROGRAM

When you have ensured that data can be successfully sent from Flash to ASP, have a record written to the database, and have the correct return string produced by your ASP script, you're 90% done. The one remaining hurdle is to make sure the mail program functions correctly.

Whatever program you normally use to send mail—whether it's a CGI script, ASPMail, or something else—is the one you should use for this application. As long as you can specify the sender address, recipient address, message body, and subject, you're set. (You'll also need to capture whatever information is returned from the script to tell if an error occurred so that you can pass that back to Flash and inform the user.) If your site is on a server that supports ASPMail, you can use the script found on the accompanying CD-ROM and just change the remote host specification.

1 Substitute whatever coding you need to tell the email program to use variables passed with a POST, as in this code:

```
Mailer.FromName = request.form("fromName")

Mailer.FromAddress = request.form("fromEmail")

Mailer.AddRecipient request.form("toName"), request.form("toEmail")
```

This code assigns the variables passed from Flash to the `Mailer` object that will be used by ASPMail.

2 Code the capture and return of any error information with code whose function matches this:

```
if not Mailer.SendMail then

    Response.write "mailError=1"

else

    Response.write "mailError=0"

end if
```

If mail is not successfully sent, the value of `mailError`, which is passed back to Flash, is set to `1`.

As previously mentioned, I suggest you test the mail program by calling it from an HTML form (sending to your own address) before trying to use it with Flash. A sample HTML form is included on the accompanying CD-ROM, and the key content is listed here. If you fill out the information, click Send, see `errorCode=0` pop up in the browser, and find a message in your inbox, you know the mail program works with the same fields your Flash movie will provide.

```
html code to verify email functionality required by Flash movie

<html>
<head>
 <title>Form for testing email</title>
</head>

<body>
<form method="POST" action="sendit.asp">
<input name="msgID" type="hidden" value=35><br><br>
from Name: <input name="fromName" type="text" size=50><br><br>
from Email: <input name="fromEmail" type="text" size=50><br><br>
to Name: <input name="toName" type="text" size=50><br><br>
to Email: <input name="toEmail" type="text" size=50><br><br>
<input type="Submit" value="Send">
</form>
</body>
</html>
```

Testing the email program using a simple HTML form with the same data that the program will be receiving from Flash is a useful first step to ensure that the program works as intended.

DISPLAYING THE CARD FOR THE RECIPIENT

Now you have a complete set of cards and a cardsender movie that works in conjunction with your server-side scripts, including one that successfully sends email to a recipient. The final piece needed is an ASP script to be run when the recipient receives an email and clicks on the link therein. Open **showmycard.asp** in Homesite or another editor. You'll note three parts to this file:

- The HTML frame for the page, with a title, standard HTML tags, and a table structure that makes sure the card will appear centered both horizontally and vertically within the browser window.

- A VBScript section that looks in the database and extracts the information about the selected card.

- The OBJECT and EMBED tags used to open the .swf with a querystring appended. This, for example, is the PARAM tag, which is part of the OBJECT that Internet Explorer will use to display the movie:

```
<PARAM NAME=movie
➥VALUE=" card<%=cardID%>.swf?fromBrowser=1&
➥toName=<%=toName%>&
➥toEmail=<%=toEmail%>&
➥fromName=<%=fromName%>&
➥fromEmail=<%=fromEmail%>&
➥message=<%=message%>">
```

PARAM tag that includes VBScript to pass ASP variables to the Flash card movie.

You create these tags by publishing the card .swf and then manually appending the information you need to pass to the movie. When **cardnn.swf** is executed, parameters passed in this way are automatically available for use as _root variables in frame 1.

```
<HTML>
<HEAD>
<TITLE>Greetings from Say It With Scenics eCards</TITLE>
</HEAD>
<BODY bgcolor="#333333" leftmargin=0 topmargin=0 marginwidth=0 marginheight=0>
<%
Set conn = Server.CreateObject("ADODB.Connection")
conn.Open "greetingsDSN","",""

sql = "SELECT * from cardInfo WHERE msgID = " & request.querystring("m")

set rs = Server.CreateObject("ADODB.Recordset")
rs.Open sql, conn, 0, 1
rs.MoveFirst

cardID = rs.Fields("cardID")
toName = rs.Fields("toName")
toEmail = rs.Fields("toEmail")
fromName = rs.Fields("fromName")
fromEmail = rs.Fields("fromEmail")
message = rs.Fields("message")

rs.Close
set rs = nothing

conn.Close
set conn = nothing
%>

<table cellpadding=0 cellspacing=0 border=0 width="100%" height="100%">
<tr>
  <td height="100%" align="center" valign="middle">
  <OBJECT classid="clsid:D27CDB6E-AE6D-11cf-96B8-444553540000"
  codebase="http://download.macromedia.com/pub/shockwave/cabs/flash/swflash.cab#version=6,0,0,0"
  WIDTH=560 HEIGHT=410><PARAM NAME=movie
VALUE="card<%=cardID%>.swf?fromBrowser=1&toName=<%=toName%>&toEmail=<%=toEmail%>&
fromName=<%=fromName%>&fromEmail=<%=fromEmail%>&message=<%=message%>">
  <PARAM NAME=quality VALUE=high><PARAM NAME=bgcolor VALUE=#000000>
  <EMBED src="natcard<%=cardID%>.swf?fromBrowser=1&toName=<%=Server.urlencode(toName)%>
&toEmail=<%=Server.urlencode(toEmail)%>&fromName=<%=Server.urlencode(fromName)%>&
fromEmail=<%=Server.urlencode(fromEmail)%>&message=<%=message%>"
  quality=high bgcolor=#000000 WIDTH=560 HEIGHT=410 TYPE="application/x-shockwave-flash"
PLUGINSPAGE="http://www.macromedia.com/shockwave/download/index.cgi?
P1_Prod_Version=ShockwaveFlash">
  </EMBED></OBJECT></td></tr>
</table>
</BODY>
</HTML>
```

The contents of **showmycard.asp**. This file was produced by publishing **card01.fla** to **card01.html**, which was then modified in Homesite to include VBScript to access the database, HTML tags for a table cell display of the card, and addition of VBScript tags to pass parameters to the card movie.

Putting It All Together

Now that you have all the pieces assembled, the only remaining task is to make sure they're all in the same directory on your web server. (Or, if a separate directory is used for the ASP files, the correct paths must be specified in the `sendAndLoad` statements in **cardsender.fla**.) The user's first stop is **cardsender.html**, which allows each of the three card files (**card01.swf**, **card02.swf**, and **card03.swf**) to be viewed, collects recipient and sender information, and calls **writetodb.asp** and **sendit.asp** to save the information and send it to the recipient. Finally, the recipient receives a link to **showmycard.asp**, which brings up one of the same card .swf's inside the browser. Voilá! You've got a fully functional eCard system that incorporates the beauty and small file sizes that Flash offers with the scripting and tracking power of a backend database.

Recently a new breed of developers has

taken on the challenge of creating applications

that enable users to create their own

content. In this chapter, you'll build one

such application—an online Movie Maker

that enables users to build short movies

from a set of premade animations.

Working on projects like Movie Maker presents

a special challenge to developers who are

learning ActionScript. This project takes

advantage of some powerful new features,

including movie clip buttons, dynamic event

handlers, and the `registerClass` method.

MOVIE MAKER

by Jason Krogh
with original audio and design by Brian Ziffer and James Lloyd of **www.systemsoular.com**

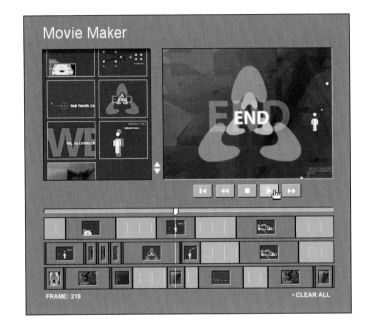

Difficulty rating: ★★★★★

Made with:
Animation created using Adobe Photoshop, Extreme 3D, LightWave, AfterEffects, ImageReady
Audio processed using Reason, Max/Nato Custom applications
Original audio and design by Brian Ziffer and James Lloyd, **www.systemsoular.com**

Final file size: 30KB (**moviemaker.swf**), 2MB (**assets_ziffer.swf**)

Modem download time: 7 seconds + time for assets

Development time: 5 days

IT WORKS LIKE THIS

The Movie Maker enables users to create a movie by arranging animated clips within a timeline. The drag-and-drop interface is designed to be easy to use while giving users a great deal of flexibility.

The Movie Maker timeline contains 480 frames and playback is set at 20 frames per second (fps). To create a movie, the user drags a timeline clip from a palette into one of three tracks. These timeline clips are visual representations that indicate when the animated clips begin and end as well as where they sit in the stacking order. (For example, items in track 1 appear on top of items in track 3.)

The movie displays in a preview window. This preview is constantly updated based on the arrangement of the timeline clips and the position of the playhead marker. The user can use the playback controls to play, stop, rewind, or fast forward through the movie.

PREPARING TO WORK

Before you get started, you need to copy the **11_Movie_Maker** folder onto your hard drive and launch Flash MX. Take a moment to try out the finished Movie Maker, and then open the starter source file.

1   From your hard drive, open the **moviemaker.html** page in your web browser. Drag timeline clips from the palette into one of the three tracks and experiment with the playback controls.

2   Open the **mm_start.fla** file from the 11_Movie_Maker folder on your hard drive.

The start file includes all the buttons, movie clips, and some of the functions needed to make things work.

3   Advance to frame 2 and examine the layer structure in the timeline.

Note: Flash MX makes it easier to take advantage of *object-oriented programming* (OOP) techniques. An *object* is just a set of shared properties (information) and methods (capabilities). The example most Flash users are already familiar with is the `MovieClip` object. All movie clips share certain properties, such as `_x`, `_y`, and `_alpha`, as well as methods, such as `getDepth` and `loadMovie`. Although a full discussion of OOP concepts is beyond the scope of this chapter, a few relevant topics are covered.

Note: This project uses two Flash files. The main file (**moviemaker.swf**) contains the interface and programming. The assets file (**assets_ziffer.swf**) contains the animation and a movie clip containing the background audio. By having the assets in a separate movie, you can more easily manage the artwork without interfering with the core of the application. The assets file contains a set of movie clips with linkage identifiers, enabling you to use the `attachMovie` method to place them on the stage programmatically. Examine the **assets_sample.fla** file to see how it is organized.

4 Open the Movie Explorer panel from the Window menu and examine the movie clips and buttons.

The interface on the main timeline is set up with four parts: the palette, the timeline area, the preview window, and the playback controls. Nearly all the code is found on the main timeline.

Note: The start file already includes most of the functions needed for the Movie Maker. These functions are located on the first keyframe of the **Functions** layer. Each function performs a certain part of the work and many correspond to the actions of the user.

5 Open the Library from the Window menu. Open the **Track Clip** folder in the Library and examine the track-clip symbol.

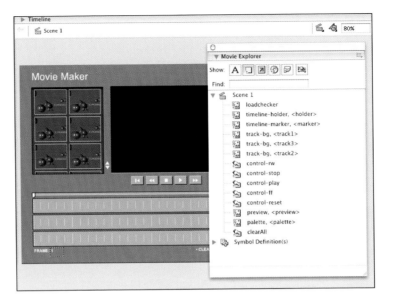

The Movie Explorer shows the movie clips and buttons that have been placed on the stage.

CREATING NEW TIMELINE CLIPS

The timeline clips are the central element of the Movie Maker. The number, type, and position of these clips represent the composition. Timeline clips are created by the spawn function, which is triggered when the user clicks an item in the palette.

1 On the main timeline, with the Actions panel open, select the keyframe in frame 1 of the **Functions** layer. Locate the spawn function in the Actions panel.

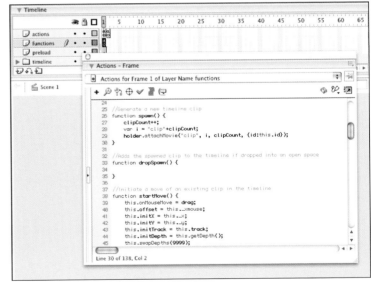

The spawn function is used to create timeline clips.

2 Add this code directly after the line defining the spawn function.

This code attaches a new instance of the timeline clip symbol to the **holder** movie clip. You use four arguments with the `.attachMovie` method: the linkage identifier `"clip"`, and then the instance name, depth value, and an `initObject`.

The code for the `initObject` argument makes use of an abbreviated syntax for creating objects. The `{id:this.id}` statement creates a simple object with a single property id.

```
clipCount++;
var i = "clip"+clipCount;
holder.attachMovie("clip", i, clipCount, {id:this.id});
```

Macromedia Flash MX: The optional `initObject` argument is a new feature of Flash MX. It enables you to assign a set of methods and properties to the clip as it is attached. In this case, you use this feature to pass the id to the newly created movie clip instance. You will see how this is used when you look at the `TimelineClip` class.

DEFINING THE TIMELINECLIP CLASS

A *class* is used to define a set of objects with common features (for instance, a class of trees or a class of kindergarten kids). In ActionScript you define a class using a function. The timeline clips added by the spawn function share certain properties (for instance, which animation segment they represent) and methods (for example, resizing themselves). Using a class enables you to define a single blueprint for your timeline clips.

Note: The distinction between a function and a method is subtle but important. A *method* is a function that has been associated with an object. The beauty of methods is that they have direct access to the properties of the object to which they are attached.

1 Locate the `TimelineClip` function in the Actions window. Add this code directly under the line marked `//Properties`.

The id used when setting the span property is passed to the object by the `attachMovie` method invoked in the spawn function. It identifies which segment of animation the timeline clip represents. (They are numbered 1–15.) The span represents the length of the clip in frames, and the `offset` is used when positioning the clip while it is being dragged.

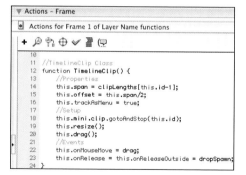

```
this.span = clipLengths[ this.id-1 ];
this.offset = this.span/2;
this.trackAsMenu = true;
```

2 Add this code directly under the line marked
`//Setup:`

These three lines are performed as soon as the new timeline clip is created. The `gotoAndStop` action changes the mini view of the animation based on the `id` of the clip. You then call the `resize` and `drag` methods right away. These two methods are defined by existing functions.

```
this.mini.clip.gotoAndStop(this.id);
this.resize();
this.drag();
```

3 Add this code directly under the line marked
`//Events:`

Here you assign callback functions to the built-in movie clip event handlers. The first line triggers the `drag` function when the user moves her mouse, and the second line triggers the `dropSpawn` function when the user drops the clip.

```
this.onMouseMove = drag;
this.onRelease = this.onReleaseOutside = dropSpawn;
```

4 Add this code directly under the line marked
`//Register Class:`

The first line tells the player that your `TimelineClip` inherits all the built-in methods and properties of the `MovieClip` class. Any of the new methods and properties you attach are added to those already available in all movie clips.

The second line makes use of a powerful new ActionScript command. You use the `registerClass` method to associate the `TimelineClip` class with the Library symbol with the linkage identifier `"clip"`. Note that you are not associating the class with an instance but rather the Library symbol. This means that all new instances of the symbol with the linkage identifier `"clip"` are members of the `TimelineClip` class and therefore have all the properties and methods defined for this class.

```
TimelineClip.prototype = new MovieClip();
Object.registerClass("clip", TimelineClip);
```

Adding a new timeline clip to the movie.

The spawn function attaches and initializes a new clip. The drag function moves the clip to follow the cursor. The dropSpawn function adds or removes the clip based on its position.

MacromediaFlash MX: In Flash 5, you used movie clip events by placing code within an onClipEvent (MovieClipEvent) statement. This approach severely limited your ability to centralize your code, because these statements needed to be placed directly on movie clip instances. In Flash MX you can assign callback functions to these events programmatically. Not only that, but there are also new handlers for button events (for instance, .onPress), which you can use with movie clips.

The ability to add button events to movie clips can simplify complex movies considerably. In Flash 5 it was often necessary to nest a button inside a movie clip. This was necessary any time you needed to catch button events while being able to manipulate visual properties of the button (such as, _x, _y, _width, and _alpha). Now we can add those events directly onto the movie clip instance. In fact, because of these new features there is very little reason for experienced developers to use button symbols.

5 Add this code directly under the line marked //Methods:

Because these methods are common to all members of the TimelineClass, you attach them to the class's prototype. By doing so, all objects created from this class do not contain their own copies of these methods but rather share the exact same set of code. The result is more efficient use of memory in the Flash player.

```
TimelineClip.prototype.dropLocationOkay = dropLocationOkay;
TimelineClip.prototype.updateQuePoints = updateQuePoints;
TimelineClip.prototype.drag = drag;
TimelineClip.prototype.resize = resize;
```

Assign functions to act as methods for the timeline clips.

Adding Drag and Drop Behavior

Now that you have your new timeline clip, you need to create some of the methods that it will use. Four methods are involved in this process: drag, dropSpawn, updateQuePoints, and dropLocationOkay. You are going to add the first two of these.

The drag method has been assigned to the onMouseMove event and is called continuously until you remove the handler. It positions the timeline clip according to the location of the cursor and provides user feedback as the clip is moved around. It does this with the help of updateQuePoints and dropLocationOkay. The dropSpawn method is called when the user releases the mouse button after having just created a new timeline clip.

1 Locate the drag function in the Actions panel. Add this code directly following the line defining the drag function:

Repositioning the timeline clip.

```
this._x = this._parent._xmouse-this.offset;
this._y = this._parent._ymouse;
this.updateQuePoints();
```

The first two lines reposition the clip based on the user's cursor position. The offset is used to handle situations where the user picks up the clip by the edge.

The updateQuePoints updates important information about each timeline clip as it is manipulated by the user. It sets three properties based on the clip's position: begin, end, and track. begin and end are set to the first and last frame where the clip is present. The track property is set to one of four values: 1, 2, 3, or null if the clip is not in a track.

2 Add this code:

Testing the location of clips.

```
if (this.dropLocationOkay()) {
    this._y = _root["track"+this.track]._y;
    this._alpha = 100;
} else {
    this._alpha = 50;
}
updateAfterEvent();
```

The dropLocationOkay method uses the new begin, end, and track values and tests to see whether they overlap with any existing clips. The dropLocationOkay method returns true if the location is acceptable.

If the method returns false, we know that the timeline clip is not in a valid location. We indicate this to the user by setting the alpha property to 50%. Otherwise you set the alpha to 100% and snap the clip to the nearest timeline.

3 Add this code directly following the line defining the dropSpawn function:

Deleting the clip when its location is unaccepatble.

```
delete this.onMouseMove;
if (!this.dropLocationOkay()) this.removeMovieClip();
this.onPress = startMove;
this.onRelease = this.onReleaseOutside = dropMove;
```

The first line removes the onMouseMove handler. This stops the drag method from being called. The next line checks to see whether the user released the clip in an acceptable position. If not, the clip is deleted (along with all of its methods and properties).

Note that when the user moves an existing clip things are treated a little differently. Because of this you have separate `move` and `dropMove` methods. The last line of code reassigns the `.onRelease` and `.onReleaseOutside` events to trigger the `dropMove` method the next time the clip is dropped.

THE DISPLAYFRAME FUNCTION

The playback of the movie is controlled by the `displayFrame` function. This function calculates the current frame and then goes through each timeline clip to see which clips are present in that frame. The flexibility in the user interface makes your work a little more difficult. You cannot assume that the movie is going to be played from start to finish. Instead you have to consider other scenarios, such as the following:

- The playhead is dragged back and forth.
- Playback is started while midway through a timeline clip.
- The `playSpeed` is set for rewind or fast forward.
- The timeline clips are being moved during playback.

In short the function must work in isolation without knowing what has happened before or after it. The user can move the clips or the playhead and always see (and hear) the correct animation in the preview display.

1 Locate the `displayFrame` function in the Actions panel. Add this code to the `displayFrame` function:

The first line declares a new array called `occupied`. You will use this later to monitor which tracks contain clips on the current frame.

The next line calls the `moveMarker` function if the movie is playing. The `moveMarker` changes the position of the playhead based on the `playSpeed` variable. Next you calculate the current frame based on the playhead marker's position.

```
var occupied = new Array(3);
if (playing) moveMarker();
frame = 1+Math.floor((marker._x-tl_left));
```

Tracking the presence of timeline clips.

2 Add this code directly following the statements added in Step 1:

The first line sets up a for-in loop. This type of loop is used to step through the contents of an object. In this case, you are checking each item inside the holder movie clip.

The body of the for-in loop checks each timeline clip within the holder to see whether the current frame lies between the clip's begin and end values. If it is not already present, the clip is added using the attachMovie method.

If the movie is playing normally and the clip is not being dragged, you let the animation segment play. If the movie is not playing back or the clip is being moved, however, you instead set the frame position of the clip based on how far into the clip you are.

```
for (item in holder) {
if (holder[ item] ._alpha == 50) continue;
if (frame >= holder[ item] .begin and frame <= holder[ item] .end) {
        var instance = "i"+holder[ item] .track;
        if (preview[ instance] .id != holder[ item] .id) {
                var linkage = "clip"+holder[ item] .id;
                var depth = 4-holder[ item] .track;
                preview.attachMovie(linkage, instance, depth);
                preview[ instance] .id = holder[ item] .id;
        }
        occupied[ holder[ item] .track]  = true;
        var isDragging = (holder[ item] .onMouseMove == drag);
        if (playing && playSpeed == 1 && !isDragging) {
                preview[ instance] .play();
        } else {
                var clipFrame = 1+frame-holder[ item] .begin;
                preview[ instance] .gotoAndStop(clipFrame);
        }
    }
}
```

3 Add this code directly after the end of the for-in loop:

First you remove any animation clips that are no longer needed.

Next you handle the playback of the background audio. The background audio is treated differently than the other elements. The background audio clip is attached in frame 2 of the Actions layer and is present throughout the movie.

If the movie is playing, the movie clip containing the audio is told to play. Otherwise you cue the movie clip to the right point so that when the movie is played, the audio starts in the appropriate place.

```
for (var i=1;i<4;i++) {
        if (!occupied[ i]) preview[ "i"+i] .removeMovieClip();
}
if (playing && playSpeed == 1) {
        preview.bgAudio.play();
} else {
        preview.bgAudio.gotoAndStop(frame);
}
```

4 Now test your movie. If it is not functioning
as expected, make sure the assets file is located
in the same directory. Use the finished file,
moviemaker.fla, to check the code you have added.

Note: It is extremely rare that a programmer writes polished code in a single pass. This is especially true for routines such as `displayFrame`.

When tackling a complex problem, it's often best to start with a diagram and then translate it into pseudo-code. The descriptions of the code in this chapter are examples of pseudo-code, or explanations in plain English of what the code does. However, real-life pseudo-code more often consists of scribbled notes on the back of a piece of paper.

You can create the framework for your projects using a combination of function declarations, comments, and trace statements. Here is a simple example:

```
//This function returns the average of two integers.
function average(a,b) {
        trace("calculating an average");
}
```

Now you can choose where to start filling in the details. Much like taking a test, it's sometimes better to start with the easy questions and return to the tough ones later. For complex routines, you often need several passes to get the exact functionality you need. Getting comfortable with this iterative approach will help you tackle all sorts of complex programming challenges.

SUMMARY

Flash MX enables developers to create sophisticated applications. However, building such applications involves more than a knowledge of ActionScript. It also requires the ability to step back, look carefully at the steps involved, and translate these steps into code.

In this chapter you looked at a few of the new features of Macromedia Flash MX that enable you to create flexible centralized code. Specifically, you made use of dynamically assigned event handlers and classes to define a blueprint for a set of objects.

Although creating applications requires a certain discipline in how you approach your work, don't ever be afraid to write, rewrite, and experiment as you go.

Your presentation requires you to move from one screen to another. How do you do it elegantly? The trick lies in applying a transition. Transitions enable you to control how you move from one page to another. A simple cut just doesn't do it anymore; you need to be able to add a little jazz. In this project, you will learn how to create transitions with ActionScript and apply them programmatically to any point within a movie. By the end of the project, you will be able to apply 18 different types of transition. Each transition can be individually taken from the script and applied to any presentation you have created.

12

TRANSITIONS

by Matthew David
with images by Jimmy Chen

Difficulty Rating: ★★★

Made With: Macromedia Flash MX

Final File Size: 27KB

Modem Download Time: 20 seconds

Development Time: 3 hours

IT WORKS LIKE THIS

The transition movie requires a lot of script. That's the bad news. The good news is that most of the script is repeated (you'll see why later), which makes the scripts you create very flexible. To view a complete version of the movie, open **final_transition.swf** from the **Projects/12_Transitions** folder on the accompanying CD. The final .swf is a movie of green leaves with 18 different buttons. Each button is a different transition.

The entire movie is controlled through the use of ActionScript. Each button on the right is script that activates a particular transitional effect on the image to the left. The transitions are all mathematically calculated with the ActionScript at the opening of the movie. The buttons on the stage trigger these scripts to affect the **slice** movie instance. The result is a transitional effect.

The transition script itself is embedded as an initialization script within the main movie. You will also be able to dynamically change the transitioning image to another image, completing the transition from one image to another.

PREPARING TO WORK

Before starting, you need to copy the **12_Transitions** folder onto your hard disk, start Flash, and open the **transition.fla** file.

This file has some of the building blocks for the project already completed. You can see that the buttons are already placed in the correct positions on the screen.

The movie has four layers, and each layer is only one frame long. All of the transitions will be programmatically created, so there is no need for lengthy animations.

These are the four movie layers:

- **Scripts.** The topmost layer. Frame 1 contains the script that is the engine that runs the entire movie.

- **Buttons.** The second layer. It separates all of the buttons from the graphics on the stage, making it easier to control the scripts for each button later.

- **Text and Background.** The third and fourth layers. These contain the text and graphical elements. Toward the middle of the left side of the movie there is a white dot, which is a placeholder for a movie clip. This placeholder identifies a movie clip with a blank first frame. This movie clip is an instance of the **slice holder** movie clip. The clip is named holder.

Open the Library (Ctrl+L/Cmd+L) and expand the Movies folder.

The six movie clips in this folder will be the triggers for the transitions: **img Holder**, **img selector**, **place_holder**, **preset selector**, **slice**, and **slice holder**.

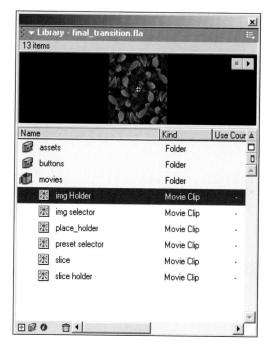

The **movies** folder in the Library contains the movie clips that will have script applied.

INITIALIZING THE MOVIE CLIPS

The movie clip instance on the stage must be named before you can add any scripts. This is because ActionScript can trigger events in a movie clip only when it can navigate to that movie clip by name. The first movie clip to be named is the empty **slice holder** movie clip.

1. Select the instance of the **slice holder** movie clip in frame 1 of the **Scripts** layer. In the Property Inspector, set the instance name to **holder**.

   This will be used to identify the movie clip with ActionScript later on. (Note that the Property Inspector does not always open by default. It only opens by default if you are using one of the default Panel layouts or if the last time you used Flash MX you did not close out the Inspector. If you did, however, the Inspector will not open by default.)

2. Locate the **slice** movie clip in the Library, right-click on it (Cmd-click on the Mac), and open its properties. Check the Export for ActionScript and Export in First Frame options, and identify the movie clip as **pic**.

3. From the Library, double-click the **img Holder** movie clip.

   This will open it into edit view. This movie clip controls which image is having the transition effect applied to it. There are three keyframes to this movie clip, and each keyframe has an image. The first has the image of the green leaves, the second has the water, and the third has the fire image.

4. Select frame 1 of the **img Holder** movie clip's timeline. From the Property Inspector, label this frame **img1**. Select frame 2 and name it **img2**, and then select frame 3 and label it **img3**.

The Property Inspector gives you immediate access to the common features of a movie clip. Here the **slice holder** movie clip has the name **holder** added to it.

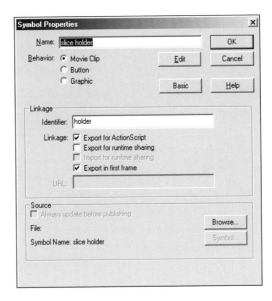

The Symbol Properties dialog box enables you to change the identifier and other features of the **slice holder** movie clip.

5 Add this code to frame 1:

This completes the functionality of this **img Holder** movie clip. The function of this script enables the movie clip to correctly navigate to a specific frame based on the value of _parent.type.

When the main movie is complete, the user sees effects being applied to an image on the stage. The effect is an illusion. The image on the screen is replaced with a movie clip that actually does the transition effect on the screen.

6 From the Library, open the **slice** movie clip. Select the mask layer and draw a rectangle on the stage that's 100 pixels high by 5 pixels wide, keeping the stroke turned off. Drag an instance of the **img Holder** movie clip onto the stage into the **img** layer and give it an instance name of **img**.

7 In the **slice** movie clip, extend the timeline to 50 frames in both layers. In the **img** layer, add a keyframe in frame 50. Select this keyframe and move the **img Holder** movie clip 100 pixels to the left of the rectangle. Add a motion tween between frames 1 and 50. Right-click (Ctrl-click) the mask layer to make it a mask and apply it to **img Holder**.

8 Select frame 1 of the **Masks** layer on the main timeline and add this code in the Actions panel:

```
gotoAndStop(_parent.type);
```

Navigating to a specific frame.

The images in the **img Holder** Holder movie clip will be jumped to with ActionScript later. To get the correct image, each frame with a new image must be identified with a short script at the beginning of the movie clip.

```
if (!once) {
    once=true;
    frame=_name.split("_");
    frame=frame[1];
    gotoAndStop(frame);
}
```

Here Flash is able to navigate to the correct label within the **img Holder** movie clip.

Essentially, this script enables Flash to navigate to the correct label within the **img Holder** movie clip and attach it to the mask. The key code here is the `name.split` method. This method breaks a string into specified parts. In this case, the part is the name that is going to be passed to it from the main movie. This prevents any confusion within the program over which portion of the image should be presented.

SCRIPTING THE IMAGE SELECTION BUTTONS

The following steps explain how to set up the buttons on the stage that will allow you to dynamically change the image being transitioned.

1   From the Library, open the **img selector** movie clip, which has a blank movie clip in the center of the screen. Select the movie clip and add this code in the Actions panel:

Here a variable called `frame` is being created. It is passing an action to the same level as the main movie and will be triggered when a user releases his or her mouse.

```
on (release) {
    _level0.setUp(frame);
}
```

This script passes the value of the frame variable to the main movie.

2   On the main stage, drag three instances of the **img selector** movie clip over the text of "Leaves," "Water," and "Fire" along the top of the movie clip.

These buttons control which image will be displayed on the screen.

3   Select the movie clip over the text "Leaves" and add this script:

By leveraging the code already embedded in the button, all you need to do is call the `img selector` variable `frame` and tell it to which frame to change the image. Here the frame is **img1**.

```
onClipEvent (load) {
    frame=" img1";
}
```

This script tells Flash to load the image in the **img1** frame into the **img_placeholder** movie clip.

4 Select the movie clip over the text "Water" and add the same script, but change `frame=" img1";` to `frame=" img2";`. Do the same for "Fire" and change the reference to `img3`.

```
onClipEvent (load) {
    frame=" img2";
}
```

This script tells Flash to load the image in the **img2** frame into the **img_placeholder** movie clip.

```
onClipEvent (load) {
    frame=" img3";
}
```

This script tells Flash to load the image in the **img3** frame into the **img_placeholder** movie clip.

5 Add this code to the instance of the **slice holder** movie clip on the stage:

This step tells Flash to execute the new effect when the movie clip with the effect is played. Line 2 of the code renders the correct image into the movie clip. The script `_level0.readPre` applies the correct transitional effect. The image is now prepared to have transitions applied to it.

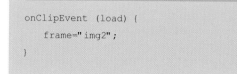

The choice of image is now controlled through ActionScript.

```
onClipEvent (enterFrame) {
    _level0.render();
}
onClipEvent (keyDown) {
    if (Key.getCode() == "45");
    {
        _level0.readPre();
    }
}
```

The Transition events will be triggered as the transitioned movie clip plays.

Setting Up the Transitions

Now that the movie clips have been set up, you have to add the guts to the movie: the transitions themselves. Each transition is created with ActionScript, so tune in the left side of your brain. You're going to need it.

1   Add this code to frame 1 of the **Scripts** layer in the Actions panel:

The first section of script identifies in order which properties will be manipulated as the transitions. Each line defines an effect, which you will create, that can be applied to movie clips on the stage. The array shown identifies the parameters that can be applied to different effects:

- waveLength. Oscillation effect on the image

- sangle. The angle at which the image will be moved in the transition

- distance. The distance the image will move

- drift. How far the image will skew

- picDrift. The skew distance of each image

- rotate. The amount that the image will rotate

- optX. How far off the X-axis the image will move

- optY. How far off the Y-axis the image will move

- optXs. How much the image will be scaled along the X-axis

- optYs. How much the image will be scaled along the Y-axis

- optR. How much the image will be scaled as it is rotated

These are the effects that will be applied to the final transition.

```
function readPre () {
    var choice=new Array()
    choice.push(_level0.waveLength);
    choice.push(_level0.sangle);
    choice.push(_level0.dist);
    choice.push(_level0.drift);
    choice.push(_level0.picDrift);
    choice.push(_level0.rotate);
    choice.push(_level0.optX);
    choice.push(_level0.optY);
    choice.push(_level0.optXs);
    choice.push(_level0.optYs);
    choice.push(_level0.optR);
}
```

Each choice identifies a different effect that can be applied to the **img Holder** movie clip on the stage.

The next step is to organize when each effect will be played back; this is achieved with the following script. Each item in this list has a number, and that number is used to determine where the specific effect is to be executed in the render script.

2   Add this code below the code you added to frame 1 of the **Scripts** layer:

This gives you 11 variables to modify. This will become more relevant when the effects are being created later in the script.

The most important event here is the linking of the transitions being created to a movie clip on the main stage. The link is made absolute with the line `stage.attachMovie("pic", "p_"+i, i)`. The link will be made absolute with a line of code that will be added later in this step. This attaches an instance of the **slice** movie clip on the stage, which you gave the identifier pic. The instance is attached with an instance name. To make the code easier, the instance name is then turned into a variable in the following line.

The math needed to calculate specific values opens with `nangle += waveLength`. Here the calculation for `waveLength` is being identified. The distance an image will move is calculated with `scale = dist*Math.sin(angle)`. Here the value of scale is equal to `dist` multiplied by the angle of `sin`.

The true value of `waveLength` is identified as the value of `waveLength + nangle`.

```
function preset (choice) {
    _level0.waveLength = choice[ 0] ;
    _level0.mwaveLength.reset();
    _level0.sangle=choice[ 1] ;
    _level0.msangle.reset();
    _level0.dist=choice[ 2] ;
    _level0.mdist.reset();
    _level0.drift=choice[ 3] ;
    _level0.mdrift.reset();
    _level0.picDrift=choice[ 4] ;
    _level0.mpicDrift.reset();
    _level0.rotate=choice[ 5] ;
    _level0.mrotate.reset();
    _level0.optX=choice[ 6] ;
    _level0.moptX.reset();
    _level0.optY=choice[ 7] ;
    _level0.moptY.reset();
    _level0.optXs=choice[ 8] ;
    _level0.moptXs.reset();
    _level0.optYs=choice[ 9] ;
    _level0.moptYs.reset();
    _level0.optR=choice[ 10] ;
    _level0.moptR.reset();
}
```

The order in this setting will be the order in which they are rendered.

3 Add this code below the script in frame 1 of the
Scripts layer:

The script initializes the 19 visual effects. The value
and movement of each effect are placed in the array
for each line. The sequence for each line matches
the order established in the function `preset`. With
the values now in place, you can actually go in and
change the values. This enables you to come up
with your own transitional styles.

Each line will be associated with a specific button.
If you take `pre9`, you can break down the effect
that will be applied as:

waveLength	-0.2
sangle	-6
dist	100
drift	0.004
picDrift	-2
rotate	0
optX	0.4
optY	0.2
optXs	0
optYs	0
optR	-0.2

```
pre0=[ 0,0,0,0,0,0,0,0,0,0,0] ;
pre1=[ -0.15,0,12.5,0.005,0,0,0,1,0,0,0] ;
pre2=[ -0.05,0,90,0.001,-2,0,0.001,0,0,0,1] ;
pre3=[ -2,0,100,0.04,0,90,0.001,0,0,1,0.01] ;
pre4=[ -0.1,0,100,0.0006,0,-91,-0.8,-1,0.3,0.3,-0.01] ;
pre5=[ -0.07,0,100,-0.002,0,0,0.2,1,0,1,1] ;
pre6=[ -0.03,0,100,0.002,0,0,0,0.04,0,1,0] ;
pre7=[ -1,0,13,0.005,0.06,-90,0,1,0,0,0] ;
pre8=[ -1.3,0,100,0.004,0,0,1,1,1,1,1] ;
pre9=[ -0.2,-6,100,0,-2,0,0.4,0.2,0,0,-0.2] ;
pre10=[ -0.1,0,100,0.004,-2,0,-1,0.7,0,-0.7,1] ;
pre11=[ -0.04,0,41,-0.005,0,0,-1,0.3,-0.2,-1,1] ;
pre12=[ -0.05,0,100,0.002,0,0,0,0,0,0,1] ;
pre13=[ -2.4,0,18,0.01,0,0,0,1,0,1,0] ;
pre14=[ -3.2,0,100,0.00345,0,0,-0.85,1,0,-0.4,0] ;
pre15=[ -0.6,0,5.6,0.03,0,0,0,0.06,0,1,0] ;
pre16=[ -1.1,0,12.5,-0.005,0,-180,0,1,0,-1,0] ;
pre17=[ -0.5,0,100,0.003,0,0,-0.1185,1,-1,-1,0] ;
pre18=[ -0.3,0,100,0,1,0,-0.08,0.2795,0,0.17,0.7] ;
```

The order and value of
each effect for the render
engine is specified.

The final effect will be to apply a snaking, undulating effect to the **slice** movie clip on the stage. Each of the 19
effects is linked directly to the `readPre` array, which in turn has each item (such as `waveLength`, `dist`, and `optX`)
mathematically calculated in the `render` function. The result is a highly customizable set of transitional effects.

Up to this point, it looks like you have a great list of variables. The only catch is that all of the variables, such
as `optR` and `picDrift`, are meaningless. What you need to do now is associate the variables with real methods
and properties.

4   Add this code:

5   Complete the script on frame 1 with a simple
    `stop()` command.

```
stop();
```

This stops the movie from repeating itself and
constantly resetting itself to the default settings.

```
function setUp (type) {
    var stage=_level0.holder;
    for (i=1; i<51; i++) {
        stage.attachMovie("pic", "p_"+i, i);
        pic = stage["p_"+i];
        pic.type=type;a
        pic._x = (i*2.9)-(25*2.9);
        nangle += waveLength;
        angle = sangle+nangle;
        scale = dist*Math.sin(angle);
        pic._yscale = 100-scale;
    }
}
function render () {
    var nangle;
    var stage=_level0.holder;
    stage._rotation=_level0.rotate;
    for (i=1; i<51; i++) {
        pic = stage["p_"+i];
        nangle += _level0.waveLength;
        _level0.sangle+=_level0.drift;
        var angle = _level0.sangle+nangle;
        var scale = _level0.dist*Math.sin(angle);
        pic._x = ((i*2.9)-(25*2.9))-(scale*optX);
        pic._y = scale*optY;
        pic._xscale = 100+(scale*optXS);
        pic._yscale = 100-(scale*optYS);
        pic._rotation = (scale*optR);
if (int(_level0.picDrift) == 0) {
myFrame=i;
} else {
pic.frame-=int(_level0.picDrift);
myframe=pic.frame;
if (myframe<1) {
myframe=50;
} else if (myframe > 50) {
myframe=1;
}
pic.frame=myframe;
}
pic.gotoAndStop(myframe);
    }
}
```

The actual visual presentation
of each effect is identified
with this script.

187

6 Finally, select frame 1 of the **Scripts** layer. Add this code:

Here you can control how the movie is presented and which image will be the first on the stage.

Line 1, `_quality`, controls the playback quality of the movie, set here to BEST. The setting can also be changed to LOW, MEDIUM, or HIGH. If the audience viewing this movie is using a slow computer, I recommend changing the quality to LOW. This makes the image and text appear grainy, but the animation is rendered much faster and more efficiently. You will have to weigh whether it is worth losing image quality to have faster playback.

Line 2 triggers the transitional effect called pre0.

In Line 3, img1 identifies the default image to be displayed on the stage.

```
_quality = "BEST";
preset(_level0.pre0);
setUp("img1");
```

ADDING THE INTERACTION

The final step is to let users choose which effect they want to apply to the final movie. The Transition buttons on the right side of the stage do this. Each title, including Reset, has an invisible button on it. The invisible button is an old trick—but a good one—for hiding code on the stage.

1 From the Library, open the **preset selector** movie clip. Select the button and add this code:

```
on (release) {
    _level0.preset(_level0["pre"+num]);
}
```

This script identifies which transitional effect is being applied when.

2 Select the button over the word "Reset." In the Actions panel, add this code to the button on the main timeline:

```
onClipEvent (load) {
    num=0;
}
```

This script is the default setting for the transitioning movie clips on the stage.

The script is telling Flash to dynamically create a preset value as pre + the variable num. For the Reset button, you see that the value is 0 (num=0). Hence, Flash must look for *pre0*. That script added to frame 1 has pre0=[0,0,0,0,0,0,0,0,0,0,0], which resets all of the values of the effects for the image to zero. Basically, nothing will happen.

3 Go back to the main movie and select the button over "Marching." Add this code.

4 Preview the movie. Select the Marching button. The image should now animate. If you don't like the animation, select the Reset button.

Every button can be associated with a preset value. To do this, add the same script applied to the Marching button with the exception of changing the value of num.

Here are the transitions with the correct num:

```
Flag          num=1
Karma         num=2
Ink Blot      num=3
Marching      num=4
Wind          num=5
Over Easy     num=6
Water         num=7
Tennis        num=8
Snake         num=9
Energy        num=10
Slinky        num=11
Waves         num=12
Chaos         num=13
In & Out      num=14
Breeze        num=15
Flame         num=16
Rain          num=17
Drum Sticks   num=18
```

```
onClipEvent (load) {
    num=4;
}
```

This script applies the Marching visual.

How to Improve

For this project, you are using static graphics. Each of the movie clips in each of the frames of the **img Holder** movie clip could be a short animation itself. You can have more than three. All you need to do is add additional frames to **img Holder** and label each new frame.

You probably have noticed that the transitioned image is a specific size. If you replace the image with a larger image, you will immediately notice that it is being cut short in size. The rectangle mask in the **slice** movie clip controls the size of the movie on the screen. Increasing the size of the rectangle will let larger images be transitioned effectively in the final movie.

Finally, the transitions can easily be pulled from this movie and applied to other movie clips to move users from one scene to the next.

Flash MX lets designers and developers create masks with animated graphics, programmatically controlled movie clips, and dynamic text. Masks can be used to reveal, cover, or create design effects. This allows so many exciting, creative opportunities that it must be considered one of the best new design features.

Programmatic, dynamic, and animated masks can be used to create animated transitions, user-controlled and user-influenced masks, games in which masks are used to hide and reveal parts of the scene, masks that reveal the inner workings of objects, masks that zoom in or out of graphics, and even new and intriguing interfaces. Using dynamic, animated masking combined with scaling, rotating, and other effects completely opens up the world of the Macromedia Flash designer to any kind of creative effect imaginable.

13

DYNAMIC MASKING

by Glenn Thomas
with images by Troy Parke

Difficulty Rating: ★★★

Made With:

    Scanned watercolors

    An HP ScanJet 6200C

    Macromedia Flash MX

Final File Size: 82KB

Modem Download Time: 10 to 15 seconds on a 56K connection

Development Time: 2 hours or less

IT WORKS LIKE THIS

The dynamic masking presented here provides a platform to understand animated and dynamic masking by creating a simple example using the fundamental attributes of this new feature, namely animation within a movie clip and the ability to access movie clips on mask layers using ActionScript. For the sake of brevity, a less complicated programmatic example is presented here that can be taken and creatively expanded by designers and graphic artists with their own different masking effects.

The goal was to develop a project that enables a user to reveal a picture by making another picture disappear through the user's mouse movement. After the new picture appears, a new mask is dynamically created, and the process of revealing another picture begins all over again. This can go on indefinitely for as many pictures as a designer wants to introduce into the project.

Macromedia Flash MX: This project could be done completely programmatically in Flash MX using only ActionScript contained in the first frame of the movie. In Flash MX, the mask could be created on-the-fly with the drawing API and be animated solely with functions. The photos could be loaded dynamically as .jpegs into the .swf from a web site and changed as needed. Although quite exciting to contemplate, it's definitely beyond the scope of this short example to explain the complexity of such a movie.

Moving the mouse over the current watercolor reveals a new one below it.

Note that there's no title or loading sequence in this movie even though there are two large photographs in the first frame. To be conscientious of users, it would be important to add a title or loading sequence to cover the 10 to 15 seconds of preload that the project requires on a 56K modem connection.

Before developing the project, it's useful to open the **dynamic masking final.swf** and play with the finished movie to understand how it works. As a viewer, the movie opens with a simple picture and a request to move around the photo with the mouse. As the user moves the mouse over the picture, that square part of the picture grows smaller and disappears. A new image shows through the parts of the picture that have disappeared. When the first picture is completely gone and the new picture is revealed, the viewer is prompted to continue moving the mouse over the picture to reveal yet another picture.

The dynamic masking project contains three main parts internal to the Flash movie:

- Photos to be revealed
- A dynamically created mask with movie clips containing buttons that trigger actions
- A function that causes events to occur

PREPARING TO WORK

Before starting, copy the **13_Dynamic_Masking** folder onto your hard disk, start Flash, and open the **dynamic_masking_START.fla** file.

The **13_Dynamic_Masking** folder contains three .jpg images and the **dynamic masking START.fla** file with layers set up and basic graphics and text defined. The folder also contains a **dynamic masking finished.fla** file and a **dynamic masking finished.swf** file, both of which are useful for comparison throughout the project.

ADDING THE MOVIE ATTRIBUTES AND PHOTO ASSETS

Because there's no character animation in this project, it's useful to set a high frame rate for both motion graphics playback and any future programmatic work that uses `enterFrame`. In this case, set the frame rate in the Property Inspector to 30fps. A higher rate will cause motion graphics to play back more smoothly and `enterFrame` actions to happen faster. When using high frame rates, it's important to test the finished movie on multiple machines to see how it plays back on slow computers.

The project movie is set up with a movie dimension of 400×350 for an intended photo size of 400×300. Although the movie dimension doesn't matter, the size of the photo area is crucial because it affects the file size of the movie and thus the download time.

Begin creating the project by adding the photos to the main movie timeline.

1 Drag the **patagonia.jpg** file from the Library and drop it onto the **mask pic** layer.

An instance of **patagonia.jpg** is placed on the **mask pic** layer.

2 Select the photo and create a new movie clip called **mcPic1**.

Convert the photo to a movie clip and name it **mcPic1**.

> **Note:** Although the programming in this example doesn't specifically use the photo movie clips, it's good practice to plan ahead and place graphic assets into movie clips. By doing so, it's easy to access them programmatically at any time. It's also much easier to swap out graphic assets if they need to be changed in the future.

3 Drag and drop **tomiya.png** onto the **mask2 pic** layer.

4 Select it and create a **mcPic2** movie clip.

> **Note:** Better aesthetic results usually occur if raster assets such as photos are resized to the exact intended usage size in an editing program prior to importing them into Flash. Resized raster images tend to contain artifacts in Flash and don't provide satisfactory image quality. Although resizing can be useful for quick comping purposes, it produces inferior final results.

5 Select **mcPic1** and **mcPic2**. Use the Align tool to align the images vertically and horizontally to the upper-left corner of the movie stage.

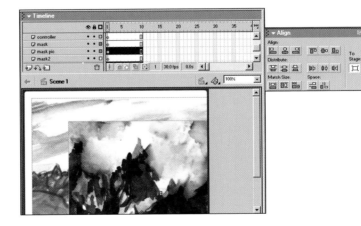

Using the Align panel, align the two clips horizontally and vertically.

6 Place a blank keyframe in frame 2 of the
mask pic layer.

The basic graphic assets are now in place. A dynamically
created mask can now be used to let the user make the top
photo (**mcPic1**) disappear and reveal the second photo
(**mcPic2**).

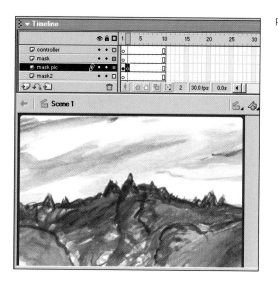

Place a blank keyframe in frame 2.

CREATING THE MASK STRUCTURE

It's now time to create the basic structure for the mask. Three symbols make up the mask
movie clip: a basic shape (in this case, a square), a movie clip containing an animated
mask effect, and a shell movie clip that contains the dynamically created mask.

1 On the **mask** layer, draw a red square with the
stroke turned off.

Not turning off the stroke causes unnecessary use of
the processor during graphic refresh because it has to
continually—and unnecessarily—redraw the line.

2 Select the square and, in the Property Inspector, make it 25×25.

Make the square 25 pixels wide by 25 pixels high.

3 Select the square and turn it into a movie clip called **mcShape**. Make sure to set the Registration point to the upper-left corner.

4 Delete this movie clip off the work area.

It will be used inside the mask effect movie clip later.

Make the square into a new movie clip called **mcShape**.

CREATING THE ANIMATED EFFECT

After the simple shape used to create the mask effect is built, it's on to creating the actual animated effect used in the project. As an effect, this movie has a square becoming smaller and disappearing that's a simple tween on the square mask shape. As the viewer rolls over the photo, square pieces of the photo appear to recede and disappear in waves. Any animated effect that a designer can think of is now possible with the new mask functionality.

1 Create a new empty movie clip and name it **mcMaskEffect**. Don't close the dialog box yet.

2 Click the Advanced button in the Create New Symbol dialog box. In the Linkage area, select Export for ActionScript. Leave Export in First Frame checked and change the identifier to **square**.

   The identifier is the name that will be used to access the movie clip programmatically with ActionScript.

3 Add three layers to this new movie clip, giving it a total of four. From the top down, these layers are **labels**, **frame actions**, **effect**, and **base**. Add 30 frames to all the layers.

Create a new movie clip and use the Advanced options to change the clip's linkage identifier and to set export options.

4 Add a `stop();` action in frame 1 of the **frame actions** layer.

```
stop();
```

5 Drag and drop an instance of the **mcShape** movie clip onto the **base** layer.

6　Align **mcShape** to the upper-left corner of the movie clip stage by using the Align tool or by setting both X and Y to 0 in the Property Inspector.

With the button placed, it's easy to create the desired animated effect. The one trick here is to make sure to compensate for the registration point on the **mcShape** movie clip being in the upper-left corner.

7　Add a blank keyframe in frame 5 of all the layers.

8　On the **label** layer, add a label named **off** in frame 5 and on the **frame actions** layer, add a `play();` action.

9　Add another instance of the **mcShape** movie clip in the **effect** layer in frame 5. Once again, align the movie clip to the upper-left corner of the stage.

10　Add a keyframe in frame 25 of the **effect** layer and a blank keyframe in frame 26 of the **effect** and **frame actions** layers. Place a `stop();` action in frame 26 of the **frame actions** layer.

11　Make the **mcShape** instance in frame 25 of the **effect** layer smaller. Make it 5% of the original size.

Note: There are no alphas in masks. However, it's now possible to simulate alpha transparencies in masks by programmatically synching a transparent movie clip with the mask movie clip. Tethering the two movie clips like this might cause playback hesitations, so test thoroughly.

Note: When resizing, the movie clip will resize to its registration point rather than to the center point. This often causes movie clips to become misaligned when they are resized. This problem can be fixed by moving the placement of the movie clips after resizing them (as is done here) or by changing the registration point to the center of the movie clip before resizing. This is done by Alt+clicking/Option+clicking on the center point when the object is selected with the Free Transform tool. This only affects the specific instance of the symbol or shape.

Note: Draggable movie clips can only be used on mask layers if they're synched with a movie clip outside the mask layer. Buttons do not stay active on mask layers, but movie clips do maintain their integrity. Use the standard `startDrag` ActionScript to make a movie clip on a nonmask layer draggable and then use `enterFrame` to synchronize the x and y coordinates of the dragged movie clip with a movie clip on the mask layer.

12 Onion skin frames 24 and 25 with the Edit Multiple Frames option. Select both movie clips and center them vertically and horizontally to each other with the Align tool. Turn onion skinning off.

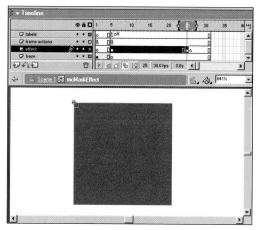

Use Edit Multiple Frames onion skinning to select both movie clips.

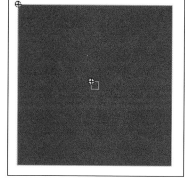

Center the clips horizontally and vertically.

13 Create a motion tween between frame 5 and frame 25 on the **effect** layer.

Add a motion tween to the **effect** layer.

DYNAMICALLY BUILDING THE MASK

In this movie, ActionScript is used to build a mask out of the **mcMaskEffect** movie clips based on a grid of rows and columns. This creates a rectangular mask with evenly spaced square masks. Using differently shaped movie clips or distinct algorithms to place the shapes would allow for the creation of an infinite variety of masks and mask effects.

1 Return to the main timeline and create a new movie clip called **mcMask**.

2 Rename the layer in the new **mcMask** movie clip to **frame actions**.

This movie clip will contain one single frame that will build the mask.

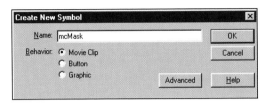

Create a new movie clip called **mcMask**.

3 Add a `stop();` action to the first frame:

```
stop();
```

4 Add the variable definitions for the mask area and the movie clip size after the `stop();` action:

It's crucial to define the total mask area and the size of each individual movie clip in the mask to calculate the number of columns and rows needed in the grid.

```
var width = 400;
var height = 300;
var maskWidth = 20;
var maskHeight = 20;
```

5 Add this code next:

This code determines the number of columns and rows needed in the grid and defines those variables, in this case `kTotal` for the columns and `iTotal` for the rows.

In building the mask dynamically, there will be 20 columns and 15 rows for a total of 300 movie clips in the mask. The rows and columns divide neatly in this example, but if they don't, it's crucial to use `int` to make the number an integer.

```
var kTotal = width/maskWidth;
var iTotal = height/maskHeight;
```

6 Add a last line of code:

```
_root.maskTotal = kTotal*iTotal;
```

This code changes the `maskTotal` variable in the root timeline to the mathematically determined number of movie clips. The `maskTotal` variable will be defined when the rollover programming for this exercise is written. This mathematically determined number, the total number of movie clips created in the mask, will be used to determine when actions occur in the movie.

With all the variables for the overall creation of the mask grid defined, it's now possible to add the code to build the mask in the current frame. The code goes step by step through each row and attaches a new movie clip in each column of the grid. When each column is filled, the code starts attaching movie clips in the next row until all the rows and columns are filled.

7 Add this code below the previously defined variables:

```
var i = 0;    //The variable for the rows.
var k = 0;    //The variable for the columns.
var l = 0;    //The variable for the movie clip level.
```

This defines the simple variables that will be used to keep track of whether the rows and columns have been filled and to what level each new movie clip will be added.

8 Add this code:

```
while (i < iTotal){}
```

This code continues doing the actions inside the brackets until the number of rows filled in the grid equals the number of total rows.

9 Inside the first `while` action, add another `while` action. Make sure the second `while` action is inside the closing bracket of the first `while` action. Add this code:

```
while (k < kTotal){}
```

Using the `k` and `kTotal` variables as the expression keeps track of the number of columns that have been filled for each row in the grid and lets actions continue until all the columns have been filled.

10 Add this code inside the second `while` action:

This defines a name for each new movie clip that is related to its position in the grid: `mcSq1_1` signifies the movie clip in the first row and first column, `mcSq1_2` signifies the movie clip in the first row and second column, and so on.

```
newMC = 'mcSq' + i + "_" + k;
```

11 Add this code inside the second `while` loop:

This code attaches a new movie clip to the stage on a new level for each column and row intersection in the grid using the `newMC` variable for a name. In this case, the movie clip that is attached is the **mcShape** movie clip with the linkage name `square`. The variable `l` assigns the attached movie clip to a unique level.

```
attachMovie('square', newMC, l);
```

12 Add this code, still inside the second `while` loop:

Each attached movie clip is first placed in the top-left corner of the movie clip **mcMask**. This code resizes the attached movie clip to the proper dimensions and then defines new x and y coordinates for the new movie clip using the row and column numbers multiplied by the size of the movie clip. This code moves the new movie clip to its proper place in the grid.

```
eval(newMC)._width= maskWidth;
eval(newMC)._height = maskHeight;
eval(newMC)._x = k*maskWidth;
eval(newMC)._y = i*maskHeight;
```

13 Add this code, still inside the second `while` action:

This code updates the column number (the variable `k`) and increases the level number (the variable `l`) by 1.

```
k++;
l++;
```

14 Add this code outside the second `while` action but still inside the first `while` action:

```
k = 0;
i++;
```

When all the columns in a row are filled, the code then moves to the next row in the grid and begins filling columns there. When that happens, the row variable needs to be reset and the current row number increased. This code accomplishes those tasks.

The code to create the dynamically built mask is now done.

15 To create a dynamically built mask in this project, it's crucial to return to the main timeline and place an instance of **mcMask** onto the **mask** layer in frame 1. Give it an instance name of **mask**. Align the movie clip with the top-left corner of the movie and turn the layer into a mask.

Macromedia Flash MX: An exciting new feature of masks is the capability to programmatically assign one movie clip as a mask to another movie clip with the `setMask` method. This enables masking to occur completely on-the-fly.

```
MovieClipToBeMasked.setMask( MovieClipThatActsAsMask );
```

To cancel a mask created in this way, pass the value `null` to the `setMask` method.

```
MovieClipToBeMasked.setMask( null );
```

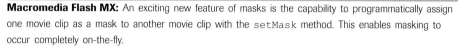

The completed code that creates the grid and attaches the mask.

```
▼ Actions - Frame
  Actions for Frame 1 of Layer Name frame actions
+ ⊘ ⊕ ✓ ≡ ⊡
var width = 400;
var height = 300;
var maskWidth = 20;
var maskHeight = 20;
var kTotal = width/maskWidth;
var iTotal = height/maskHeight;
_root.maskTotal = kTotal*iTotal;

//Create Grid and Attach Mask
var i = 0;
var k = 0;
var l = 0;
while (i < iTotal){
    while (k < kTotal){
        newMC = 'mcSq' + i + "_" + k;
        attachMovie('square', newMC, l);
        eval(newMC)._width = maskWidth;
        eval(newMC)._height = maskHeight;
        eval(newMC)._x = k*maskWidth;
        eval(newMC)._y = i*maskHeight;
        k++;
        l++;
    }
    k = 0;
    i++;
}
Line 29 of 29, Col 2
```

CREATING THE CONTROLLER MOVIE CLIP

Because Flash MX doesn't allow buttons to maintain state within the mask, it's now necessary to create a movie clip structure identical to the **mcMask** movie clip that contains a rollover button to trigger the mask effect.

The basic structure for the controller movie clip is made up of an invisible button, a movie clip containing the rollover button, and a shell movie clip that contains the dynamically created movie clip structure.

1   On the **controller** layer, draw a red square with the stroke turned off.

2   Select the square and, in the Property Inspector, make it 25×25.

3   Select the square and turn it into a button symbol called **btn_Square**. Make sure to set the registration point to the upper-left corner.

4   Delete this button off the work area.

The next movie clip that needs to be made is one that contains a rollover button that can cause actions to occur on the movie clips in the mask.

5   Create a new empty movie clip and name it **mcMaskEffect_Control**. Don't close the dialog box yet.

6   Click the Advanced button in the Create New Symbol dialog box. In the Linkage area, select Export for ActionScript. Leave Export in First Frame checked and change the identifier to **control**.

7   Add two layers to this new movie clip, giving it a total of three. From the top down, these layers are **labels**, **frame actions**, and **button**. Add eight frames to all the layers.

8   Add a stop(); action in frame 1 of the **frame actions** layer.

9   Drag and drop an instance of the **btn_Square** symbol onto the **button** layer.

10   Align **btn_Square** to the upper-left corner of the movie clip stage by using the Align tool or by setting both X and Y to 0 in the Property Inspector.

11   Make the **btn_Square** symbol transparent by selecting Color equal to an Alpha of 0% in the Property Inspector.

Making the button transparent is more processor intensive than using a button containing only a hit area (making it also transparent to the user). Unfortunately, a symbol containing a button without a hit area doesn't resize properly so it can't be used here.

12   Add a blank keyframe in frame 5 of all the layers.

13   On the **labels** layer, add a label named **off** in frame 5; on the **frame actions** layer, add a stop(); action.

The last part of the controller structure that needs to be created is a movie clip that mimics the grid structure in the mask movie clip. Because the controller movie clip will contain the exact same structure as the mask movie clip, it's easiest to duplicate the movie clip, rename it, and then revise the code as needed.

14   In the Library, select **mcMask** and then right-click (PC) or Opt+click (Mac) to bring up the Duplicate command.

15   Select Duplicate and name the new movie clip **mcMask_Control.**

16   Open the Actions panel for frame 1 inside the **mcMask_Control** movie clip.

17   There is now one word in one line of code that must be changed to make the controller structure synchronize properly with the mask movie clip. Replace the word "square" with the word "control" in the attachMovie action.

The full code looks like this:

```
attachMovie('control', newMC, 1);
```

The **mcMask_Control** movie clip attaches the movie clip with the rollover button rather than the animated effect movie clip that's used in the mask movie clip.

By keeping the instance names of the dynamically attached movie clips the same in both of the shell movie clips, the rollover movie clips can be directly synchronized to the animated effect movie clips.

18   To synchronize the controller and mask movie clips in this project, it's important to return to the main timeline and place an instance of **mcMask_Control** onto the **controller** layer in frame 1. Align the movie clip with the top-left corner of the movie and give it the instance name **controller**.

DEFINING THE ROLLOVER EFFECT FUNCTION

The function that the button inside the controller triggers on rollover does two things. First, it causes an action to occur within the proper movie clip within the mask instance of the **mcMask** movie clip. Second, it checks to see if all of the movie clips that make up the mask have been acted on. After they've all been acted on, another action defined in the function occurs.

Note: In this project the function contains simple actions, but it could contain numerous other actions. These actions could act on individual movie clips in the mask, on the mask as a whole, or even on completely different parts of the movie.

1 Open the Actions panel for frame 1 of the main movie timeline and add a `stop();` action in the **frame actions** layer.

```
stop();
```

The next steps initialize the variables that will be used to check whether the mask has completely disappeared.

2 Add this code below the `stop();` action in the same frame:

```
var maskTotal = 0;
```

This variable keeps track of the total number of movie clips in the mask. The `maskTotal` variable will be redefined when the mask is built.

3 Add this code:

```
var curMaskTotal = 0;
```

The `curMaskTotal` will be used to see if the number of individual movie clips acted on within the mask equals the total number of movie clips in the mask.

4 Add this code:

```
function changeMask(curName) {}
```

This code starts the function that will always be called to create interactivity within the mask. To let the function act on a specific movie clip within the mask, it's crucial to pass the name of the movie clip into the function. In this case, it's the variable `curName`.

5 Add this code inside the function brackets:

This code defines the path to the mask movie clip. Because the rollover action is being triggered from the controller movie clip (**mcMask_Control**), this is a very important line of code to add. In this project, the name of the mask movie clip will be set in advance, but this could be set dynamically every time a new mask is created.

```
curPath = "_root.mask."+curName;
```

6 Add this code inside the function:

This code evaluates the path to get the name of the movie clip to act on. It then tells that movie clip to do something, in this case to go to a specific label.

This small piece of code will cause an action to occur inside of every single movie clip within the mask when a user rolls over the button in the controller movie clip (**mcMask_Control**). It's easy to do but allows for any number of exciting, creative effects.

```
eval(curPath).gotoAndStop('off');
```

Note: The example presented here requires only a simple `gotoAndStop` command, but it's been set up to dynamically know and use the name of the movie clip containing the button inside the mask. It can thus be infinitely expanded to cause any other complex programmatic change to the movie clips inside the mask.

The other goal of the function is to check whether all of the movie clips in the controller have been triggered and then do something when that is true.

1 Add this code inside the function:

This `if` statement checks whether all of the movie clips in the mask have triggered.

```
if (curMaskTotal == maskTotal) {}
```

2 Add this code inside of the `if` statement:

If the expression evaluates to true, this code resets the value of `curMaskTotal` to 0 and does something (in this case, play).

```
curMaskTotal = 0;
play();
```

3   Add this code:

For testing purposes, add a `trace` action inside the `if` statement to see if it works.

```
trace("The mask has been cleared.");
```

The code is now complete. It causes the movie clips inside the mask to disappear and causes the movie to play when all the movie clips have been cleared away. Check to make sure the code is valid ActionScript using Ctrl+T/Cmd+T. If there are errors, an explanation will appear in the Output window; otherwise, a dialog box saying "The script has no errors" will appear.

The completed `changeMask` function controls the individual masks.

```
stop();

//INITIALIZE VARIABLES
var maskTotal = 0;
var curMaskTotal = 0;

//FUNCTION TO CREATE INTERACTIVITY
//The changeMask function runs what happens to the individual masks
//In this example it starts a simple gotoAndStop command, but it's
//infinitely expandable to do much more complex operatons on the masks

function changeMask(curName) {
    curPath = "_root.mask."+curName;
    eval(curPath).gotoAndStop('off');
    if (curMaskTotal == maskTotal) {
        curMaskTotal = 0;
        play();
    }
}
```

THE ROLLOVER CODE, CURSOR, TESTING, AND MORE PICTURES

A few steps remain to complete the dynamic mask example, the most important of which is to add the rollover code to the button in the controller movie clip to make it appear that the mask is disappearing.

1   Return to the **mcMaskEffect_Control** movie clip and select the button.

2   In the Actions panel, add this code:

```
on(rollOver){
    _root.curMaskTotal++;
    _root.changeMask(this._name);
}
```

The curMaskTotal variable keeps track of the number of movie clips that have been triggered and allows the function to check whether the entire mask has been cleared. The changeMask line passes the name of the current movie clip to the function and then triggers the function. Because this name is synchronized to the instance name inside the mask movie clip, it will appear as if the mask is disappearing on rollover.

3   Return to the main timeline and drag an instance of the movie clip **brush** onto the **cursor** layer.

4   Select the **brush** movie clip and add this code:

When the movie clip loads, this code hides the regular mouse cursor and then makes the movie clip draggable. In this case, the movie clip is confined to a 400×300 rectangular area that starts in the upper-left corner (0,0). It can't be dragged outside that area.

```
onClipEvent (load) {
    Mouse.hide();
    startDrag(this, true, 0, 0, 400, 300);
}
```

5   With the movie clips, code, cursor, and pictures added to the movie, it's time to see how the movie works. Select Test Movie. Move the mouse cursor over the photo and see how the movie clips within the mask animate and then disappear. Move over every square in the mask until they've all disappeared. The Output window should show the sentence "The mask has been cleared."

Once the parts of the dynamic mask work, it's easy to continue adding new photos or graphics to the project. In the finished movie .fla available for download, it's possible to review how a new mask and photo are added in frame 6 of the main timeline by adding stop(); commands, a new mask layer containing all of the preceding elements, and a new graphic. This could go on indefinitely with many more graphics being added.

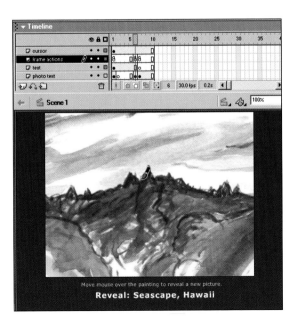

New graphics can be added by using the same steps already described.

Note: Although it's possible to create a one-frame movie with all the masks and photos sitting on top of each other in layers, it's better for downloading and streaming if they're spread out over a timeline. This enables a user to begin playing with the movie before all the photos have downloaded, even on slow connections. Always remember that most of the world is still on dial-up modems.

With Flash MX, it's possible to use the new Load JPEG feature to manage downloads and bandwidth, but the programming is significantly more complex than this example.

208

Summary

The dynamic masking project presented here provides a movie and knowledge foundation that can be used to develop more sophisticated effects and uses of dynamic, programmatic masks. The new mask feature makes masks an incredibly powerful tool for designers and developers.

With the capability to create complex animated masks and to programmatically affect so many features of a mask, the realm of possible effects and uses is wide open. This feature provides the most exciting possibilities for creative expression of any of the new features in this version of Flash. What designers and developers do with this feature is likely to amaze us all.

How to Improve

Flash's new drawing API lets developers create shapes programmatically. These shapes can be animated over time as movie clips or by redrawing them using the drawing API. When shapes are created as movie clips, it's also possible to use the new setMask method to create completely programmatic masks.

Although it's not possible to go into the drawing API here, the following code draws a triangle in a triangle movie clip and a circle in a circle movie clip. The setMask method is then used to make the triangle movie clip mask the circle movie clip. That's exciting.

```
_root.createEmptyMovieClip ("triangle", 10);
with (_root.triangle){
        beginFill (0x0000FF, 100);
        moveTo ( 0, 0);
        lineTo ( 0, 0);
        lineTo (100, 0);
        lineTo (50, 100);
        endFill();
}


_root.createEmptyMovieClip( "circle", 5 );
with ( _root.circle )
{
    beginFill( 0xFF0000 );
    moveTo( 100, 100 );
    curveTo( 150, 100, 150, 50 );
    curveTo( 150, 0, 100, 0 );
    curveTo( 50, 0, 50, 50 );
    curveTo( 50, 100, 100, 100 );
    endFill();
}

this.circle.setMask(this.triangle);
```

This project covers building a database-driven (MySQL, in this case) online user poll that can easily be customized and integrated into any site. Why an online user poll? Gathering feedback is just one reason. A user poll could be integrated into a customer feedback section where visitors to your site could vote on certain features they would like to see revised or integrated into your product line, or they could possibly provide feedback on the site itself.

This information could prove invaluable when planning and deploying next year's latest and greatest widget. What better way to deliver it than via Macromedia Flash with instant user feedback, quick integration to your site, and rapid customization of look and feel?

14

DYNAMIC DATABASE USER POLL

by Robert M. Hall

with images by Bromide73

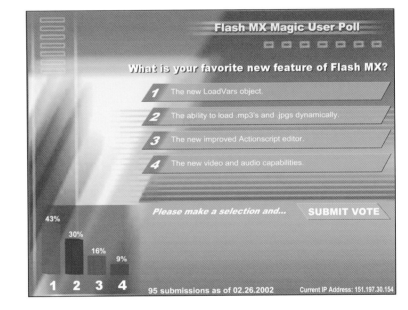

Difficulty Rating: ★★★

Made With:

    Macromedia Flash MX

    BBEdit for developing PHP files (any text editor would suffice)

Final File Size: 48KB

Modem Download Time: With a 56k modem, 14 to 18 seconds for complete load with data from server; with DSL/cable modem or higher, 1 to 2 seconds with data depending on server load

Development Time: 4 to 5 hours

It Works Like This

You will be using PHP as the web scripting language on the server side in combination with a MySQL database.

> **Note:** With the release of Flash MX, Macromedia has also made good on its promise to deliver a Mac OS X native version of Flash. This is an ideal environment to work under because Mac OS X comes with Apache and PHP ready to go by default, and MySQL is only a download away. (Mac OS X Server comes with MySQL preinstalled and configured.) Macromedia Flash MX developers working with a Microsoft Windows-based platform should not be concerned because PHP and MySQL are both open-source projects that are available as free downloads. They are easy to install and get going and work well with the built-in web server on most Microsoft operating system installations.
>
> Having PHP and MySQL installed locally alongside a web server like Apache or IIS, you have everything you need to build this project and test it before it is ever actually placed on a live Net-connected server. Included with the project is a folder called **testmode**. This folder contains dummy data PHP files that can be pointed to during the construction of this project to allow the Macromedia Flash work to be completed and partially tested before proceeding with the MySQL and PHP installations or configurations. The dummy PHP files do not contain actual PHP code; instead, they contain the data that would be returned from an actual functioning installation of the database and PHP files for this project. This does not allow you to experience the full scope and functionality of the project but should be sufficient to get the Flash MX portion completed. You will also still need a web server of some sort that you can place the dummy PHP files on.
>
> This project will go step by step through the creation of a Flash user poll that interacts with PHP to store and retrieve information about the poll from a MySQL database. The questions, responses, totals, and several configuration options for the poll are stored in a MySQL database. The advantage of the database approach is that any time the poll needs to be changed, it can be done without having to make modifications to the published .swf files. The basics of the project are as follows: building the shell Flash file, creating the interface elements, adding the ActionScript that interacts with the PHP and MySQL, adding the ActionScript that presents the information retrieved from the database and allows the user to interact with it, and installing the PHP files and MySQL database that the project relies on.

Preparing to Work

Before you get started, you need to copy the **14_Dynamic_Database** folder onto your hard drive and launch Flash MX.

BUILDING THE FOUNDATION

The first step is to create a new blank document for the project. Because this project will take a moment or two to load, you will create a preloader. This will give the user a visual indicator of the loading progress when this project is accessed via the web. Manipulation of a text field as if it were a movie clip is a new functionality introduced with Flash MX. It will be utilized for the preloader.

1   Start a new document. Set the size to 640×480 with a background color of ff6600 and a frame rate of 20.

> **Note:** For this project, you are going to skip the step of making the individual symbols. From the **14_Dynamic_Database** folder on the accompanying CD-ROM, open the **user_poll_mx.fla** file as a Library. All the movie clips and symbols you need can be dragged from this Library.

2   Use the Scene panel to rename scene 1 to **Preloader**. Make an additional scene named **Poll**.

3   Switch to the Preloader scene and rename layer 1 as **actions**.

4   Make three additional layers beneath **actions** named **loadbar**, **loadbar_bg**, and **background**.

These four layers will contain the elements necessary for the preload status indicator.

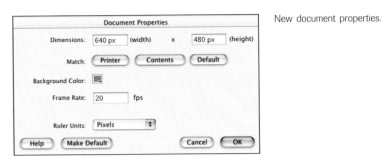

New document properties.

Scene panel properties.

Making the Preloader scene keyframes.

212

5 Add a `stop();` action to the **actions** layer in frame 1.

Shortcut to the `stop();` action.

6 From the **user_poll_mx.fla** Library, drag the loadbar symbol to the center of the stage and into the **loadbar** layer.

Locating the loadbar symbol.

7 Using the Property Inspector, give the loadbar symbol you just placed on the stage an instance name of **preload_bar**.

Aligning the loadbar symbol.

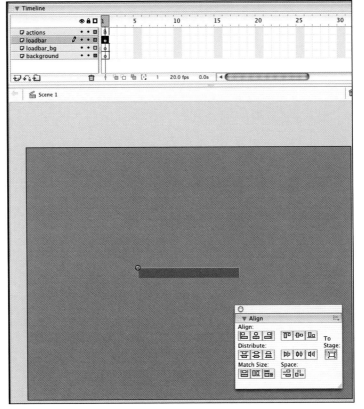

8 Use the Align panel to center the instance of the loadbar symbol on the stage vertically and horizontally. Use the Transform panel to apply a 36.0-degree skew horizontally to the symbol and a 123% scale on the height.

Applying the Transform properties to the **loadbar** movie clip.

9   Use the Property Inspector to apply a tint
    to the symbol.

    Here, it's red: RGB 255, 0, 0.

10 Copy the instance of the loadbar symbol, switch to
    the **loadbar_bg** layer, and do a paste in place.

    You should now have a duplicate instance of the
    loadbar symbol on the **loadbar_bg** layer.

11 Hide the **loadbar** layer. Select the new duplicated
    loadbar and give it a new instance name of
    loadbar_bg.

    You will not be referencing this movie clip, but you
    need to differentiate it from the first one.

12 Using the Property Inspector, change the tint on this
    item to a yellow: RGB 255, 204, 0.

13 Use the Transform panel again to set the percentages
    for the size of this symbol to: 101.4 and 138.9.

14 Unhide the **loadbar** layer and use the cursor keys to
    nudge the symbol on the **loadbar_bg** layer so that a
    little bit of it is evenly showing around all the sides
    of the loadbar symbol on the **loadbar** layer.

15 With the Text tool, make a dynamic text box on the
    loadbar layer. It should have the following settings:
    _sans, 12 point, white, single line, nonselectable,
    width = 38.0, and height = 20.1. Assign it an instance
    name of **load_indicator**.

Property Inspector settings
for the **loadbar** movie clip.

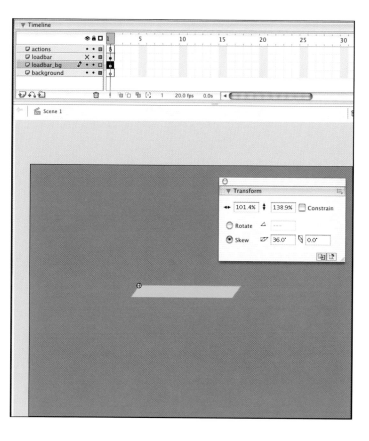

Applying the Transform properties
to the **loadbar_bg** movie clip.

16 Make **amount** the variable name for this text field. Use the Property Inspector to position the text field at X = 181.6, Y = 230.2.

This puts it just to the left of the loadbar on the **loadbar** layer. It will be the percentage-loaded numerical indicator.

Now might be a good time to save your work.

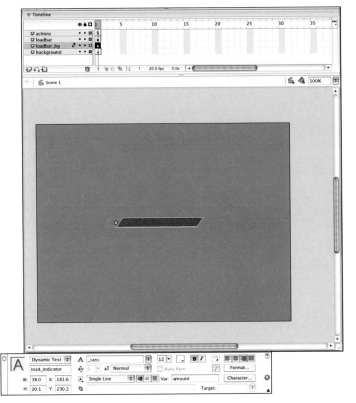

Properties for the load_indicator dynamic text field.

INSERTING THE PRELOADER CODE

All of the elements are in place for the preloader, so now you can assign the
ActionScript that actually does the work.

1 Click on the `preload_bar` instance of the loadbar
symbol in the **loadbar** layer, open the Actions panel,
and add this code to that instance:

Here you're evaluating how much of the
movie has been loaded thus far, using an
`onClipEvent(enterframe)` that will work
continuously as you load. To figure out how much
of the movie is left to load, divide the amount of the
movie's `getBytesLoaded` property by the total
amount of bytes for the movie (`getBytesTotal`)
and multiply by `100`. This percentage can then be
used to change the scale of the loaderbar so that it
gives you a visual representation of the amount
loaded.

Then you set that same value of the amount variable
in the `load_indicator` text field as another visual
representation. Now that you can manipulate text
fields in a manner similar to movie clips in Flash
MX, you can also dynamically change their position
because they have _x, and _y properties as well. As
the percentage loaded value increases, multiply the
text field's original position on the stage by `2` and
add it back, which will move the load bar along as
the movie continues to load.

The `if` statement constantly evaluates whether you
are completely loaded. If the movie has been loaded,
you jump to the next frame. It does this by comparing the actual amount of `getBytesLoaded` thus
far to the `getBytesTotal`. If they are equal,
you are finished.

```
onClipEvent (load) {
// determine our initial position of the loadbar
    this.percent_xpos = _root.load_indicator._x;
}
onClipEvent (enterFrame) {
    // set the size of our movieclip based on the amount of our movie loaded
    this._xscale=((_root.getBytesLoaded()/_root.getBytesTotal())*100);
    _root.amount = 1+int((_root.getBytesLoaded()/_root.getBytesTotal())*100);
    _root.load_indicator._x = (this.percent_xpos+(this._xscale*2));
    // if we have loaded everything then jump to the next frame and do our
    ➥fade out
    if (_root.getBytesLoaded() == _root.getBytesTotal()) {
        _root.gotoAndPlay(2);
    }
}
```

Determining the amount of the movie's download.

MAKING A TRANSITION

Now you need to make transition frames so that you move smoothly from the preloader to the content.

1 Make a new keyframe for the **background** layer in frame 2 of your timeline.

2 From the Library, drag the background movie clip to frame 2 of the **background** layer and position it at X = 0, Y = 0. Using the Property Inspector, set its Alpha to 0% so that it will be invisible at first. Give it an instance name of **background** and apply this code:

This gradually increases the alpha level of the back-ground movie clip over time.

3 Insert a frame in frame 20 of the layer.

This extends the timeline out to frame 20 for the **background** layer.

```
onClipEvent (enterFrame) {
        setProperty(this, _alpha, _alpha+= 10);
}
```

Setting the alpha level.

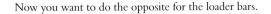

Adding frames to the **background** layer.

4 Insert keyframes on frame 2 for the **loadbar** and **loadbar_bg** layers and extend them to frame 20. Remove the `load_indicator` text field from the **loadbar** layer in frame 2.

Because the movie's frame rate is 20 frames per second, after the preloader is finished, it will jump to frame 2. For about 1 second, it will play the transition from preloader to content.

The background movie clip increases back to 100% visible thanks to the ActionScript assigned to it.

Now you want to do the opposite for the loader bars.

Adding frames to the **loadbar** and **loadbar_bg** layers.

5 Apply this code to the loaderbar and the **loaderbar_bg** movie clip instances in frame 2. Replace any existing code on those movie clips that was used in frame 1.

This reduces the alpha property over time, making the **loaderbar_bg** movie clips invisible. This gives a nice, smooth transition to the next scene.

```
onClipEvent (enterFrame) {
    // over the next 19 frames do a fade out of the preloader bar
    setProperty(this, _alpha, _alpha-= 10);
}
```

Reducing the alpha level to fade the movie clips.

THE POLL SCENE AND FUNCTIONS

In this section, you will create a new scene that will contain the user interface and ActionScript used to display it based on what is retrieved from the database. This first portion covers the creation of all the functions used to talk to the database and to retrieve the information needed for the next section. In this first frame, you use the LoadVars object in your functions several times.

1 Switch to the Poll scene and rename the default layer 1 as **actions**.

2 Select frame 1 of the **actions** layer. Assign this frame the name **start**.

3 Open the Actions panel and place it into Expert mode.

4 Use the Import From File option from the Actions panel to import the **main_funcs.as** file from the **14_Dynamic_Database** folder on the accompanying CD-ROM.

Note: For the following steps you should look at and examine the ActionScript to familiarize yourself with its functionality and operation. To save you from trial and error in keying in all this code, it has been placed into the previously mentioned .as files that you import from the ActionScript Editor window.

Note: By importing the **main_funcs.as** file, you have "entered" all the code for this section. To break it down and explain it one section at a time, however, you will continue to follow steps, even though you won't have to enter more code.

The ActionScript in frame 1 of the poll scene is used for setting up variables, objects, and functions. The new LoadVars object is used to retrieve and store all the information you gather from PHP and MySQL.

The first section of code prevents the casual user from hijacking your content and using it on another server or even locally on his or her computer without going to a lot of trouble.

You do this by taking advantage of the _url property that is set whenever a movie is played. The _url property contains the exact path—whether it's a web server or local file directory path—from which the .swf document is currently being played. You establish your base directory on your server for the final .swf file. Using this, you can compare where the file should be playing from with where it actually is playing from. If the two do not match, you can load in an alternate .swf file as a warning or indicator that the movie is not being served from the correct location.

5 You need to set the `_global.base_URL` variable to the full path where the PHP scripts will be located. This would be the full path on your server from where your PHP files will be served. The url that exists there now is only an example of the syntax.

For testing during the development of this project, you may place the dummy PHP files from the testmode directory found on the accompanying CD on your web server. These will return dummy data to allow you to complete the project before having to delve into MySQL and PHP. There will also be a companion resource site for this chapter, which will contain further tips, testing files and resources for PHP and MySQL at **www.impossibilities.com/mxmagic/**.

```
// BASE URL:
_global.base_URL = "http://www.impossibilities.com/mxmagic/";
url_loc = this._url;
//
// Also we can setup some basic security by checking to make sure the URL where
// this is being served from matches the _root._url property. Uncomment the lines in
➡between the // *** START UNCOMMENT *** and // *** END UNCOMMENT *** lines
// to enable this and then specify a movie to load that would be located
// relative to your base_URL. This movie would contain a warning or other message for
➡the user. In this case a movie called stolen.swf is loaded that displays a message
➡indicating the file is playing from an unauthorized location. Substitute any movie
➡of your own here. Make sure it is stored relative to the base_URL we set, if not
➡make sure you provide an absolute URL to its location.
// I like to actually tie it to a .php script that will page me with the users IP and
➡the referring URL
// so i can track down the culprit. :)
// *** START UNCOMMENT ***
// if (url_loc != base_URL +"user_poll_mx.swf") {
// loadMovieNum(base_URL+"stolen.swf", 0);
// }
// *** END UNCOMMENT ***
```

Setting the `_global.base_URL` variable.

6 The next section of ActionScript in this frame does some preliminary work on the date information you will need.

You create a new date object and retrieve the values of the current month, day, and year. You then format the date so that it follows a format similar to how you store data information in your MySQL database and for display in your interface.

Now you start to work with some new features of Flash MX. One that is essential to this project is the `LoadVars` object.

Note: Even though Flash has support for reading the date and time from a user's computer, you cannot fully rely on the user having their computer set with correct date and time, especially when you will be relying on that information to insert accurate voting results in your poll database. Therefore, you also handle the date function directly in PHP and MySQL where the server is your master source of date and time.

The PHP scripts will handle the date used for insertions into the database and make sure a user hasn't voted more than once in 24 hours. We do, however, use the date returned from Flash for presentment on the user's screen, since it's not critical for the displayed date to be 100% accurate. Considering that users may be using your site from all over the world, in varying time zones, a good exercise for you to pursue when this project is complete, would be to use the knowledge you gained from Project 4, "Time Zones." Then revisit this section to pull the time in from the server and adjust it to GMT time for the user, showing the difference between their time zone and settings and the servers time zone and settings.

```
// Setup the date information.
myDate = new Date();
myMonth = (myDate.getMonth())+1;
myDay = myDate.getDate();
myYear = myDate.getFullYear();
// Add beginning zeros in Flash so we wont have to strip off or
// work further with the dates in PHP or mySQL.
if (myMonth.length<2) {
    myMonth = "0"+myMonth;
}
if (myDay.length<2) {
    mDay = "0"+myDay;
}
mySQL_formatted_date = myYear+"-"+myMonth+"-"+myDay;
// Format the date for display on poll page.
dateTextField = "submissions as of "+myMonth+"."+myDay+"."+myYear;
```

Retrieving date information.

7 This first function defines how you initially retrieve information from your database about the current poll question and its various attributes.

First you create a new `LoadVars` object called `userpoll_main_mySQLdata`. This is where all the results from the **current_poll.php** file are stored.

After the object is created, you use the `load` method combined with your base URL to query the **current_poll.php** file.

The `onLoad` event handler is used to trigger another function when you have received the info from your database. Part of that information is the `poll_id`. Each poll has its own unique `poll_id`, and that is how it is referenced in the database. It also has a name, which is the actual poll question, and a `total_qs` value, which indicates how many possible responses are stored for the particular poll in question.

The **current_poll.php** file also returns the IP address of the browser or user visiting your poll. This is critical to prevent a user from voting more than once per day and artificially manipulating or skewing the poll results. In your PHP source, you use the environment variable `$REMOTE_ADDR` to get the user's IP address from the server.

For display, a text field variable called `current_IP` is set to show the current user's IP address.

```
// Load the current active poll question from the server.
// This is stored in the poll table in the user_poll mySQL database
// and the current_poll.php file returns the results:
// poll_id, pollname, total_qs
// Placing results into userpoll_main_mySQLdata object
function current_Poll() {
    userpoll_main_mySQLdata = new LoadVars();
    userpoll_main_mySQLdata.load(base_URL+"current_poll.php");
    userpoll_main_mySQLdata.onLoad = function(success) {
        // set the IP address field on the display screen for debugging
        // the IP is returned in the first query we do to current_poll.php
        current_IP = "Current IP Address: "+userpoll_main_mySQLdata.current_IP;
        // Once we know the data is loaded call the current_Questions function
        // to get the list of questions for the currently active poll.
        // Also retrieve the current number of votes for each question,
        // along with the hex value of the bar for each questions.
        pollquestionRetrieve();
    };
}
```

Retrieving database information.

Note: Now might be a good time to take a quick look through the .php files. Though this book deals specifically with Flash, this project depends upon PHP for retrieving and inserting information from the database and it might be a good time to start familiarizing yourself with its functionality. For reference to the functions and commands used in the .php files, visit the official PHP web site: **www.php.net**.

8 Then the `pollquestionRetrieve();` function is defined with the following code:

This section uses the `LoadVars` object again, but you make a new object to contain more information from a different file. A great feature of the `LoadVars` object is that you can load and send information into it, and you can do it again and again. If you load data in more than once, any existing values that are pulled in again are overwritten. Anything new that is found is added, but nothing is taken away.

> **Note:** You could have actually used a single `LoadVars` object for this entire project, but instead you make multiple `LoadVars` objects for the purposes of this project so that you can isolate each different function and PHP file and the values it returns.

In the `pollquestionRetrieve` function, the `poll_id` info stored in the `userpoll_main_mySQLdata LoadVars` object is passed to the **current_questions.php** file. The PHP file queries the MySQL database for the currently active set of responses where the `poll_id` matches the `question_id`. In the example database, you have only one active poll and one active set of questions, so the value for `poll_id` would be 0 and so would the `question_id`. The PHP script finds all the responses that match `poll_id=0`. You pull them into Flash, along with how many votes for each have already been submitted and the `item_id` so that you have a number to identify and refer to each question in ActionScript.

```
function pollquestionRetrieve() {
    // Load the current active poll question from the server where the
    // questions are active and the poll_id matches the active poll we
    ➥loaded in
    // the userpoll_main_mySQLdata function.
    // question_id, questionX, total_submitsX, item_idX, barcolorX
    // are all placed into userpoll_main_mySQLdata object
    // each of the above have the X replaced with an iteration number
    ➥depending on
    // how many rows or questions have been assigned to the particular poll
    userpoll_sub_mySQLdata = new LoadVars();
    userpoll_sub_mySQLdata.load(base_URL+"current_questions.php?question_id=
    ➥"+userpoll_main_mysqldata.poll_id);
    userpoll_sub_mySQLdata.onLoad = function(success) {
        // If we were able to load both sets of data then tell the main
        ➥timeline
        // to move forward to the display frame where the interface is
        ➥created from
        // the data we retrieved from PHP and mySQL.
        gotoAndStop("display");
    };
}
```

The color preference for each bar on your chart for the current question is also retrieved. PHP returns those values in a sorted order so that, starting with `question0` and going up, the most popular responses are returned first. This serves several purposes. First, the charts will always be easy to read because they will display in descending order from left to right. This also makes the section of ActionScript for generating your bar charts much easier to do when you know that the first bar in your chart and the first response to your poll will always be the one with the greatest amount of submissions.

After the information is pulled into the new `LoadVars` object from the **current_questions.php** file, you tell the movie to jump to the display frame on the main timeline in the poll scene. In your steps that frame has not yet been made, but it is the main interface frame.

Notice in the `.load` method for this `LoadVars` object that you appended some variables to be sent onto the end of the URL.

Note: Alternatively, the `sendAndLoad` method could be used after populating your object with values for `poll_id`, but in this case, you simply chose to append them to the URL. Either way is valid, but because this entails using the `GET` method, limitations are imposed as to the length of a `GET` request. Using the `send` or `sendAndLoad` `LoadVars` method enables you to send a much greater amount of information using the `POST` HTTP method. For this project we are not working with enough data to run into the limitation of the `GET` HTTP method.

9 Review this next section of ActionScript:

Here, a function is defined that relies on the LoadVars object. This function is querying the **vote.php** file. The date that the user's computer is set to, as determined by Flash, is sent for comparison to the server's date, along with the poll_id for the currently active poll. This function is looking in your database in the ip_tracking table. Every time a user successfully submits a vote for a particular poll, his or her IP address, the poll_id he or she voted on, and the date on which he or she submitted the vote are recorded. This prevents a user from voting more than once a day.

Note: A further extension to this particular .php file would be to also use a cookie to get around the problem that more than one user could have the same IP address. Many corporate LANS, or even broadband routers for the home, use a single IP address to communicate with the outside world. A typical dialup account from an ISP such as AOL, Earthlink, and so on doles out IP addresses dynamically from a pool of available addresses. This can potentially cause a problem because IP addresses are constantly being reused and are not specifically linked with any particular account. Thus, a user might be restricted from voting if he or she happens to get assigned an IP address that was used earlier in the day by another user to place a vote.

To surmount this problem, an area to explore would be a new feature of Flash MX called *SharedObjects*, which could be used similarly to a cookie but specifically for Flash. SharedObjects enable you to save information on a user's hard drive that can be reused each time he or she visits the same site or file. This feature could be used to store the time and date when the person last voted and evaluate this information either as a replacement to this function or as an enhancement.

```
// This function is used on the submit button to determine its state and
➥whether
// or not the user can vote today. It tells the submit movie to jump to the
➥right
// frame or not. We use the $REMOTE_ADDR feature in PHP on the server side to
// determine the users IP Address.
function canVote() {
    userpoll_canVote_mySQLdata = new LoadVars();
    userpoll_canVote_mySQLdata.load(base_URL+"vote.php?today="+_root.mySQL_
    ➥formatted_date+"&poll_id="+_root.userpoll_main_mySQLdata.poll_id);
    userpoll_canVote_mySQLdata.onLoad = function(success) {
        if (userpoll_canVote_mySQLdata.vote_result == "vote_exists") {
            _root.submit.gotoAndStop(3);
        } else if (userpoll_canVote_mySQLdata.vote_result ==
        ➥"vote_did_not_exist") {
            _root.submit.gotoAndStop(4);
        }
    };
}
```

10 The next function handles sending in the actual vote after a user has made a selection and clicks to submit it:

The `poll_id`, the `item_id`, and the date are passed to the **vote_submit.php** file using yet another `LoadVars` object.

If a successful response is received, the function tells the Submit button to jump to a new frame, and you make sure the response that the user clicked stays highlighted. The function turnoff is also called. This function goes through and turns off the capability for the user to make any further input on the response buttons after he or she has clicked the Submit button.

```
// if the user can vote, the vote is sent in and their IP address is added to the
➥database
// with the current date tacked on so we know which day they voted.
function votesubmit(item_id, question_id) {
    // Set the specific values we want to send. These are pulled from the submit
    ➥button
    // on frame 2 of the main timeline. These values have been set by the user after
    // they made their selection from the list presented to them in the main
    ➥interface.
    appendvars = "poll_id="+_root.userpoll_main_mySQLdata.poll_id+"&item_id=
    ➥"+item_id+"&date="+escape(_root.mySQL_formatted_date);
    userpoll_sendvote_mySQLdata = new LoadVars();
    userpoll_sendvote_mySQLdata.load(base_URL+"vote_submit.php?"+appendvars);
    userpoll_sendvote_mySQLdata.onLoad = function(success) {
        // If we have a successful insert into the database tell the submit button
        // to jump to the exit state and change its label
        _root.submit.gotoAndStop(6);
        // invoke the turn off function -- see the next function below
        turnoff();
    };
    // the next two lines make sure that when a user submits their choice
    // that the movieclip indicating their choice stays highlighted
    targ = question_id-1;
    _root["poll_input"+targ].tab.gotoAndStop(3);
}
```

11 The `ip_insert` function handles placing the date, `poll_id`, and `ip_address` into your `ip_tracking` MySQL table.

The `poll_id` and the `ip_address` of the user are passed and inserted into the database. Because this is the last step in the poll, a success sound is played. (This is defined a bit further down in this frame.)

```
function ip_insert() {
    // This function inserts the IP address into the database after a
    // successful entry of their selection into the database. This is where
    ➡you might want to place your
    // cookie code. The ip_insert.php file could be modified to set a cookie
    ➡on the users
    // browser to expire after 24 hours. It would not need to contain their
    ➡IP simply
    // is presence would indicate they have already voted. you would also
    ➡want to modify the
    // php file that checks for their IP which is: to use that cookie.
    userpoll_sendip_mySQLdata = new LoadVars();
    userpoll_sendip_mySQLdata.load(base_URL+"ip_insert.php?poll_id=
    ➡"+_root.userpoll_main_mySQLdata.poll_id);
    userpoll_sendip_mySQLdata.onLoad = function(success) {
        _root.success_sound.start();
    };
}
```

12 Here is the turnoff function that turns off the response buttons after a user has clicked the Submit button:

All of the response buttons on the next frame have instance names that start as `poll_inputX`, where the X is a number starting at 0 and increases depending on how many possible responses are available for this currently active poll.

> **Macromedia Flash MX:** Buttons now have an enabled property that can be either true or false. By default, a button's enabled property is set to `true`.

```
// the turnoff function sets all our input buttons to inactive after the user
// has submitted their vote to prevent the chart from changing further or the
// user from changing their current choice.
function turnoff() {
    for (i=0; i<_root.userpoll_main_mySQLdata.total_qs; i++) {
        _root["poll_input"+i].inputButton.enabled = false;
    }
}
```

13 The last few items remaining in this section of ActionScript define the sounds for clicks and for success, and to initiate the loading of the poll information.

To use the `sound` object and the `attachSound` method properly, make sure to set the linkage property for the sounds in the Library. Right-click/Ctrl-click on the **click_sound** in the Library and select the linkage properties. Assign the asset an identifier. Often it is easiest to remember if the identifier is the same as the Library name. You also want to make sure that the Export for ActionScript and Export in First Frame check boxes are selected. They should already be set properly in the included file, but keep this in mind for further projects.

```
oversound = new Sound();
oversound.attachSound("click_sound");
oversound.setVolume(100);
success_sound = new Sound();
success_sound.attachSound("submit_sound");
success_sound.setVolume(100);
//
// done with all our function definitions...lets start er up!
// invoke the current_Poll function to get the ball rolling.
current_Poll();
// Stop here...our functions that load data will move us along if everything is cool.
stop();
```

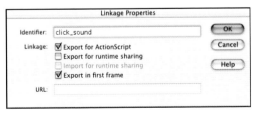

Setting and viewing the Linkage Properties for the click_sound.

14 In the **user_poll_mx.fla** Library, select all the sounds from the **!sounds** folder and drag them to the Library of your new document.

If the Library window is stretched out, the linkage properties for the two sound files are visible, indicating that they will be exported. This enables them to be used anywhere in the project, even if they never make it onto the stage at any point in the movie.

The last thing to do is call the `current_Poll()` function defined earlier. This starts the ball rolling, pulling in the values from the database.

The `stop();` ActionScript is there so that the movie will stay put until you have enough data to build the interface on the next frame.

Library - user_poll.fla			
29 items			

Name	Kind	Use Cou	Linkage
!audio_sounds	Folder		
click_sound	Sound	0	Export: click_sound
submit_sound	Sound	0	Export: submit_sound

BUILDING THE USER INTERFACE

This section covers the actual placement of movie clips, text fields, and graphics on the stage that will be used for the interface and acted on by the ActionScript in frame 2 of this scene.

First you need to add several more layers to the poll scene.

1 Add the following layers below the **actions** layer:

title_bar

text_labels

responses

buttons

barchart

barchart_bg

background

2 In the **background** layer, drop in the background movie clip from your Library. Position it at X = 0, Y = 0. Assign it an instance name of **background**.

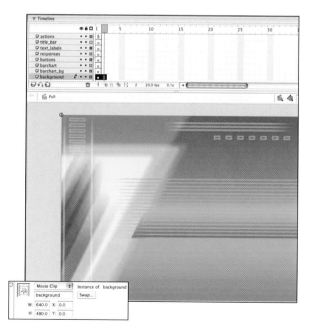

Adding the layers to the poll scene.

3 Add a frame to the **background** layer.

4 Drag the titlebar graphic symbol from the **!user_interface_items** folder in the **user_poll_mx.fla** Library to the top-right of the stage of your new document and onto the **title_bar** layer on frame 1.

Placing the titlebar symbol on the stage.

5 Add an additional frame to the **title_bar** layer. Then add an additional keyframe to all the remaining layers that don't have anything in frame 2 yet.

Adding the layer keyframes.

230

6 Select frame 2 of the **text_labels** layer. Drag the barpercent symbol from the **!movie_clips** folder in the **user_poll_mx.fla** Library to the stage and position it at X = 17, Y = 199. Assign it the instance name **barPercent**.

7 Drag the indicators graphic from the **!user_interface_items** folder in the **user_poll_mx.fla** Library to frame 2 of the **text_labels** layer. Position it at X = 149.8, Y = 459.5.

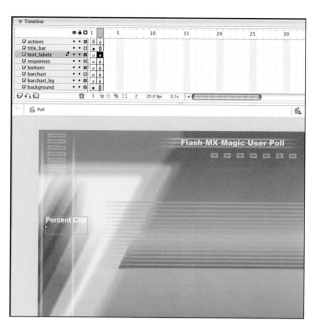

Placing the **barpercent** movie clip on the stage.

8 In the Actions panel, add this code to **barPercent**:

This tells the movie clip to jump to frame 2 the second it appears on the stage. You do this because you have placed some text labels in the barpercent symbol so that you can work with it more easily on the stage and identify it more quickly, but you don't want the labels to appear in the movie, so you tell the movie clip to jump to the second frame.

Note: If you double-click on the **barpercent** movie clip, you will see that there is a text field inside it with an instance name of **percentField** and a variable name of **percent**.

This movie clip will be duplicated several times on the stage to display the varying percentage amounts for the barchart you will generate from your poll information.

```
onClipEvent (load) {
    this.gotoAndStop(2);
}
```

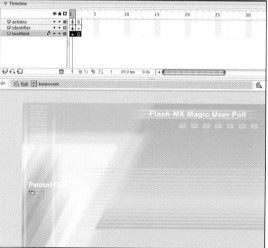

Viewing the **barPercent** dynamic text field properties.

9 Select frame 2 of the **barchart** layer. Drag the bar symbol from the **!movie_clips** folder in the **user_poll_mx.fla** Library to the stage. Scale it to a width of 30.6 and a height of 200.0. Position it at X = 23.0, Y = 243.0. Assign it the instance name **poll_bar**.

Adding and setting the properties of the bar symbol.

10 In the Actions panel, add this code to the poll_bar instance:

This sets the alpha value to 85. The movie will be duplicating this clip several times to draw the bar chart.

```
onClipEvent (load) {
    // Set each occurrence of the bars to an initial transparency or alpha value
    this._alpha = 85;
}
```

11 Select frame 2 of the **barchart_bg** layer. Drag the dynamask symbol from **!user_interface_items** folder in the **user_poll_mx.fla** Library to the stage. Scale it using the Property Inspector to a width of 76.5 and a height of 54.0. Position it at X = 13.4, Y = 421.0. Also set the color to Advanced and apply the following values: Red: -10% x R)+ 255, Green: 100% x G)+ -255, Blue: -100% x B)+ -237and Alpha: 51% x A)+ -5. Assign it the instance name **dynamask**.

This symbol will be dynamically resized as the background area for the barchart. Its size will be determined by how tall the bars grow and how many bars are actually drawn, which in turn is determined by the number of possible responses for a particular poll.

Resizing the dynamask symbol.

12 Select frame 2 of the **text_labels** layer and drag the bar_id_clip symbol from the **!movie_clips** folder of the **user_poll_mx.fla** Library to the stage. Position it at X = 20.0, Y = 438.0. Assign it the instance name **bar_id_MC**.

Placing the bar_id_clip symbol on the stage.

13 Place the following code on the `bar_id_MC` instance:

This is identical to the code placed on the **barPercent** instance. The **bar_id_MC** movieclip contains a text field that displays the item or ID number associated with a particular bar on the chart. This helps the user correlate visually the numbered response selections and their visual representation in the bar chart.

```
onClipEvent (load) {
    this.gotoAndPlay(2);
}
```

14 With the **text_labels** layer selected, make a text field that is approximately 526 pixels wide. Set the font to Arial Black (or something similar) with a point size of 18 and set the color to #FFFFFF. Make it a dynamic text field, which is not selectable, with no border/background. Assign it the instance name **pollNameText**. For the variable name, assign **pollname**. Place it at the coordinates of: X = 104.0, Y = 81.0.

Setting the **pollNameText** dynamic text field properties.

This text field will contain the actual question for the poll. If you plan to make long, elaborate questions for your poll, you would be wise to make this a multiline text field and position it appropriately for your layout to accommodate the length of your questions. For this example's purposes, the single line setting is fine.

15 Select frame 2 of the **responses** layer. From the Library, drag the **item_clip** movie clip from the **!user_interface_items** folder in the **user_poll_mx.fla** Library to the stage and position it just below the **pollNameText** text field. Use the Align tool to position it so that it lines up along the right side.

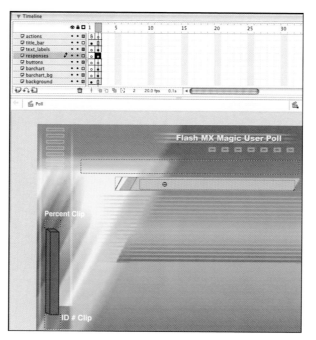

Placing the item_clip symbol on the stage.

16 Assign the item_clip symbol an instance name of **poll_input** and place the following ActionScript code on this instance:

This **poll_input** instance is what will be duplicated to make the various response selections for the poll. The preceding code helps the button embedded in this symbol to determine its selection state. This code works in conjunction with the next symbol you will add to the stage. You will revisit this symbol after you place your final symbol on the stage.

```
onClipEvent (load) {
    this.mousestat == false;
}
onClipEvent (enterFrame) {
    if ((_root.submit.question_id != this.question_id) && (this.mousestat ==
    ➥false)) {
        this.tab.gotoAndStop(1);
    }
}
```

17 Select frame 2 of the **buttons** layer and drag the Submit button from the **!user_interface_items** folder in the **user_poll_mx.fla** Library to the stage. Assign it the instance name **submit**. Position it anywhere below the poll_input symbol as long as its right edge aligns with the right edge of the poll_input symbol already on the stage.

This clip will be moved programmatically to be below the last poll_input item you duplicate on the screen, so the Y positioning does not matter at this point.

Placing and setting properties for the **submit** movie clip.

18 Place the following ActionScript on the submit symbol on the stage:

Here's what this does: Whenever the Submit button is first viewed, the canVote function that you defined in frame 1 of the **Actions** layer is invoked. This function loads information from a .php file using the LoadVars object and determines whether or not the current user can vote today. This section also makes sure that the two variables that will be used in the interface and on this submit instance are set to null.

```
onClipEvent (load) {
    this.question_id = null;
    this.item_id = null;
    // call the canVote function to see if a users IP is in the
    // database and the date in which it was inserted so we can
    // determine if they are permitted to vote or not.
    _root.canVote();
}
```

All of the items and symbols you will need for this project have all been placed on the stage now.

PRESENTING THE INTERFACE AND RESULTS

This next section goes over the ActionScript used to build your interface and to present the data retrieved from the database.

1 Select frame 2 of the **actions** layer. Assign this frame the name **display**.

2 Open the Actions panel. Use the Import From File option from the Actions panel to import the **poll_funcs.as** file from the **14_Dynamic_Database** folder on the accompanying CD-ROM.

Now you will go through the imported code and break it down section by section.

3 Take a look at the first part of the ActionScript. There are some variables set to be equal to values you have stored in the userpoll_main_mySQLdata LoadVars object. This will enable you to reference them a little more easily. Then you define the function pollcalc(). This function is what calculates the total number of submissions for the current active poll and also adjusts the size of the bar chart and its elements when the interface is first loaded. It is also called whenever the user makes a selection that would alter those results. See the comments in the ActionScript itself for further detail.

Note: This section of ActionScript will be broken down into chunks and individually explained. It is imported from a file to save you the time it would take to manually key in all the code, possibly introducing errors.

```
// This contains all the ActionScript to create the bar chart and display
➥and format the
// data we retrieve from the mySQL database for the current active poll.
//
// Set the total # of questions to the main timeline to access easier
total_questions = _root.userpoll_main_mySQLdata.total_qs-1;
// Set the name of the poll question into the display textfield on our
➥interface
_root.pollname = _root.userpoll_main_mySQLdata.pollname;
// Define the function used to draw the bar chart from our data
// and to also update it on clicks of the input fields and trigger a little
// animation of each item when they are clicked.
function pollcalc() {
    // create the array we need for sorting the order and determine height
    this.tallest = new Array();
    // loop through the items and duplicate a bar chart movie clip along
    // with the item id textfield and a percentage indicator
    for (item=0; item<=total_questions; item++) {
        // Calculate the individual percentage results for each question
        xx = int((_root["poll_input"+item].result/_root.total_submits)*100);
        // If its less than 0 make it 0
        if (xx<=0) {
            xx = 0;
```

continues

continued

```
        }
        // If its greather than 2000 make it 100 (just in case)
        if (xx>=2000) {
            xx = 100;
        }
        // Set the up and down or yscale of each bar to the percentage its votes tally to.
        // Plus multiply by 2 for extra height on our bar for the right proportions for our layout
        _root["poll_bar"+item]._yscale = xx*2;
        // This line triggers some clip events contained on the bar to do their
        // animation when one is clicked or when they are first loaded.
        _root["poll_bar"+(_root.submit.question_id-1)].bar_sub.bounce = true;
        // Set the position of the percentage indicator. If you reposition the
        // percentage indicator in your layout or resize them you might have to tweak the
        // values in the next line. Try playing with the 187 first. The 200 represents the
        // actual height of the bar at 1005 scale that it will be tied to.
        _root["barPercent"+item]._y = (425-(xx*2));
        // Set the percentage value for the display textfield
        _root["barPercent"+item].percent = xx+"%";
        // Populate our array to keep track of the heights
        this.tallest[item] = xx*3;
    }
    // If you remove the ORDER by total_submits DESC in the $query in the
    // current_questions.php file you must uncomment the following line
    // which does the sorting on the bar charts height. We put the
    // heights into an array so we can sort them and determine the tallet item
    // that item we use as a guide to change the height of the background behind the charts.
    // If we dont let PHP do the sorting, we must allow Flash to. If PHP does the sorting
    // we dont need to sort it as we will always know that tallest[0] contains the tallest.
    // this.tallest.sort(); // <-- uncomment this line!
    _root.dynamask._width = (65+(40*total_questions));
    _root.dynamask._height = (Number(this.tallest[0])+20);
}
```

4 This next section is responsible for duplicating all the various movie clips on the page that make up the bar chart, including the bar chart bars, the percentages above them, the indicators below them, and the actual coloring of the bars based on the hex values pulled in from the database.

```
// Get our original positions of the input bars and the submit button
// that we are about to duplicate to build the interface
positiony = _root.poll_input._y;
positionx = _root.poll_bar._x;
// Loop through the data and duplicate the clips and populate them with all
➥the
// information we pulled in from the database.
for (i=0; i<=total_questions; i++) {
    // This line duplicates the label under each bar
    _root.bar_id_MC.duplicateMovieClip("bar_id_MC"+i, depth++);
    // This line duplicates the bars for the chart
    _root.poll_bar.duplicateMovieClip("poll_bar"+i, depth++);
    // This line duplicates the percentage indicator above each bar on the
    ➥chart
    _root.barPercent.duplicateMovieClip("barPercent"+i, depth++);
    // This line makes a new color object for each bar of the chart.
    _root["barColor"+i] = new Color(_root["poll_bar"+i]);
    // This line converts the string containing the hex value to an integer
    ➥hex value
    barcolordata = parseInt(eval("_root.userpoll_sub_mySQLdata.barcolor"+i),
16);
    // This line sets the color of each bar based on the data we pull in
    ➥from mySQL
    _root["barColor"+i].setRGB(this.barcolordata);
    // set the initial height of each bar to 0
    _root["poll_bar"+i]._yscale = 0;
    // set the x axis position of each bar, identifier and percentage
    // the value will increase as we loop through for each iteration
    _root["poll_bar"+i]._x = positionx;
    _root["bar_id_MC"+i]._x = positionx;
    _root["barPercent"+i]._x = positionx;
    // each time we make a new indentifier at the bottom increase it by 1.
    _root["bar_id_MC"+i].bar_id = i+1;
    // This value affects the spacing between the bars. If you want to use a
    ➥new symbol or
    // image you might have to play with this value to adjust your layout.
    positionx += 40;
}
```

5   This section of ActionScript handles the duplicating and population of data into the response input areas and the positioning of the Submit button below the last response.

```
// Loop through our data and create the input bars for the user to respond with
for (i=0; i<=total_questions; i++) {
    // Duplicate the initial movie for each iteration
    _root.poll_input.duplicateMovieClip("poll_input"+i, depth++);
    // Make the number of submits for each item into a number from a string and
    // add them together to get the total number of votes thus far
    _root.total_submits += parseInt(eval("_root.userpoll_sub_mySQLdata.total_
    ➥submits"+i));
    // populate each iteration with its own number of votes
    _root["poll_input"+i].result = eval("_root.userpoll_sub_mySQLdata.total_
    ➥submits"+i);
    // populate each input with the value for the user response to select from
    _root["poll_input"+i].question = eval("_root.userpoll_sub_mySQLdata.question"+i);
    // populate each iteration with an identifier from the database so we can
    ➥associate
    // each vote with the correct entry in the database
    _root["poll_input"+i].item_id = eval("_root.userpoll_sub_mySQLdata.item_id"+i);
    // Give the interface a corresponding identifier to allow a correlation between
    ➥the
    // response presented to the user and the bar chart on the bottom left.
    _root["poll_input"+i].question_id = i+1;
    // Position the response bars a bit apart from each other for each iteration
    _root["poll_input"+i]._y = positiony;
    // keep moving the input button down below the last response bar
    _root.submit._y = positiony+80;
    // increment the spacing for the y axis between each iteration.
    positiony += 40;

}
```

6　Finally, the original movies on the stage are made invisible. The `pollcalc` function is called to do the initial calculations from the data pulled in, and then the movie stops and waits for user input.

Now all the large sections of ActionScript have been covered.

```
// Set our original movieclips to invisible and clean up our setup.
_root.poll_bar._visible = false;
_root.poll_input._visible = false;
_root.barPercent._visible = false;
// run through the charting routine one time and setup all our variables and
➥chart
pollcalc();
// We are all done with this frame...go have a nice roast beef sandwich. :)
stop();
```

User Interface Elements

There are a few bits of code in some of the clips, however, that need to be revisited to understand how they work. These are the input areas and the Submit button.

1 Double-click on the `poll_input` instance on the **questions** layer to edit it in place and examine its structure.

2 Select the **invis button** instance on the **inviso_button** layer. You will see the following code:

This code is used for determining the current selection and its state. It then transmits the values to the **submit** movie clip, which handles the execution of the proper functions after an item has been pressed. This code also handles adjusting the responses from active to inactive if a user makes a selection and then, before hitting submit, changes his or her response.

```
on (rollOut, dragOut) {
    this.mousestat = false;
    if (_root.submit.question_id != this.question_id) {
        this.tab.gotoAndStop(1);
    }
}
on (rollOver, dragOver) {
    this.mousestat = true;
    if (_root.submit.question_id != this.question_id) {
        this.tab.gotoAndStop(2);
    }
}
on (press) {
    this.last_question = _root.submit.question_id;
    this.last_item = _root.submit.item_id;

}
on (release) {
        if((this.last_question == this.question_id) && (this.click != "off")) {
            _root.submit.question_id = null;
            this.click="off";
            this.tab.gotoAndStop(1)
            this.result--;
        _root.total_submits--;
        } else {
            _root.submit.question_id = this.question_id;
            this.tab.gotoAndStop(3);
            if ((this.last_question != this.question_id) && (this.last_question != null)) {
            _root["poll_input"+(this.last_question-1)].result-;
            _root.total_submits--;
            _root.submit.item_id=null;
        }
        this.click="on";
    this.result++;
    _root.submit.item_id=this.item_id;
    _root.total_submits++;
        }
    _root.oversound.start();
_root.pollcalc();
}
```

3   Go back to frame 2 of the **buttons** layer of the main timeline in the poll scene and select the **submit** movie clip. Double-click it to edit it in place.

You will see the frames that enable the Submit button to have various states. Initially, the Submit button is off and nonfunctional while waiting for the IP address check. If a user has voted within the past day, it goes to the "sorry" state and prevents the user from voting. If a user hasn't voted in the past 24 hours, it goes to the "submit" state while waiting for a selection and input. It also has a transferring data state, "sending," when the Submit button is actually pressed and has an "exit" state after a successful insert into the database. In each of these states, the tab clip has its own states for mouseovers, mouseouts, and hits. When You are integrating this project into your site, you should edit the "exit" state so that it will jump back to the next section of your site.

Note: For more information on setting up PHP and installing MySQL for OS X, please see the file **setup_install.pdf** in the 14_Dynamic_Database folder on the accompanying CD.

```
1  on (rollOut, dragOut) {
2      this.tab.gotoAndStop(1);
3  }
4  on (rollOver, dragOver) {
5      this.tab.gotoAndStop(2);
6  }
7  on (press) {
8      this.tab.gotoAndStop(3);
9  }
10 on (release) {
11     if (this.question_id) {
12         this.gotoAndStop(5);
13         _root.votesubmit(this.item_id, this.question_id);
14     }
15 }
```

Submit button ActionScript for sending a vote.

SUMMARY

This project covered the integration of Flash MX with middleware talking to a database to deliver a user poll. The capability of Flash MX to communicate and retrieve information from external sources enables developers to deliver dynamically changing content. A web site that delivers more than static information is the first step in building a truly interactive experience, one that viewers will continue to visit regularly.

The concepts covered in this project can be extrapolated and applied to using a database to store personalization information for return visitors, shopping carts, game scores, and so on. Don't think of this project as simply a user poll—think of it as a building block of knowledge that can be applied to other projects. The key element used in this project is the new `LoadVars` object. Further experimentation on its use, methods, and properties will provide you with an excellent method for retrieving data that does not have to be as rigidly structured as XML. It is excellent for rapid development of Flash MX projects that rely on sending and retrieving data from external sources.

HOW TO IMPROVE

This project could be adapted to other web scripting languages (like ColdFusion/ASP/JSP/Perl) and be used in conjunction with any other database system, such as Microsoft SQL. The web scripting middleware has been divided into specific tasks to enable you to tackle them one at a time if you do decide to port them to another language. For this project's purposes, the focus was not on the PHP and MySQL, which in and of themselves could command an entire book. Rather, it provided a foundation to build on and explore as you concentrate your efforts on the Flash and ActionScript concepts rather than having to also become a MySQL database guru.

A poll could be used for a news site where visitors can vote on the types of topics and stories covered. It could also be used to gather information about the demographics of your users. In turn, this information could help you to refine and tailor your site to the audience you are trying to reach. You might even help Floridians in West Palm Beach during the next election year by providing a simulated voting booth experience for the elderly to practice with. (It's okay. I am a Florida native, so I am allowed to poke fun at them.) There are hundreds of variations on what you could do with a user poll on your site.

One area to explore beyond making an administration tool in Flash and PHP, would be to modify the structure of the database and the Flash MX project so that you can support having more than one active poll. This might be accomplished by modifying the MySQL queries in the PHP files so that additional criteria are used to determine which active poll to return to Flash.

You might also consider modifying the project so that a pie chart is displayed instead of a bar chart. If you have polls that require many responses, having a pie chart to display the percentages and results will enable you to know the exact size the chart will take up, allowing you to refine the layout for your site. Conversely, you might further refine the existing bar chart routine to take advantage of the new ActionScript-based drawing API in Macromedia Flash MX. This would enable you to create very elaborate charts with a great degree of control over their placement and sizing.

A working example of this project will be accessible from the author's site, along with any errata, future enhancements, or modifications like those previously mentioned will be available at the following URL: **www.impossibilities.com/mxmagic/**.

Have fun exploring and modifying!

Flash has been used to create games ever since it has carried the name Flash. Over the years, along with the evolution of Flash, games have become more and more complex. This has opened the doors more and more to use Flash to create "real" applications. Each version of Flash not only has enabled new possibilities to create entirely new things, it also has made it easier to create what you could before.

Flash MX follows this direction, and one might say it is probably the biggest step in the evolution of Flash yet. This project will focus on the new way in which you can program in Flash MX and how you will benefit from it.

15

PROGRAMMING A GAME

by Andreas Heim
with contributions from Troy Parke

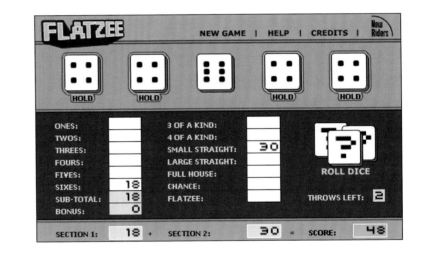

Difficulty Rating: ★★★★

Made With: Graphics created using Macromedia Flash

Final File Size: 240 KB project files, 25KB for the game.

Modem Download Time: 60 / 6 seconds

Development Time: 4 hours

It Works Like This

In this project, you'll create a game named Flatzee, a Flash version of Yahtzee. You'll start by analyzing the board game to determine what elements it contains, then you'll create these elements in Flash, and finally you'll make them work together as a game. Basing the game on a real-world board game makes it easier to talk about objects because, for the most part, an object in Flash represents a real-world object. Flatzee is played with five dice. You can roll the dice up to three times per turn. Using the dice, you try to create combinations much like those in poker. At the end of each turn, you enter the score of your combination in a scorecard. After 13 turns, your scorecard is full and the game is over.

Here are the main elements you need for this game. Because this project is targeted toward programming, all the artwork has been provided for you.

- Five dice.
- A scorecard with slots to enter your scores.
- A table, floor, or board on which the game is played.
- A roll button to roll the dice.
- Because the game is played on a computer, you will need a few navigational elements, such as a help button and a button to start a new game.

Preparing to Work

Before starting, you'll need to copy the **15_Game_Programming** folder onto your hard disk. Open the Extension Manager and install **flatzee_prefixes.mxp**. Then start Flash MX and open the **flatzee_tut1.fla** file. If you have Flash already open, you might have to close it and reopen it to activate the extension.

Note: Throughout this project, I use a naming convention that is based on prefixes, such as mc for "movie clip" in mcFoo. The extension you just installed includes a Custom Actions XML file. This extension makes the ActionScript Editor recognize the types of the names used so that, for example, if you type in mcFoo, the code hints for the movie clip will appear.

CREATING A DIE

Defining a die is a simple task at first. It has six sides, you can roll it, and after rolling it, it shows you a value. In Flatzee, you can do a bit more with it. You can choose to hold a die after you first roll it, and you can change your mind and release it again.

Note: All code in this project is to be created in Expert mode. To switch to Expert mode, open the options for the Actions panel with the icon in the upper-right corner and select Expert Mode.

1   Double-click on the die that is already on the stage to enter Edit in Place mode.

Inside are two layers, named **AS** (for ActionScript) and **mc sides**. The **mc sides** layer holds a movie clip with the instance name **mcSides**. If you explore the movie clip, you'll see that it consists of six frames, each representing one side of the die.

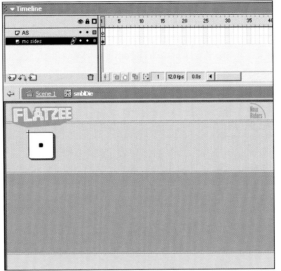

The inside of a die.

2   Select Window > Library. Find **smblDie** in the **Die Parts** folder. Open the library's Options menu and select Linkage.

smblDie is set as the identifier, and Export for ActionScript is selected.

Another check box, Export in first frame, is unchecked, which means you have to place an instance of the symbol on the stage before you can use it with `attachMovie`.

The linkage settings for the die.

Note: This might seem backward at first, but it solves a huge problem that this feature had in Flash 5. In that version, a symbol would always be exported for frame 1 if you chose to export it. This could lead to a huge overhead before the user could see anything when viewing a Flash movie that used this feature extensively. It was designed that way because Flash can't anticipate when you would actually make use of the symbol. Now you are given control over the load order of exported symbols. You simply have to place an instance on the stage, and from that frame on, you can use it via `attachMovie` wherever you want.

3 Select the empty frame in the **AS** layer and open the Actions panel if it's not already open. Add this code:

Flash MX introduces the concept of movie clip classes, and this is an example of defining one. The code between #initclip and #endinitclip executes only once for each movie clip symbol that uses this construct. It runs before the first instance is placed on the stage and is used to define the behavior of all instances of it.

Note: Because the code between #initclip and #endinitclip is supposed to run before anything else in a movie clip, it needs to be defined in frame 1 of a movie clip before anything else is defined.

---

clssDie is the constructor method used for the smblDie symbol. It runs once for every instance of it and takes care of all initialization. It is called "constructor" because it is used to create an instance of the class. In OOP terms, something that used to be called a function is referred to as a *method*. Also, anything that an object "owns" is a *property*. This usually means the same as a variable. However, behind such a property there can be almost anything: a number, a string, an array, or any type of object, even a method.

In the fifth line, the prototype of clssDie is being used as the template to create an instance. Here it's set to a new instance of MovieClip. This is used to implement a concept called *inheritance*. Without it, you'd only create a new object solely based on clssDie. What you want, however, is a die that's still a movie clip. You can achieve this by creating a new MovieClip object as a prototype of clssDie. Now every instance of clssDie inherits everything that makes it a movie clip, like the gotoAndStop method.

```
#initclip
clssDie = function () {
    this.init();
}
clssDie.prototype = new MovieClip();
Object.registerClass("smblDie", clssDie);
#endinitclip
```

Defining a movie clip class.

Note: A *class* is a term used in object-oriented programming (OOP). It is a template to create objects with a certain behavior. Here it means that you can now define movie clips in this manner.

The sixth line is a magic line of code that creates the link between the symbol `smblDie` and the `clssDie` constructor method. Now when you create an instance of `smblDie`, Flash knows that the class from which to create it is `clssDie`. So `clssDie` is the name of the class as well as the constructor method.

Note: You can choose Window > Actions (or press F2) to arrange your workspace. Here I've docked the timeline to the stage so that I can toggle between viewing the stage and viewing the Actions panel to create the maximum space for scripting on a small screen (800×600).

Spend a few minutes exploring the all-new Actions panel. The actions tree to the left has been reorganized. At the top of the editor, you will find shortcut icons to important tools and settings such as code hints and displaying line numbers. Above that there is the script chooser, which enables you to edit scripts applied to any frame or scriptable object in that frame. This is especially useful when you can't see the stage. You can also pin a script with the button to the right of the script chooser. A pinned script will stay in the editor, even if you select other frames or objects.

In the Panel Options menu, you will find more options. One leads you to the preferences for the Actions panel. There you can, for example, choose the font, font size, and color scheme for the editor.

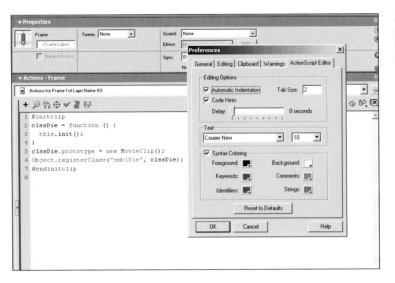

Arranging the workspace and customizing the ActionScript Editor in the Preferences dialog box.

4   Add two methods to `clssDie.prototype`,
    `init` and `reset`. Do this after
    `Object.registerClass("smblDie",`
    `clssDie);` and before `#endinitclip`.

The `clssDie` constructor calls the `init` method
when the instance is created, which takes care of all
initialization. In this case, it makes `mcSides` stop.

Note: You might wonder why the constructor doesn't
take care of what `init` does. By moving the actual
initialization into an `init` method of its own, the first
part of defining a movie clip class can always remain
the same. Simply change the name of the constructor
and the symbol name in the call to
`Object.registerClass`.

The `reset` method is called at the beginning of each
turn, resetting all values. The value of the die is set to
`null` because it doesn't have one yet. Then it makes
sure the die is unlocked.

In this game, users can hold a die after it's rolled. For
them to hold it, they need to be able to click on it,
but at this point, the die hasn't been rolled so you
don't want the user to be able to click on it. The
ninth line of the code prevents this by setting
`enabled` to `false`.

```
clssDie.prototype.init = function () {
    this.mcSides.stop();
    this.reset();
}


clssDie.prototype.reset = function () {
    this.iValue = null;
    this.unlock();
    this.enabled = false;
}
```

Adding the first two methods to the die class, `init` and `reset`.

Macromedia Flash MX: A lot of things have happened to buttons.
Buttons are now objects, almost like movie clips. Movie clips can also
act as buttons but the developer has more control over them.

5 Enter two new methods for `clssDie.prototype`, `lock` and `unlock`:

These two methods act as a toggle: `lock` is equivalent to holding the die, and `unlock` reverses that action. First you lock the die, and then you have to unlock it before you can lock it again. Line 5 of the code triggers this.

When `lock` is called, the `onPress` event handler of this movie clip is set to `unlock`. From here on, the movie clip acts like a button. When the user clicks on the die, the `onPress` event is invoked. This points to the `unlock` method, so `unlock` gets called and this action happens:

```
this.onPress = this.lock;
```

Line 12 reverses the previous setting. The remainder of these two methods keeps track of the current locking state in `bLocked` and also does a visual representation of the two states by moving `mcSides.mcBg` between frames 1 and 2. The `lock` method makes sure it only runs if the die has a value before locking it.

```
clssDie.prototype.lock = function () {
    if (this.iValue != null) {
        this.bLocked = true;
        this.mcSides.mcBg.gotoAndStop(2);
        this.onPress = this.unlock;
    }


}
clssDie.prototype.unlock = function () {
    this.bLocked = false;
    this.mcSides.mcBg.gotoAndStop(1);
    this.onPress = this.lock;
}
```

Methods to lock and unlock the die.

USING THE ROLL METHOD TO ROLL A DIE

Now that you can lock and unlock the die, it's time to think about rolling it. Create a roll method that first checks whether the die is locked. Only if this is not the case do you actually roll the die. Use `Math.random` to create a random result and set this result as the value of the die.

Because it could be boring or confusing if the die showed the result right away, you'll want to keep the die rolling for a bit before actually displaying the result.

1   Add this code:

The fifth line defines an `onEnterFrame` handler, which will get called in every frame and point to a rolling method.

Because you don't want the die to roll until the end of time, you need to define a random roll time. In the seventh line, `setInterval` is a new callback timer that works like this: After `iRollTime`, the function with the name `endRoll` will be called in the object `this`, which represents the die. By default, `setInterval` makes this call not only once but every `iRollTime` milliseconds until you clear the interval again. To clear it, you need an interval `id`, which is returned when you set up the interval.

After it's set up, make sure the die can be clicked on by setting its `enabled` property to `true` and return the result. Although it doesn't show the result yet, that's what the value will be.

```
clssDie.prototype.roll = function () {
  if (!this.bLocked) {
    var iResult = Math.floor (Math.random()*6) + 1;
    this.iValue = iResult;
    this.onEnterFrame = this.rolling;
    var iRollTime = Math.floor (Math.random()*800) + 300;
    this.iIntervalId = setInterval (this, "endRoll", iRollTime);
    this.enabled = true;
  }
  return this.getValue();
}
```

Start rolling the die with the `roll` method.

Note: You can add parameters that are passed on to the function after the interval has elapsed. Simply add them after the interval time.

There is a second, default way to call `setInterval`:

```
setInterval ("methodName", intervalTime);
```

The difference is that it calls only the method passed to it, but it doesn't call it in any timeline or object. This means that `this` inside the method will be undefined.

253

2 To keep the die rolling for the set time, create this `rolling` method:

This picks a random side and shows it. Because `rolling` is the `onEnterFrame` handler, this happens every frame until the end of the roll is determined.

```
clssDie.prototype.rolling = function () {
    var iSide = Math.floor (Math.random()*6) + 1;
    this.mcSides.gotoAndStop (iSide);
}
```

Keep the die rolling with the `rolling` method.

3 Define the function that is called when the random roll time is up:

By setting `onEnterframe` to `null`, you ensure that the die stops rolling. You clear the interval of calling `this` method by calling `clearInterval` with the stored interval `id`. Last but not least, the actual result is shown.

```
clssDie.prototype.endRoll = function () {
    this.onEnterFrame = null;
    clearInterval (this.iIntervalId);
    this.mcSides.gotoAndStop (this.iValue);
}
```

Stop rolling.

4 Define a method that returns the value of the die:

Although you could read the value of `iValue` from the outside, that's bad style. The properties on an object or a movie clip are supposed to be private. You should only access them from the outside with an access method. This is part of a concept called *information hiding*.

For example, you might decide later on to not return a value while the die is still rolling. If `iValue` is exposed, you need to set it to `null` first so that it doesn't show the old value and only define it at the end of the roll. If you use an access function like `getValue`, you can ensure that the result that is returned is what should be returned at that moment.

```
clssDie.prototype.getValue = function () {
    return this.iValue;
}
```

The `getValue` getter method to get the value of the die.

5 Go back to the main timeline where you'll see the die. Make the invisible layer **btRoll** visible to show a roll button. In frame 1 of the **AS** layer, assign this code:

First you define a `roll` method that calls the `roll` method of the die. Later, this will roll all buttons.

Next you create a reference to the main timeline as `refmcMyself`. Then you create an `onPress` event handler for the `roll` button, which calls the `roll` method in the main timeline.

That's it for the die. It's all set and defined. Try it out to see if it's all working.

6 Save your file if you haven't done so already and select Control > Test Movie.

At first you shouldn't be able to click on the die, but you can click on the roll button to roll the die. After you do that, you can lock and unlock the die. Try to roll it after you lock it—it shouldn't roll.

Macromedia Flash MX: In Flash 5, a method looks up properties other than local method properties in the timeline in which the code is running. You can still do this in Flash MX, but to access those properties, you need to prefix them with `this`. Otherwise, Flash will look those properties up where the method was defined. This is how you can set `refmcMyself` here in the method and the roll button still finds it when you press it.

```
function roll () {
   this.mcDie.roll();
}
var refmcMyself = this;
this.btRoll.onPress = function () {
   refmcMyself.roll();
}
```

Assigning an `onPress` handler to the roll button.

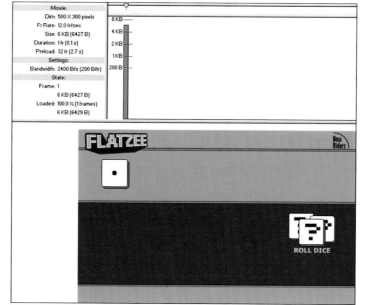

Checking out the die.

PLACING THE DICE ON THE TABLE

Now that you can roll a single die, you'll need to place five dice on the table and roll them together. You'll also need to set the number of rolls to only three times and then start over again. Finally, you'll lay the foundation to integrate the scorecard with the dice on the table.

1 Open **flatzee_tut2.fla**.

The elements from the previous part have been moved into a movie clip: The instance name is `mcTable`, and the symbols export identifier is `smblTable`. Instead of one die there are now five, named `mcDie0` to `mcDie4`. There is a new game button and a "Throws Left" display.

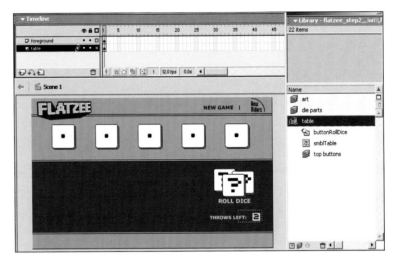

Five dice are on the table.

2 Double-click on an element of `mctable` to enter Edit in Place mode. Select the script in the **AS** layer and open the Actions panel.

The constructor definition for `clssTable` is already prepared for you.

The constructor of the table class.

> **Note:** As with the previous creation of the die movie clip class, all the following method definitions need to be placed after `Object.registerClass("smblTable", clssTable);` and before `#endinitclip`.

```
1  #initclip 10
2
3  clssTable = function () {
4    this.init();
5  }
6
7  clssTable.prototype = new MovieClip();
8
9  Object.registerClass("smblTable", clssTable);
10
11 #endinitclip
12
```

Line 6 of 12, Col 1

3. As with the die, the first method you create for the table is `init`:

First define the maximum number of throws per turn as 3 in `cMaxTries`. The `c` prefix is an abbreviation for "count."

Then store references to all dice in an array called `aDice` (the `a` prefix stands for "array"), which makes it easier to access them as a whole later on. The number of dice on the table is stored in `cDice` (for "countDice").

The roll button gets its `onPress` handler assigned in the same way as before. The new game or reset button gets an `onPress` handler as well, this one calling the `reset` method of the table.

Finally, the game gets started with a call to `startTurn`.

```
clssTable.prototype.init = function () {
    this.cMaxTries = 3;
    this.aDice = [];
    this.cDice = 0;
    while (this["mcDie"+this.cDice] != null) {
        this.cDice = this.aDice.push( this["mcDie"+this.cDice] );
    }
    var refmcMyself = this;
    this.btRoll.onPress = function () {
        refmcMyself.roll();
    }
    this.btReset.onPress = function () {
        refmcMyself.reset();
    }
    this.startTurn();
}
```

Initializing the table.

4. Now create the `startTurn` method:

At the beginning of each turn, the throw counter needs to be reset to 3. This is stored in a count variable `cTriesLeft`. This will be a number and will be used for calculation. You also need a visual representation for the user to see. Here, a dynamic text field is used.

Text fields are now objects, too, and can be modified programmatically in many ways. The application here doesn't make use of those ways; all you do is set the text field's `text` property to what you want to display.

```
clssTable.prototype.startTurn = function () {
    this.cTriesLeft = this.cMaxTries;
    this.tfThrowsLeft.text = this.cTriesLeft;
    this.mcScoreCard.deactivate();
    this.resetDice();
    this.btRoll.enabled = true;
}
```

A `startTurn` method for the table class.

Note: You could use the value of `tfThrowsLeft.text` as your counter. Even though what you see is a number, the `.text` property is a string. Although Flash does an automatic type conversion depending on how you use a variable, it's generally a good idea to be sure of the type of a number. Otherwise, you can sometimes get unexpected results.

The next line of code calls the scorecard's `deactivate` method. You don't have a scorecard yet, so it doesn't do anything at this point. Later on, this ensures that you can't click on the scorecard until you've first rolled the dice.

Finally, reset the dice and make sure the roll button is active.

5 Create the `resetDice` method of the `table` class:

Because you stored references to all dice when the table initialized in an array, you just need to loop through this `aDice` array and can call each die's `reset` method.

> **Note:** As logical as it might sound, the first time this is run, these calls won't reset the dice. Due to Flash's execution order, the table's constructor gets called first—before the dice's constructor—because the dice are placed in the table's timeline. Before the constructor is called, the movie clip class is not initialized, and the newly defined methods don't exist yet.
>
> In this case, that doesn't hurt you; you have set up the dice so that they will reset themselves when initializing.

```
clssTable.prototype.resetDice = function () {
  for (var i=0; i<this.cDice; i++) {
    this.aDice[ i] .reset();
  }
}
```

Reset all dice from the table.

6   Improve the `roll` method you created before and make it a method of the `table` class as well:

If you have tries left, you will roll all the dice. Dice that you are holding will ignore this. If this was the first throw of the turn, you'll activate the scorecard—from now on you have a score that you could enter.

Next, decrement the number of tries left. At 0, turn the roll button off. Finally, update the "Throws Left" display.

After you play a game (or when you're not happy with your progress), you'll probably want to reset the game to start a new one.

```
clssTable.prototype.roll = function () {
  if (this.cTriesLeft > 0) {
    for (var i=0; i<this.cDice; i++) {
      this.aDice[ i] .roll();
    }
    if (this.cTriesLeft == this.cMaxTries) {
      this.mcScoreCard.activate();
    }
    this.cTriesLeft--;
    if (this.cTriesLeft == 0) {
      this.btRoll.enabled = false;
    }
    this.tfThrowsLeft.text = this.cTriesLeft;
  }
}
```

Roll all the dice together, and keep track of how many tries you have left.

7   Add a `reset` method:

All you need is to reset the scorecard and start a new turn.

```
clssTable.prototype.reset = function () {
  this.mcScoreCard.reset();
  this.startTurn();
}
```

Reset the table.

CALCULATING THE VALUES OF THE DICE

You now have everything to control the dice and limit the user to three throws per turn, but you have no idea yet what to do with the combinations you threw.

1 Capture the values of the dice with this method:

Do a quick check to determine whether you rolled the dice already for that turn. If so, loop through the `aDice` array again and store each die's value in an `aDiceValues` array. That array is then returned to the caller.

If you haven't rolled yet, it returns `null` because there are no values to return.

```
clssTable.prototype.getDiceValues = function () {
  if (this.cTriesLeft < this.cMaxTries) {
    var aDiceValues = [];
    for (var i=0; i<this.cDice; i++) {
      aDiceValues.push( this.aDice[ i ].getValue() );
    }
    return aDiceValues;
  }
  else {
    return null;
  }
}
```

Fetch the values of all dice on the table.

2 Even though you don't have a scorecard yet, select Control > Test Movie.

At first, all you can do is roll the dice. They will roll for slightly different amounts of time. The "Throws Left" display will count down. You can now hold dice as you please and roll again. After three throws, the roll button becomes inactive.

Because you can't enter your score just yet, you have to use the New Game button to start over.

Rolling the dice.

Set up arrays and counters for the slots on the left and the right. Each of these two columns has a distinctively different behavior and its own sum, so treat them as separate entities but keep a total count of all slots so that you know when the scorecard is filled out and the game is over.

Next, push references to the slot movie clips into the respective arrays, much like the dice were organized before. Finally, call `reset`.

Stop. Rewind. What is `oSlotInit` doing there? You might have noticed that none of the constructors expects any arguments to be passed in. If you've created constructors before—either in JavaScript or in ActionScript other than for movie clips—you know that you can usually pass arguments to the constructor.

> **Note:** In movie clip classes, you can't pass arguments to a constructor directly because you can't call the constructor yourself directly. Due to Macromedia Flash's execution order, the constructor of the slots will be invoked after the scorecard's `#endinitclip` has passed.

The slot movie clips, however, are already there, and you can access them. So you can set properties in a slot's timeline, and the slot's constructor can look out for them and then use them as if they were arguments that got passed in.

Although you don't want to fill up the slot's timeline with different properties, it's the only way. You can do this more gracefully, however, by creating an `init` object, which can be passed to the slot. The slot's constructor can then look at the `init` object and do with it whatever it needs. This is a voluntary way of creating a fairly clean passage to passing arguments to a child movie clip upon initialization.

Here, you pass a reference to the `table` movie clip and a numeric ID to each slot's `oInit` object.

> **Note:** Another benefit of using an `init` object—and you use it consistently in the same way expected of retrieving arguments—is that you don't run the risk of accidentally overwriting a passed argument during initialization, which is what happened in the following example:
>
> ```
> this.mcFoo.bar = "hello";
> ```
>
> In the constructor of `mcFoo`, not knowing that `bar` is passed in:
>
> ```
> this.bar = 100;
> ```
>
> Now `mcFoo.bar` is 100, and setting it to `hello` was a waste of time. If you set properties directly inside a movie clip, you have to know exactly how that movie clip will deal with them. Unless you are programming within a movie clip directly, you usually don't want to mess with its properties because this can quickly lead to conflicts. The best way to interact with a movie clip is through its methods. The `init` object is an exception because the methods are not available at the time.

> **Note:** As in Flash 5, you can dynamically create instances of movie clips by using `attachMovie` or `duplicateMovie`. Both of these methods now have another argument you can specify, an `init` object. The properties of the `init` object get set in the new movie clip's timeline. You can also pass an object as a property of that argument to achieve the same format as earlier.
>
> Here's an example, assuming you have a symbol in your Library set to export with the linkage ID `smblFoo`:
>
> ```
> var oFooInit = { iZip : 98133 };
> this.attachMovie ("smblFoo", "mcFoo", 1, { oInit: oFooInit} );
> trace (this.mcFoo.oInit.iZip);
> ```
>
> Unlike instances of movie clip classes placed on the timeline, the constructor of dynamically created movie clips gets invoked right away. So by the time you call the trace action, the new movie clip has already initialized.

4 Now that the skeleton of the `init` method is
defined, add this code in the first loop for the left
slots. Do so after `oSlotInit = ...` and before
`refmcSlot.oInit = oSlotInit;`.

All slots behave in a similar way. On every slot, you
can click and it then displays a score. However, each
slot needs to calculate its score in a different way. The
slot class, as defined later, is incomplete and it needs
to be passed a method to calculate a score from the
dice's values.

The `id` is what was already passed to the `oSlotInit`
object; the slot's constructor stores all data parameters
passed with it in an `oCalculate` object for
`calculateScore` to use.

`aValueCount` is an array in which you counted the
number of times each value has been thrown.
Another method of the slot calculates this.

5 The slots on the left were easy to calculate, but the
slots on the right need special treatment. Add this
code in the second loop for the right slot's `init`
method. Again, do so after `oSlotInit = ...` and
before `refmcSlot.oInit = oSlotInit;`.

Flash MX now has a `switch` statement
implemented, just like in JavaScript. Internally, it's
much the same as a series of "if-then-else-if-else…".

First there is an expression after `switch`. That can
be anything you would normally use on the left side
when checking something, such as the `bFound` in
`bFound==true`. It can even be something returned
from a function call. Here, `iSlot` is used because
you want to do different things for the different slots
on the right side.

```
oSlotInit.calculateScore = function (aValueCount) {
    var iScore = aValueCount[ this.oCalculate.id] * this.oCalculate.id;
    return iScore;
}
```

Tell the slots on the left how to calculate their scores.

```
switch (iSlot) {
    case ( this.checkRange (iSlot, 0 ,1 ) ) :
        // 3 or 4 of a kind
        break;
    case this.checkRange (iSlot, 2 ,3 ) :
        // small or large straight
        break;
    case 4 :
        // full house
        break;
    case 5 :
        // chance
        break;
    case 6 :
        // flatzee
        break;
}
```

Setting up a `switch` statement to define the slots in the right column.

Each case statement holds another expression, the right side of the comparison. If the left and right side match, the code after the colon executes until it hits `break;`.

You see the `checkRange` method being used there. You don't want to do completely different things for each slot, but do something similar for slots 0 and 1, and 2 and 3. So when `iSlot` is 0 or 1, the result of the expression for the case statement needs to be exactly the same as the one in the `switch` statement. That is why `checkRange` returns the number that is passed in.

All along, I've said that a `switch` statement is the same as if-then-else, but that's not completely true. `switch` uses true equality, which now can also be used in the form of a triple equal sign (===) in other expressions. So although (`"1"`==1) will return `true`, (`"1"`===1) will return `false`. Not only the value will be taken into consideration but also the type.

6 The right slots are split into different sections. Now it's time to create `calculateScore` methods for each. Assign the following code after the comment line `// 3 or 4 of a kind` and before `break;`:

First determine, depending on which slot, whether you need to check for 3 or 4 of a kind. Pass a `cSame` property to the slot. The `calculate` method then checks whether it can find `cSame` number of dice. If yes, the score is the sum of all dice; otherwise, it's 0.

Note: It is important that you use `break;`. Otherwise, all the other code in all other case statements executes as well. You can make use of this if you know what you are doing. In most cases, however, it will cause unexpected and unwanted results.

For the code here, you could also do the following:

```
case 0 :
case 1 :
  // 3 or 4 of a kind
  break;
```

This is only suitable for small ranges, however, because you have to create a case for every number in the range, and it also only works with integers. Using the `checkRange` method should prove to be more useful in the long run.

Note: After the `break;` of the last case statement, you can use a `default :` statement to catch anything that didn't match any of the cases, like the last `else` in a long if-then-else chain. I didn't need to use it here.

```
oSlotInit.cSame = ( iSlot == 0) ? 3 : 4;
oSlotInit.calculateScore = function (aValueCount) {
  var bFound = false;
  var cSum = 0;
  for (var i=0; i<aValueCount.length; i++) {
    if (aValueCount[ i] >= this.oCalculate.cSame) bFound = true;
      cSum += aValueCount[ i] * i;
  }
  var iScore = 0;
  if (bFound) iScore = cSum;
  return iScore;
}
```

Calculate the score for the 3- and 4-of-a-kind slots.

7 Creating the `calculateScore` methods for the other slots reveals nothing new. They calculate the score either by adding all values or by giving you a certain set score if you threw a certain combination. You can either create them as an exercise on your own, or you can open **flatzee_tut3_switch.as** in a text editor or import it into the ActionScript editor and add the completed `switch` statement.

8 Open **flatzee_tut3_methods.as**. This file includes a few more methods to be added to `clssScorecard.prototype`:

- `reset`. Takes care of resetting all slots and the score displays as well as the internal score variables.

- `activate` and `deactivate`. Loops through all slots and activates or deactivates them.

- `updateScoreLeft`, `updateScoreRight` and `updateScore`. These methods add up the scores of both columns, check whether you have done well enough to get the bonus, and calculate the total score.

- `scoreEntered`. Gets called by the slots after you've clicked on one to enter a score. Updates all score displays. Keeps track of the number of filled slots and lets you roll the dice again if you still have slots open.

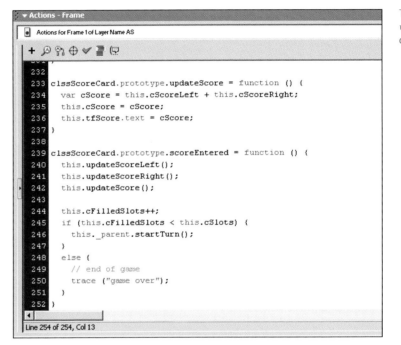

The `scoreEntered` and `updateScore` methods of the scorecard class.

```
232
233 clssScoreCard.prototype.updateScore = function () {
234   var cScore = this.cScoreLeft + this.cScoreRight;
235   this.cScore = cScore;
236   this.tfScore.text = cScore;
237 }
238
239 clssScoreCard.prototype.scoreEntered = function () {
240   this.updateScoreLeft();
241   this.updateScoreRight();
242   this.updateScore();
243
244   this.cFilledSlots++;
245   if (this.cFilledSlots < this.cSlots) {
246     this._parent.startTurn();
247   }
248   else {
249     // end of game
250     trace ("game over");
251   }
252 }
```

Line 254 of 254, Col 13

CREATING THE SLOTS

Everything is now defined except for the slots. I have mentioned them a lot, but I haven't told you anything about the insides of a slot, other than it gets a custom calculateScore method.

There is nothing really magic about a slot, so go ahead and take care of creating it.

1 Open **flatzee_tut4.fla**. Edit the scorecard and double-click on any of the slots with the white background to edit it.

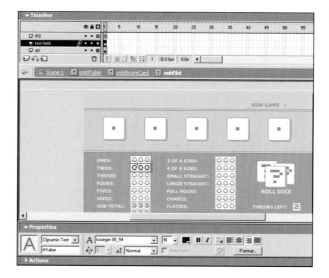

Inside the timeline of a slot.

2 Select the **AS** layer and open the Actions panel.

The slot class constructor is already defined as are some methods: reset, activate, deactivate, getValue, and setValue. These are simple in structure and do just what their names suggest.

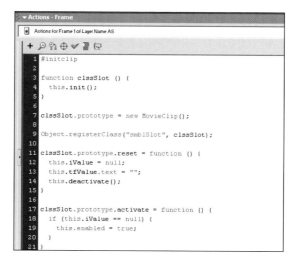

The slot's constructor.

```
1  #initclip
2
3  function clssSlot () {
4    this.init();
5  }
6
7  clssSlot.prototype = new MovieClip();
8
9  Object.registerClass("smblSlot", clssSlot);
10
11 clssSlot.prototype.reset = function () {
12   this.iValue = null;
13   this.tfValue.text = "";
14   this.deactivate();
15 }
16
17 clssSlot.prototype.activate = function () {
18   if (this.iValue == null) {
19     this.enabled = true;
20   }
21 }
```

3 Enter the missing `init` method after `Object.registerClass("smblSlot", clssSlot);`.

Here you look for the `oInit` object that was passed on by the scorecard. With a `for...in` loop, look at each property in `oInit`. If the property name is either `refmcTable` or `calculateScore`, assign them as properties of this slot. Everything else is to be used by the `calculateScore` method, so it's placed in an `oCalculate` object.

> **Note:** Alternatively, you could create an `oCalculate` object in the `oInit` object. Then you'd have just three arguments to check for. This would require a bit more effort to set up the structure of `oInit` in the score-card, and because the `init` method of the scorecard is already complex enough, I'd recommend leaving it like this.

```
clssSlot.prototype.init = function () {
  var arg;
  this.oCalculate = {};
  for (var sArg in this.oInit) {
    arg = this.oInit[ sArg];
    if (sArg == "refmcTable" || sArg == "calculateScore" ) {
      this[ sArg] = arg;
    }
    else {
      this.oCalculate[ sArg] = arg;
    }
  }
  this.reset();
}
```

Initializing a slot that received an `init` object.

4 I've already mentioned that the `calculateScore` methods receive their data input in the form of an array with counted values. Add the `countValues` method at the bottom of the script but before `#endinitclip`:

Here you take an array with dice values, loop through it, and create another array with each position representing a dice value and with the value of the position representing the count. Afterward, you return the newly created array.

```
clssSlot.prototype.countValues = function (aDiceValues) {
  var aValueCount = [];
  for (var iDie=0; iDie<aDiceValues.length; iDie++) {
    aValueCount [ aDiceValues[ iDie] ]++;
  }
  return aValueCount;
}
```

Count how often each value has been thrown.

> **Note:** The table from which you get the dice values could have counted them this way already. However, the table doesn't know and doesn't need to know how a slot in the scorecard calculates a score. It's better to do the main part of the work where it needs to be done and keep it as simple as possible on the table.

5 The slot needs to react to a press event. Add this onPress method at the end of the script, again before #endinitclip:

Now the magic comes together. By creating an onPress handler, the slot becomes clickable unless deactivated. When invoked, you first get the dice values from the table. The reference to the table was set in the slot's init method.

If something is returned, the countValues method counts the dice. You can then calculate the score with the calculateScore method that the scorecard created and passed on to the slot template. Of course, you'll want to set and display the value. Finally, you tell the parent (the scorecard) that a score has been entered, and the scorecard takes care of the rest.

6 Save your file if you haven't done so already. Select Control > Test Movie. Your Flatzee game is now fully functional. Enjoy!

```
clssSlot.prototype.onPress = function () {
  var aDiceValues = this.refmcTable.getDiceValues();
  if (aDiceValues != null) {
    var aValueCount = this.countValues (aDiceValues);
    var iScore = this.calculateScore(aValueCount);

    this.setValue (iScore);
    this._parent.scoreEntered();
  }
}
```

Defining an onPress handler for the slot.

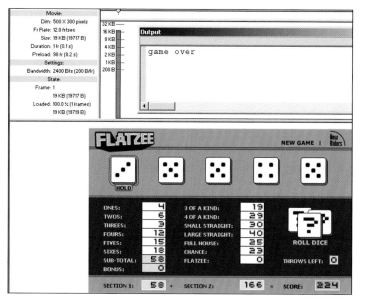

Flatzee is working.

269

Summary

You created an entire game from scratch, step by step, element by element, with the new features that Flash MX offers. Some of these new features might take time to get used to, but once you understand them, you realize how much more powerful Flash has become while at the same time actually making your life easier—and now you can play Flatzee all day long!

How to Improve

In this project, you created a fully functional game, yet there might be some things you'd like to add to it. Open **flatzee_complete.fla** to see a few additions.

The game now has a loader screen.

There is now a help screen that makes use of the scrollbar component that ships with Flash MX.

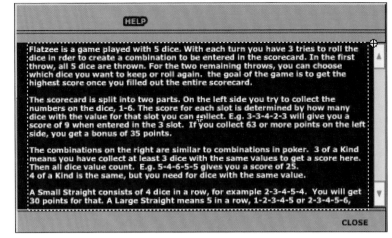

A help screen explaining the rules of Flatzee.

To prevent accidental clicks on buttons behind the help screen, the background is turned into a button that has a dummy `onPress` handler and that doesn't show the hand cursor because its `useHandCursor` property is set to `false`.

I also added sound to the buttons, including the movie clip buttons.

Adding button state frame labels to a movie clip button.

There is no _hit label, in case you were looking for such a thing. By default, the hit area is defined by the real estate that the movie clip button uses. If you want to use a different hit area, you need to point the .hitArea property of the movie clip to a movie clip that represents the area you want. This movie clip can be any movie clip. It doesn't have to be in the same timeline, and it can even be invisible with its _visible property set to false.

MORE INHERITANCE

The game includes not only a help screen but also a quit screen. Both have a very similar basic behavior: They open when you click their opener button and close again with their close button. Instead of duplicating the ActionScript to take care of that in each movie clip, I created a generic screen class, which can only be found in the Library as **smblScreenGeneric**. Both the help screen and the credits screen use the generic screen class as a super class with the following lines:

```
clssScreenCredits.prototype = new clssScreenGeneric ();
clssScreenHelp.prototype = new clssScreenGeneric ();
```

Unlike the other class prototypes you defined, these are not directly based on MovieClip. Yet they inherit from MovieClip because clssScreenGeneric does:

```
clssScreenGeneric.prototype = new MovieClip ();
```

If you look at the ActionScript in either the help screen or the credits screen, you will see the following:

```
#initclip 1
```

You haven't seen a number in this spot before, have you? Well, this is the first time it is needed. As explained at the beginning of the project, the code between #initclip and #endinitclip runs before the frame in which the movie clip is first used on the timeline (or before the first frame if you set that in the linkage settings). If you have several movie clip classes initialize before the same frame, they run in an order you can't control unless you use an integer number after #initclip. The higher the number, the further it will be pushed back in the execution order. If you don't specify a number, that is equivalent to using a 0.

The 1 here is necessary because both the help and the credit screen use screen generic as a super class. Thus, they need to initialize after screen generic does, and the 1 ensures that. You can use the same number more than once; you just can't predict which script with the same priority will run first.

You already know how much fun it is to create with Flash, moving and mixing graphics, text, and audio on your own digital palette like a major film director. Flash MX now permits you to add video to any Flash project, expanding your palette with a major new creative element.

The new video features in Flash MX include:

- Importing video
- Accepting multiple file formats
- Higher quality compression
- Importing video clips as embedded files
- Linking QuickTime files

This appendix covers the tricks of importing and exporting, quality settings, and the new Sorenson Spark "codec" (short for coder-decoder). It also explores methods for optimizing audio, synchronizing the runtime, and embedding video into the timeline. Compatibility has always been a big feature with Flash, and now with MX, importing and exporting into the various video formats is a multicodec joy. Also covered is how to link QuickTime files and how to publish a Flash movie with embedded video.

You'll want to spend plenty of time playing with these new video features and experimenting with exporting your projects, not only into .swf files but also into QuickTime 4 movies as well. Being a Flash film director never had so many advantages.

A
WORKING WITH VIDEO

by Joe Tripician

with graphics by Chip Ruhnke
video courtesy of Simon Grome, **www.shootasia.tv**

Note: You'll find four video files (created with MovieCleaner 5) on the accompanying CD-ROM. These are from two videos ("Spots" and "Fashion") created by cinematographer Simon Grome, and they come in two versions each of Windows Media Format (100K and 56K.) They are examples of this ubiquitous streaming video format in modem speed (56K) and in ISDN or low-end broadband speed (100K). These files will be useful in experimenting with importing and exporting video with Flash because they represent the most commonly used speeds of Internet video.

Test them with different quality settings and see the results. Look for file size as well as quality; as one increases, so does the other. The goal is to get the highest quality at the smallest file size. With both modem and broadband versions, you'll be able to experience what typical Internet users experience. Wow them.

IMPORTING VIDEO INTO FLASH

When you want to incorporate a video into your Flash site, there are a few things to watch out for: supported file formats, runtime, and—most importantly—proper quality settings. Because video behaves differently than vectors, optimizing settings for all the different codecs is a must.

Video File Formats

Flash can import several video formats. You can also import .flv files (without QT or DirectX required). .flv files are Flash video format, and they are created during export in an application called Sorenson Squeeze.

Video File Format	Supported by QuickTime 4	Supported by DirectX 7 or Higher (Windows Only)
.asf		Yes
.avi	Yes	Yes
.dv	Yes	
.mpg (without audio)	Yes	Yes
.mpeg (without audio)	Yes	Yes
.mov	Yes	
.wmv		Yes

Note: .avi files can be created with a variety of video and audio codecs. Your computer must have the same video and audio codecs installed as were used to create the .avi file.

Sorenson Spark Codec

A codec is a piece of software that compresses data and then decompresses or "decodes" the data.

When you import a (already compressed) video file, it is decompressed using the video's native codec and then is recompressed using the Sorenson Spark codec. Spark includes smoothing of artifacts from the video's native codec. This improves the quality of the imported streaming file by helping to eliminate some of the square tiling artifacts typical of low–bit-rate streaming video.

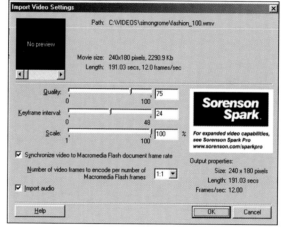

The Import Video Settings dialog box displays Sorenson Spark settings.

Note: Video keyframes (also known as "I-frames") are internal to the video data stream and contain the entire picture information of one frame. Don't confuse video keyframes with Flash movie keyframes that appear on the timeline.

Spark also performs automatic keyframes. Video codecs compress the file size by just recording the differences from one video frame to the next, but keyframes have absolute values for the pixels. When scenes change, Spark detects this and generates a video keyframe at that point.

Following is a list of the settings found in the dialog box, and what they do:

- **Quality (compression level).** The default Quality is 75%. This creates a file size that is somewhat larger than other streaming formats but smaller than raw .avi files or .mpeg files. You can reduce file size by setting the quality to a lower level. You would typically select a low Quality level (25%) for your low–bit-rate audience and a high Quality level (75%) for your broadband audience.

- **Keyframe Interval (forced keyframe every so many video frames).** This determines how many frames pass before a video keyframe is generated, in addition to the automatic keyframes that Spark generates. Normally you don't need to increase the number of keyframes (also known as forcing keyframes) because automatic keyframes do the job nicely. If, however, the video has no or few scene changes but there are changes in the picture, such as moving objects, these moving objects might get a little blurry over time. By forcing a keyframe, you can clear up the blurring. Some experts suggest forcing a keyframe every two seconds to be safe (that's a keyframe interval of 24 frames if your movie is set for 12 frames per second) and forcing more frequent keyframes if the video contains a lot of motion. Be aware that additional keyframes will make the file size larger.

- **Scale (size).** Scale changes the screen size of the video. This might be useful if your video is smaller than your stage and you want to enlarge the video to fill the stage.

Optimizing Video and Audio for Import

When optimizing your video's audio, make sure it's clear and loud but not too loud. You should never let your audio levels exceed 100% (or zero db). Audio compression keeps the volume in a small range with little difference between the softer passages and the loudest crescendos.

After compression, normalize for 90%. Normalizing is an adjustment of the volume to keep the loudest passages at a particular level. Because there is no way to adjust the audio in Flash, make sure your audio levels on your video are correct before you import the video.

After you've created your video at the desired size, you can use free encoding software from Microsoft (Windows Media Encoder for Windows Media formats) or RealNetworks (RealProducer for RealVideo formats). Conversely, you can use an encoding program like Media Cleaner 5 for Real and Windows or Sorenson for QuickTime (the best way to encode for QT).

When encoding the original video, prior to importing, try this table's recommended settings for various target audiences:

Target Audience	Size	Frames/Sec	Sec/I-frame	Audio Format
For 28.8 modem (22kbps actual)	160×120	2 or 3	10	8kbps, 8KHz for voice; 8kbps, 11KHz for music
For 56 modem (37kbps actual)	160×120	6	8 or 10	10kbps, 11KHz
For dual-ISDN (80–100kbps)	176×144	9	8	16kbps, 16KHz
For Broadband (300kbps)	320×240	15	8	32kbps, 22KHz stereo

Note: Making the video's screen size smaller is best done in the original video file using your chosen video-editing software. Spark scaling automatically smoothes the video image. Enlarging a video's screen size requires softening so that the added pixels have halftones. Otherwise, the added pixels have the exact same color as the original pixel that fathered them, resulting in one big pixel with aliased jaggies. When downsizing, softening is unnecessary, so you might get a clearer picture if you reduce the video's screen size in the original video-editing software before importing to Flash. If your video is extra crisp, such as from a Firewire capture, add a slight amount of blurring, softening, or contrast reduction. Just a little goes a long way to reduce blocky artifacts.

Also try reducing the number of transitions in your video. This works wonders in eliminating unwanted pixel artifacts.

Importing and Embedding

After you select your video file, it is imported directly to the stage and is placed on the highlighted layer in the timeline, or it can be imported into the Library via File > Import to Library. If you do not have a **Timeline** layer ready for the video, you can instead import video clips to the Library (File > Import to Library).

Next, insert a layer for the video. While that layer is highlighted, drag the video from the Library to the stage. This places the video into the highlighted layer, and once there, it can be moved and placed anywhere, just like any other graphic element.

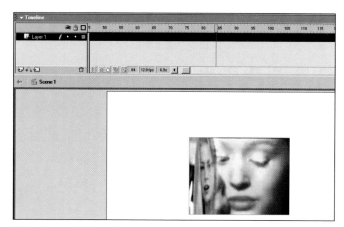

Video clip on timeline and stage.

By default, the new layer you create for the video has a keyframe at the beginning, and the video plays from that point. If you want the video to begin someplace other than at the beginning of the Flash movie, insert a keyframe at the point at which you want the video to begin *before* you import the video.

When the video is longer than the existing Flash timeline (which is likely if the video is one of the first elements you add), you'll be prompted to extend the timeline. Click Yes to extend the length of the timeline or No to keep it the same. If you choose to keep the timeline length the same, frames in the imported clip that exceed the frames in the timeline are not displayed unless you add frames subsequently to the timeline.

The Embedded Video Properties dialog box lets you update and change the embedded video clip. From the library, just click on the Options menu and choose Properties. Then click Update or Import.

Note: Some video formats do not preview within Flash. If you right-click/Ctrl-click on the video file in the Library and choose Edit With, you can open the file in the application associated with the file type. For example, .asf and .wmv files will open the file in the Windows Media Player.

Update and replace video clips from the Library window.

Synchronizing Runtime

When you import video, select the Synchronize Video to Flash Document Frame Rate option in the Import Video Settings dialog box. Otherwise, Flash maps one frame of video to one frame of Flash. If you don't select this option, Flash might slow the imported video down so that it matches its frame rate.

Importing Audio

You can import the audio from a video file by selecting the Import Audio option in the Import Video Settings dialog box. Imported audio must be in a codec that is installed and recognized by your computer.

> **Tip:** If you import multiple video files that run concurrently or that overlap, you most likely will only want the audio from one of the videos and should deselect audio for the others.

> **Note:** When previewing your video from the timeline, you will not hear the audio. You must export the file to .swf to hear the audio. Just choose Control > Test Movie for a preview.

Positioning the Video on the Stage

If the video is smaller than the stage, you can drag it to place it where you like, just like any graphic element. You can also change its location by adding keyframes to the **Timeline** layer and moving the location of the video on the stage to correspond to the keyframe, just as you would with any other graphic object.

You can import multiple videos and position them as you like, even on top of each other.

You can apply transforms to the video image in the same way you transform other graphic elements, except you cannot insert keyframes into the middle of the video to create a transform that would alter its behavior at that point. Any keyframe you insert will restart the video from its beginning. You can, however, add a keyframe at the end of the video and create a tween from the beginning keyframe to the ending keyframe.

Importing multiple video clips.

Linking QuickTime Files

To link a QuickTime movie, publish the Flash movie as a QuickTime movie, which will include a Flash track.

Import the QuickTime movie as you would any other video clip (File > Import or File > Import to Library). In the Import Video dialog box, select Embed Video in Flash Movie. Note that you cannot display a linked QuickTime movie in .swf format.

When you import a linked QuickTime movie, only the first frame of the movie is displayed. To view additional frames of the movie, you must add frames to the timeline so that the duration of your Flash movie encompasses the duration of the QuickTime movie. Your Flash movie itself cannot be viewed until you export it as a QuickTime movie.

To preview a linked QuickTime movie, choose Control > Play.

PUBLISHING A FLASH MOVIE WITH EMBEDDED VIDEO

You can publish a Flash movie that has embedded video just as you would any movie. ActionScript commands supported in embedded movies are `gotoAndPlay`, `gotoAndStop`, `toggleHighQuality`, `stopAllSounds`, `getURL`, `FScommand`, `loadMovie`, `unloadMovie`, `ifFrameLoaded`, and `onMouseEvent`.

File Formats

You can export video as .mov, .wav, and .avi in Flash by selecting File > Export Movie.

You will see a dialog box that enables you to select Compress Video. You must select this to gain access to the various video codecs that might be installed on your computer. Next, another dialog box will enable you to choose the codec you want to use and the audio quality level you want.

Exporting video.

Note: When you export your Flash movie into a video format, it automatically loses its interactivity. Native video interactivity functions are available after export, depending on the chosen video format. Some include SMIL for RealVideo, Windows Media Player 7 for Windows formats, and Sprites for QuickTime. EventStream is an authoring tool in Media Cleaner 5 for adding interactive features to video formats.

Optimizing Video and Audio for Export

QuickTime and .avi formats are bitmap based and are useful in an external video-editing application. The resulting file sizes of .avi formats are generally larger than QuickTime formats.

Exporting video into QuickTime.

Exporting video into .avi.

Tip: 44KHz audio is a sampling rate for quality similar to an audio CD. For most computer work, however, you rarely need to use a sampling rate any higher than 22KHz.

Exporting Video Into:

Settings	QuickTime	.avi
Dimensions	Enter a width and height in pixels or select Match Movie to maintain the same dimensions as the Macromedia Flash movie.	Enter a width and height in pixels. When you specify either the width or the height, the other dimension is automatically set to maintain the aspect ratio of your original movie. To set both the width and the height, deselect Maintain Aspect Ratio.
Format	Enter a color depth: black and white; 4-, 8-, 16-, or 24-bit color; or 32-bit color with alpha (transparency).	Enter a color depth. There are many applications that do not yet support the Windows 32-bit image format. You can select the older 24-bit format if compatibility issues arise.
Compressor/Compress Video	Use this function to choose a standard QuickTime compressor. For more information, refer to your QuickTime documentation.	Choose from a selection of standard .avi compression options.
Smooth	Select Smooth to apply antialiasing for a higher-quality bitmap image. Smooth might cause a halo of gray pixels to appear around images when placed over a colored background. Deselect Smooth if halos appear.	
Quality/Amount	Select the amount of compression to apply to the exported movie. Results vary according to the compressor selected.of Compression	
Sound Format	Select the export rate for sounds in the movie. The higher the rate, the better the fidelity and the larger the file size. The slower the rate, the worse the fidelity and the smaller the file size.	

Summary

Working with video in Flash begins with choosing the correct supported file format. Paying attention to the proper quality settings is the main trick. The new Sorenson Spark codec helps maintain high quality and low file size. Be aware of how keyframes, compression level, and scale affect your final results. After you have your video file embedded, it can easily be manipulated like any other graphic element. Pay attention to the length of your video file and the timeline and adjust accordingly. Synchronization has its benefits and pitfalls, so it's best to plan your fps before you import. Finally, have fun importing multiple clips and exporting into your final output, whether it's .swf or your favorite video format.

With the Cell Animation tool, a user can create primitive drawings frame by frame and then view them as an animation. This project demonstrates Flash's new Application Programming Interface (API) tools. You can now create art inside Flash entirely with ActionScript. You can also make the drawing tools accessible to the user for drawing and animation capabilities. One of the remarkable features of this API is that it creates files that are extremely small; hence, this particular project is only a few kilobytes in size. The tool you will develop consists of two parts: creating the interface and scripting its interactivity.

DRAWING BY NUMBERS

by Véronique Brossier

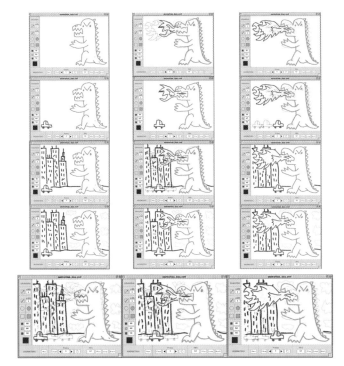

This is the kind of animation you can create with this application. The three rows show the building of each individual drawing, and the bottom column shows the drawings in sequence with onion skinning turned on.

Difficulty Rating: ★★★

Made With: 100% Macromedia Flash ActionScript

Final File Size: 4KB

Modem Download Time: 1 second

Development Time: 3 hours

IT WORKS LIKE THIS

The scripting of this project uses a different framework than the timeline-based environment inherent to Flash. The use of virtual layers and their visibility will be the concept as opposed to frame-based animation.

The project consists only of scripts. The lack of any preexisting assets demonstrates that you can create art, interactivity, and sophisticated applications using only programming.

This project first introduces the drawing methods and then covers the building of the interface and finally the incorporation of interactivity.

Before diving into the project itself, familiarize yourself with the location of the drawing methods in the Actions toolbox: Objects > Movie > Movie Clip > Drawing Methods.

PREPARING TO WORK

Before you begin, copy the movie called **animation_box.swf** onto your hard drive and launch it to familiarize yourself with the project. Experiment with the drawing tools and create some art. Then create a new "frame" by clicking on the plus (+) sign (the rightmost icon in the Frame section) and make a new drawing. After you are done drawing, click Play to see your drawings playing as an animation sequence. Experiment with the different animation options. At any time, you can go back to a drawing and edit it.

Now, copy the movie called **animation_box.fla** onto your hard drive. Open the movie and note that there is no art in the library or on the stage. Click each one of the three frames in the timeline to see the code. On the first frame, functions are declared; on the second frame, the interface is created; and on the third frame, a couple of functions are called to set up the project and make it ready for user interactivity.

For this appendix, you don't need to enter any code. Instead, you will go over the script step by step to understand how the project was built. Each section of this appendix is going to break down the ActionScript and discuss it in detail. You should keep the movie open as you read. To help you find the code easily, its frame and line numbers are specified when it is introduced. Make sure to have the option View Line Numbers on, which you can set in the top-right corner of the Actions toolbox panel.

DRAWING AND COLORING BASIC SHAPES

The new API tools allow for the creation of basic shapes, including lines, squares, and circles.

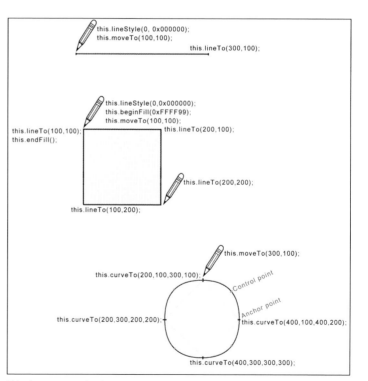

This demonstrates the drawing and color methods for a line, a square, and a circle.

To draw a line, go to Objects > Movie > Movie Clip > Drawing Methods > lineStyle. Simply select a line style (the equivalent of your pen) by specifying line thickness, RGB, and alpha. Then define the point at which the line starts by using the `moveTo()` method and select the endpoint of the line by using the `lineTo()` method. Both methods take an x and y coordinate as parameters. Flash will take care of "connecting the dots."

The drawing methods are movie clip methods, so the drawing occurs within the movie clip. Be sure to make a reference to it by using "this" or the instance name of the movie clip if the drawing is to occur within another movie clip.

To add a new line, use the `moveTo()` method to reposition the cursor to a new location and then reinvoke the `lineTo()` method once more. To draw a square, simply connect four adjacent lines by ending with the same coordinates you started with.

> **Note:** The default settings for the lineStyle are thickness = 0 (hairline), color = 0x000000, and alpha = 100. Only the thickness is a required parameter.

Creating a circle is a little more complex. It uses the `curveTo()` method, which takes four parameters. The first two are the coordinates of the control point, and the second two are the coordinates of the next anchor point.

Color can be added to your drawing by defining a fill color using the `beginFill()` method. For the script to properly execute, use of the `endFill()` method is required at the end of your statement block. Although it is not used in this particular project, you can use the `gradientFill()` method to add another exciting color option.

Finally, the `clear()` method is the equivalent to an eraser. It deletes all drawings created as well as their line style: `this.clear();`.

Now that you know how to create basic shapes, you can start looking at the project itself and how it was built.

FUNCTIONS FOR BASIC SHAPES

Drawing using the API tools can be tedious and repetitive, so writing a couple of functions will help streamline the process. Creating a function is convenient because it is reusable and prevents writing the same lines of code over and over. It is written in a generic way with variables as placeholders. When it is invoked, only specific information needs to be passed. (See frame 1, line 5: `// Functions for basic shapes`.)

You will need one function to create squares and another to draw circles. Each function has the option to draw a filled shape, a hollow shape, or a filled shape with stroke. A parameter is passed to the function to specify one of these three options: `sf` for a shape with a fill and a stroke, `f` for a shape with only a fill, and `h` for a shape with only a stroke.

For the square function, I've used the width and the height of the shape (variables `w` and `h`) instead of x and y coordinates. By using the width and height, only four parameters are needed: the coordinates for the starting point and the width and height of the shape. The function calculates the different points, step by step, based on these values. (See frame 1, line 6: `// Square function`.)

```
function square(myClip, mode, x, y, w, h, primaryColor,
➥secondaryColor) {
    with (myClip) {
    if (mode == "f") {
        beginFill(primaryColor);
} else if (mode == "h") {
        lineStyle(0, primaryColor);
    } else if (mode == "fs") {
        lineStyle(1, secondaryColor);
        beginFill(primaryColor);
    }
    moveTo(x, y);
    lineTo(x+w, y);
    lineTo(x+w, y+h);
    lineTo(x, y+h);
    lineTo(x, y);
    if (mode == "f" || mode == "fs") {
        this.endFill();
        }
    }
}
```

Drawing and coloring a square.

Similar to the square function, the circle function only needs the x and y coordinates of the circle center point and its radius. Using these values, it calculates the cosine (u) and the sine (v) and determines the different points and curves, step by step, based on these values.

Note that in this circle function, the circle is made of eight points (the `curveTo()` method is called eight times), which creates a more circular shape than one made of fewer points. (See frame 1, line 28: `// Circle function`.)

```
function circle(clip, mode, x, y, r, primaryColor,
➥secondaryColor) {
    var u = r*0.4086;
var v = r*0.7071;
with (clip) {
    if (mode == "f") {
        beginFill(primaryColor);
    } else if (mode == "h") {
        lineStyle(0, primaryColor);
    } else if (mode == "fs") {
        lineStyle(1, secondaryColor);
        beginFill(primaryColor);
    }
    moveTo(x-r, y);
    curveTo(x-r, y-u, x-v, y-v);
    curveTo(x-u, y-r, x, y-r);
    curveTo(x+u, y-r, x+v, y-v);
    curveTo(x+r, y-u, x+r, y);
    curveTo(x+r, y+u, x+v, y+v);
    curveTo(x+u, y+r, x, y+r);
    curveTo(x-u, y+r, x-v, y+v);
    curveTo(x-r, y+u, x-r, y);
    if (mode == "f" || mode == "fs") {
        endFill();
    }
    }
}
```

BUILDING THE BACKGROUND FOR THE INTERFACE

The background is made of two panels, and the square function is used to create them. (See frame 2, line 2: `// Building the background for the interface`.)

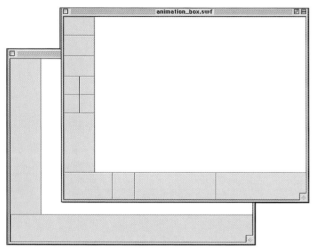

The API drawing tools are used to create the interface, which is composed of squares.

The following code creates the drawing panel (see frame 2, line 4):

```
square(this, "fs", -1, -1, 70, 342, 0xCCCCCC, 0x666666);
```

This code creates the animation panel (see frame 2, line 5):

```
square(this, "fs", 0, 340, 550, 160, 0xCCCCCC, 0x666666);
```

Finally, a series of colored lines—from white to dark gray—are created to divide the panels. These add clarity and give a sense of dimension to the interface. (See frame 2, lines 6 to 69.)

DYNAMICALLY GENERATED MOVIE CLIPS

The code on the next page creates icons for your drawing panel and your animation panel. These icons will function similar to buttons and can be created dynamically.

Before Flash MX, art (including movie clips) needed to be created first and then kept in the Library (or imported) before being used on the stage. Now an empty clip can be created dynamically using the `createEmptyMovieClip()` method, which works in a similar way to the `attachMovie()` method. It creates the movie clip as a child of the movie clip from which it is called, giving the new movie clip a registration point of (0,0) or the top-left corner of its parent. Note that additional frames cannot be added to an empty movie clip.

The movie clips are created in two steps: first, by defining each movie clip's particular setting, and then by actually creating them. For better organization, I've used a multidimensional array. Each individual movie clip has its own array that keeps track of storing its particular settings. The array `emptyClips` stores all of these arrays of settings. (See frame 2, line 72: `// Creation of "icon" movie clips`.)

```
var drawIconW = 20;
var drawIconH = 20;
var animIconW = 30;
var animIconH = 25;
var iconColorF = 0xffffff;
var iconColorS = 0x666666;
var iconSThick = 0;
var emptyClipS = new Array();
emptyClipS[ 0]  = new Array("pencilTool", "fs", 8, 55, drawIconW, drawIconH, 0xCCCCCC, iconColorS);
emptyClipS[ 1]  = new Array("lineTool", "fs", 8, 101, drawIconW, drawIconH, 0xCCCCCC, iconColorS);
emptyClipS[ 2]  = new Array("sHollow", "fs", 8, 181, drawIconW, drawIconH, 0xCCCCCC, 0x333333);
emptyClipS[ 3]  = new Array("sFill", "fs", 42, 181, drawIconW, drawIconH, 0x999999, 0x333333);
emptyClipS[ 4]  = new Array("red", "fs", 12, 225, 10, 10, 0xff0000, 0x333333);
emptyClipS[ 5]  = new Array("green", "fs", 12, 250, 10, 10, 0x00ff00, 0x333333);
emptyClipS[ 6]  = new Array("blue", "fs", 12, 275, 10, 10, 0x0000ff, 0x333333);
emptyClipS[ 7]  = new Array("newproject", "fs", 120, 364, animIconW, 20, iconColorF, iconColorS);
emptyClipS[ 8]  = new Array("remove", "fs", 175, 364, animIconW, 20, iconColorF, iconColorS);
emptyClipS[ 9]  = new Array("previousF", "fs", 213, 364, 18, 20, iconColorF, iconColorS);
emptyClipS[ 10] = new Array("nextF", "fs", 275, 364, 18, 20, iconColorF, iconColorS);
emptyClipS[ 11] = new Array("colorSwatch", "fs", 20, 300, 30, 30, 0xff00ff, 0x333333);
```

A multidimensional array used to store the icons' movie clips' individual information.

Next, the movie clips for all the icons of your interface are created. Note that dynamically created movie clips live on a depth and require a depth number. The variable myDepth is used throughout this whole project and is incremented every time a new item is created for which a depth is required. This is to avoid reusing the same depth number. Using the same depth twice would delete the existing content before replacing it by the new content.

I've used a for loop to generate these movie clips and to apply individual settings to them.

```
for (var i = 0; i<emptyClipS.length; i++) {
this.createEmptyMovieClip(emptyClipS[ i][ 0], myDepth);
square(this[ emptyClipS[ i][ 0]], emptyClipS[ i][ 1],
➥emptyClipS[ i][ 2], emptyClipS[ i][ 3], emptyClipS[ i][ 4],
➥emptyClipS[ i][ 5], emptyClipS[ i][ 6],
➥emptyClipS[ i][ 7]);
myDepth++;
}
```

Creation of the icon movie clips.

An empty movie clip, like any movie clip, can be the parent of other movie clips. For the icons corresponding to onion skinning, playback, looping, and reverse, a child movie clip is created. It is used to provide visual feedback when the setting is selected. The child movie clip holds a drawing, made of a couple of lines, that looks like a checkmark. (See frame 2, line 99: `// icons with a checkmark`.)

```
var iconCheckMarkYPos = 364;
var emptyClipSC = new Array();
emptyClipSC[ 0]  = new Array("onion", "fs", 300);
emptyClipSC[ 1]  = new Array("playback", "fs", 414);
emptyClipSC[ 2]  = new Array("looping", "fs", 452);
emptyClipSC[ 3]  = new Array("reverseplay", "fs", 490);
for (var i = 0; i<emptyClipSC.length; i++) {
        this.createEmptyMovieClip(emptyClipSC[ i][ 0], myDepth);
        square(this[ emptyClipSC[ i][ 0]], emptyClipSC[ i][ 1], emptyClipSC[ i][ 2], iconCheckMarkYPos, animIconW, 20, iconColorF, iconColorS);
        this[ emptyClipSC[ i][ 0]].createEmptyMovieClip("checkMark", 1);
        with (this[ emptyClipSC[ i][ 0]].checkMark) {
                lineStyle(0, 0x333333);
                moveTo(emptyClipSC[ i][ 2] +12,iconCheckMarkYPos-10);
                lineTo(emptyClipSC[ i][ 2]  + 15, iconCheckMarkYPos-5);
                lineTo(emptyClipSC[ i][ 2]  + 20, iconCheckMarkYPos-15);
                _visible = false;
        }
        myDepth++;
}


this.createEmptyMovieClip("cHollow", myDepth);
circle(cHollow, "fs", 19, 151, 10, 0xCCCCCC, 0x333333);
myDepth++;
this.createEmptyMovieClip("cFill", myDepth);
circle(cFill, "fs", 53, 151, 10, 0x999999, 0x333333);
myDepth++;

this.createEmptyMovieClip("selectedTool", myDepth);
        with (selectedTool) {
        beginFill(0xffffff);
        moveTo(14, 42);
        lineTo(24, 42);
        lineTo(19, 48);
        lineTo(14, 42);
        endFill();
        }
myDepth++;
```

Creation of icon movie clips using a checkmark visual feedback.

286

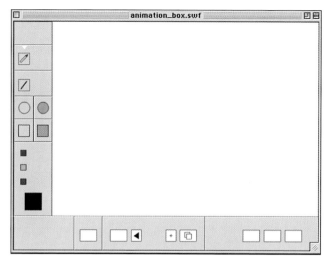

Programmatically drawn icons provide the tools for the
drawing and animating panels.

Text labels can also be created programmatically.

Next I created the icons for the circle tools and the Selected Tool icon that indicates which tool is the current setting. (See frame 2, line 119: `// circular icons` and frame 2, line 126: `// Selected tool icon`.)

Some of the icons, such as the Pencil tool, have a customized look, and individual drawings are created for them. (See frame 2, line 137: `// additional drawings on specific buttons`.)

DYNAMICALLY GENERATED TEXT FIELDS

This project requires two types of text fields: plain text to label the icons (we will refer to them as "label" text fields) and input text fields, which enable the user to change the settings of the drawing and animation tools.

In both cases, the text fields are generated dynamically using the new `createTextField()` method. Flash also enables you to set text format using the new `TextFormat()` method and the `setNewTextFormat()` method. The latter is used to format text after the text field content has been modified.

First create the label text fields. (See frame 2, line 185: `// Creation of "label" text fields`.)

First, the text setting is defined for the "label" text fields.

```
myLabelStyle = new TextFormat();
with (myLabelStyle) {
        font = "Verdana";
        color = 0x333333;
        size = 9;
}
```

Text formatting for the "label" text fields.

The text fields are created in two steps. First each text field's particular setting is defined and stored in an array.

```
lTextSize = 40;
var labelText = new Array();
labelText[ 0]  = new Array("drawing_txt", "DRAWING", 7, 15, 60);
labelText[ 1]  = new Array("animating_txt", "ANIMATING", 20, 367, 70);
labelText[ 2]  = new Array("pencilW_txt", "width", 35, 45, lTextSize);
labelText[ 3]  = new Array("lineW_txt", "width", 35, 91, lTextSize);
labelText[ 4]  = new Array("new_txt", "New", 123, 367, 40);
labelText[ 5]  = new Array("clear_txt", "Clear", 175, 367, 40);
labelText[ 6]  = new Array("frame_txt", "Frame", 236, 348, 40);
labelText[ 7]  = new Array("frameRateL_txt", "FPS", 376, 348, 40);
labelText[ 8]  = new Array("play_txt", "Play", 417, 367, 40);
labelText[ 9]  = new Array("loop_txt", "Loop", 453, 367, 40);
labelText[ 10] = new Array("reverse_txt", "Back", 491, 367, 50);
```

Using a multidimensional array to store label text fields' information.

Then, the label text fields are created. Using a `for` loop, you can generate the new text fields and apply properties and formats to them.

```
for (var i = 0; i<labelText.length; i++) {
    this.createTextField(labelText[ i][ 0], myDepth,
    ➥labelText[ i][ 2],labelText[ i][ 3], labelText[ i][ 4],
    ➥lTextSize);
    with (this[ labelText[ i][ 0]]) {
        selectable = false;
        text = labelText[ i][ 1];
        setTextFormat(myLabelStyle);
    }
    myDepth++;
}
```

Creation of the label text fields.

Dynamically created text fields are added to the interface to allow user input.

Finally, the input text setting and the input text fields are created using the same organizational system. (See frame 2 line 217 // `Creation of "input" text fields`.)

Hurray! The project interface is now completed.

METHODS FOR THE INPUT TEXT FIELDS

Now that the interface is built, the interactivity is created to track the user's selection. Text fields can now have an onChanged() event handler, which returns true if the content of the text field is changed. Use this option to track the user choice for the input text fields.

Conditions are set to control the range of values for each particular text field. (See frame 2, line 259: // Functions for the input text fields.)

For the rValue_txt (as well as the gValue_txt and bValue_txt) input text field, the range of values is 0 to 255, which corresponds to RGB values. If the user enters an out-of-range value, it is automatically set to the closest number within the range. Note that the adjustColor() function is also called. This function is defined in the next section of this project. (See frame 2, line 260: // red value.)

```
rValue_txt.onChanged = function() {
if (this.text == "" || Number(this.text)<0) {
this.text = 0;
} else if (this.text >255) {
this.text = 255;
}
adjustColor();
}
```

Function of the red value input text field.

For the pencilWidth_txt (and the lineWidth_txt), the range of values is between 0 and 15, which represents the thickness of the line. The value of the text field is passed to the variable pencilThick. (See frame 2, line 287: // pencil width.)

```
pencilWidth_txt.onChanged = function() {
if (this.text == "" || Number(this.text)<0) {
this.text = 0;
} else if (this.text >15) {
this.text = 15;
}
_root.pencilThick = Number(this.text);
}
```

Function for the Pencil tool.

For the frameRate_txt input text field, the range of values is between 1 frame per second and 30 frames per second. (See frame 2, line 305: // frame rate.)

```
frameRate_txt.onChanged = function() {
if (this.text == "" || Number(this.text)<1) {
this.text = 1;
} else if (this.text >30) {
this.text = 30;
}
_root.speed = Number(this.text);
}
```

Function for the frame rate input text field.

METHODS FOR THE DRAWING ICONS

For the icons, I've used the new event model, which lets you define a method for a movie clip that is called whenever an event (such as a mouse event) occurs. For this project, I am tracking the `onRelease()` event. Because all your scripts can now be placed on one single frame instead of the object itself, this new model represents a great organizational enhancement. (See frame 2, line 315: `// Functions for the "icon" movie clips - Drawing panel`.)

The icons for the drawing tools set the drawing variables and position the Selected Tool indicator. The `tool` variable defines the drawing tool (`pencil`, `line`, `circle`, or `box`) selected, and the `fill` variable defines the fill style (`true` or `false`) selected. Note that I called the square tool "box" because it can create a square or a rectangle.

```
pencilTool.onRelease = function() {
    tool = "pencil";
    selectedTool._x = 0;
    selectedTool._y = 0;
}

lineTool.onRelease = function() {
    tool = "line";
    fill = false;
    selectedTool._x = 0;
    selectedTool._y = 45;
}

sFill.onRelease = function() {
    tool = "box";
    fill = true;
    selectedTool._x = 34;
    selectedTool._y = 130;
}

cHollow.onRelease = function() {
    tool = "circle";
    fill = false;
    selectedTool._x = 0;
    selectedTool._y = 90;
}
```

Functions for the Pencil tool, the Line tool, the filled box and the hollow circle.

METHODS FOR THE ANIMATION ICONS

The icons for the animation panel call functions that will be defined in the final step in this project. (See frame 2, line 357: `// Functions for the "icon" movie clips- animation panel`.)

```
newproject.onRelease = function() {
    newProjectFunction();
}
```

Function for the New Project icon.

The following is a list of the icons and the name of their individual functions. When one icon is pressed, its function is called and executes a piece of code:

remove	removeAnimFunction ()
previousF	previousDrawing()
nextF	nextDrawing()
onion	onionSkin()
playback	showtime()
looping	loopFunction ()
reversePlay	reverseFunction()

FUNCTIONS FOR THE DRAWING TOOLS

The Drawing palette contains the Pencil tool (freestyle drawing), the Line tool, the Circle tool (fill or stroke), the Box tool (fill or stroke), and the RGB color fields.

tool	Stores the selected tool
fColor	Stores the fill color
sColor	Stores the stroke color
r, g, and b	Store the red, green, and blue values
lineThick	Stores the line tool width
pencilThick	Stores the width of the pencil tool

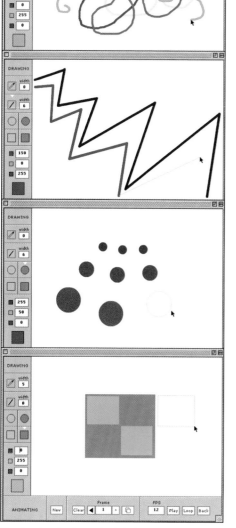

Showing the drawing tools, including marquees.

Upon the start of the movie, variables are initialized: the `tool` is assigned the value of `"pencil"`, and both `lineThick` and `pencilThick` are assigned a value of 0. The `adjustColor()` and `drawingTools()` functions are invoked. (See frame 3, lines 1 to 22.)

Now go back to frame 1 of the movie where all the functions that are the mechanisms of the drawing and animation tools are set up.

The `adjustColor` function takes the values stored in the input text fields called `rValue_txt.text`, `gValue_txt.text`, and `bValue_txt.text`. It converts these RGB values to a hexadecimal value and sets the `fColor` and `sColor` variables to it. Finally, it clears the `colorSwatch` icon and redraws it to the new color to provide a visual feedback. (See frame 1, line 56: `// Color function`.)

Every time the user modifies the content of any one of the color text fields, the `adjustColor()` function is called again, and both the fill color and stroke color are adjusted accordingly.

```
function adjustColor() {
    r = rValue_txt.text;
    g = gValue_txt.text;
    b = bValue_txt.text;
    myColor = (r << 16 | g << 8 | b);
    fColor = myColor;
    sColor = myColor;
    colorSwatch.clear();
    square(colorSwatch, "fs", 20, 300, 30, 30, fColor,
    ➥0x333333);
}
```

The `adjustColor()` function is used to define the fill and stroke color, and the look of the color swatch.

Look at the other function which was called upon the start of the movie: `drawingTools()`. (See frame 1, line 68: `// Drawing tools`.)

This function is the core of the drawing aspect of this project and enables the user to draw on the stage.

In addition to the variables previously introduced, this function uses four variables:

`myDepth`	Assigns a depth level to the new objects
`cell`	Stores the drawing currently in display
`d`	Is a counter used between drawings and represents the drawing number
`totalDrawings`	Stores the total number of drawings created

The function `drawingTools()` first increments the `d` variable and the `totalDrawings` variable.

```
function drawingTools() {
    d++;
    totaldrawings++;
```

The text field content is updated to reflect the frame number.

```
currentFrame_txt.text = d;
```

An empty movie clip is created. (Note how the `myDepth` variable is used to determine the depth number and gets incremented.)

```
this.createEmptyMovieClip("drawing"+d, myDepth);
    myDepth++
```

Another empty movie clip is created, and a square is drawn on it. This clip will be used as a mask for the **drawing** movie clip to prevent the user from drawing on the tools area.

```
this.createEmptyMovieClip("masking"+d, myDepth);
myMask = this["masking" + d];
square(myMask, "f", 70, 0, 480, 340, 0xffff00);
```

The `cell` variable is set to the name of the movie clip currently in display.

```
cell = this["drawing"+d];
```

The **masking** movie clip is now set as a mask for the **drawing** movie clip.

```
cell.setMask(myMask);
```

The **drawing** empty movie clip gets assigned new methods for two mouse events: mouse down and mouse up.

```
cell.onMouseDown = function() {
        cell.active = true;
        origX = this._xmouse;
        origY = this._ymouse;
        cell.moveTo(OrigX, OrigY);
        eval(tool+"Down")();
}
    cell.onMouseUp = function() {
            cell.active = false;
            eval(tool+"Up")();
    }
```

The `mouseDown()` and `mouseUp()` functions for the new **drawing** movie clip.

onMouseDown, the variable `active` is set to `true`, the `moveTo()` method is set to the current position of the cursor as the starting point of any drawing, and one of the tool functions is called.

Depending on the value of the `tool` variable, either `pencilDown()`, `lineDown()`, `squareDown()`, or `circleDown()` is called. For example, if the selected tool is the Pencil tool, `eval(tool + "Down")()` calls the `pencilDown()` function.

onMouseUp, the variable `active` is set to `false`. It is used as a Boolean so that the drawing capability is disabled when the mouse is up and moving.

For all the tool functions (`pencilDown()`, `lineDown()`, `boxDown()` and `circleDown()`) which are called from the `drawingTools()` function, the `onMouseMove()` function is called within the `onMouseDown()` function because it only needs to be tracked when the mouse is down and the user is actually drawing.

Except for the Pencil tool, a marquee is created as a visual aid while the mouse is moving and then disappears to be replaced by the appropriate colored shape when the mouse is released. To achieve this effect, a child movie clip called **s** is created when the mouse is first pressed down and constantly clears and redraws itself based on the mouse location.

Here is a sample look at the Line tool functions. (See frame 1, line 108: `// Line tool functions`.)

```
function lineDown() {
    cell.lineStyle(lineThick, sColor);
    cell.createEmptyMovieClip("s", 1);
    cell.onMouseMove = function() {
        if (this.active == true) {
            cell.s.clear();
            cell.s.lineStyle(0, 0xCCCCCC, 100);
            cell.s.moveTo(OrigX, OrigY);
            cell.s.lineTo(_xmouse, _ymouse);
            updateAfterEvent();
        }
    }
}
function lineUp() {
    cell.s.removeMovieClip();
    cell.lineTo(_xmouse, _ymouse);
}
```

Drawing functions for the Line tool.

If the current tool selected is "line," the function `lineDown()` is called when the user puts his or her cursor down and creates an empty movie clip called **s**. Every time the mouse moves, it clears itself and redraws itself. Its starting point is the original x and y coordinates where the mouse was first put down, and its ending point is the current mouse position. The function `lineUp()`, which is called when the user releases the mouse, erases the marquee line and creates a colored line instead.

FUNCTIONS FOR THE ANIMATION TOOLS

Look at some of the controls on the animation panel. (See frame 1, line 190: `// Animation controls.`)

After the user has created a drawing, he or she might choose to add another one and start building an animation one drawing at a time. Clicking the Forward button calls the `nextDrawing()` function (frame 1, line 192), which hides the drawing just created and calls the `drawingTools()` function again to create a new one using the same drawing functions previously discussed. Note that the Forward button will only create a new drawing if the d variable is equal to the `totalDrawings` variable. This mechanism gives the Forward button two purposes: to navigate between drawings if the one currently displayed is not the last one created (d <totalDrawings), and to create a new drawing if the one currently displayed is the last one created (d = totalDrawings).

During the drawing process, the user can go back to view earlier drawings by clicking on the Previous Frame button. This calls the `previousDrawing()` function. (See frame 1, line 213.)

Selecting the Onion Skinning icon displays all drawings at once to review the progress of the animation. Note that the checkmark created earlier becomes visible as visual feedback when the icon is pressed. (See frame 1, line 228.)

To erase a particular drawing, the `removeAnimFunction()` function is called to clear the frame. (See frame 1, line 257). Finally, to start a new animation, the `newProjectFunction()` does the proper housecleaning. (See frame 1, line 263).

The animation can be viewed by clicking the Play icon, which calls the `showtime()` function (see frame 1, line 276), with the option to loop (`loopFunction()` function; see frame 1, line 333) and play in reverse (`reverseFunction()` function; see frame 1, line 343). Here, too, the checkmarks created for visual feedback appear when their corresponding icon is pressed. The user can also change the frame rate.

The new `setInterval()` method is used to create the time delay between the display of each drawing, and it repeats a script over time. You need to give it a function and a time. The `setInterval()` calls the function over and over at the time increment specified. (See frame 1, line 284.)

```
function showtime() {
    if (playing == false) {
        playing = true;
        playback.checkMark._visible = true;
        if (onionMode == true) {
            onionHide();
        }
        go = setInterval(animation, 1000/speed);
    } else {
        cell = this["drawing"+d];
        if (d == totalDrawings) {
            nextF.cross._visible = true;
        } else {
            nextF.cross._visible = false;
        }
        playing = false;
        playback.checkMark._visible = false;
        clearInterval(go);
    }
}
function animation() {
    if (reverseMode == false) {
        _root["drawing"+d]._visible = false;
        if (d < totalDrawings) {
            d++;
        } else {
            d = 1;
        }
        currentFrame_txt.text = d;
        _root["drawing"+d]._visible = true;
        if (loop == false) {
            if (d == totalDrawings) {
                clearInterval(go);
                playing = false;
                playback.checkmark._visible = false;
                nextF.cross._visible = true;
            }
        }
```

```
        }
    } else {
        _root["drawing"+d]._visible = false;
        if (d > 1) {
            d --;
        } else {
            d = totalDrawings;
        }
        currentFrame_txt.text = d;
        _root["drawing"+d]._visible = true;
        if (loop == false) {
            if (d == totalDrawings) {
                clearInterval(go);
                playing = false;
                playback.checkmark._visible = false;
            }
        }
    }
}
function loopFunction() {
    if (loop == false) {
        loop = true;
        looping.checkMark._visible = true;
    } else {
        loop = false;
        looping.checkMark._visible = false;
    }
}
function reverseFunction() {
    if (reverseMode == false) {
        reverseMode = true;
        reverseplay.checkMark._visible = true;
    } else {
        reverseMode = false;
        reverseplay.checkMark._visible = false;
    }
}
```

FORWARD ON

This project is just one of the many applications you can make using the new drawing API. You can create randomly generated motion graphics, for example, or template designs for web sites with very small loading times. A writing and drawing tool, not unlike this one, can be used on cellular phones, pocket PC, or any device without a keyboard to fill out forms, sign documents, and write messages.

Also, many more options can be added to this cell animation box, such as:

- The option to copy and paste drawings
- One level of undo
- A gradient color tool
- The option to create and save textures as a fill option
- Imported images and sounds to create a multimedia project
- The capability to save the completed animation and send it to others via a network.

INDEX

curveTo() method, 282
customizing
    Flash sites, 87
        building JavaScript functions, 92-96
        completing movies, 91-92
        scripting movies, 89-90
        setting up movies, 88
    scrollbars, 156-157

D

data. *See also* results
    assigning, 124-125
    error checking data, 164
databases, structure of greeting card sites, 159
Date object, 41, 47-48
    advantages of, 53
    analogue clocks
        setting, 54-55
        setting rows of clocks, 56
    extending with prototypes, 50-51
    proleptic, 58
    real-time, updating, 52
    static values, 49
dates, 41, 221
    daylight saving time, 58
    Gregorian calendar, 58
    improving, 59
    online user polls, 221
    time zones, 58
    years, defining, 58
daylight saving time (DST), 57
    dates, 58
debugging programs, 161
decreaseSpeed function, 81
default : statement, 265
designing shell interfaces, 107-109
    adding dynamic components, 109-111
dice
    calculating values of, 260
    creating, 248-252
    placing on tables, 256-259
    throw counters, 257
dimensions
    exporting video, 278
    of movies, 193
disabilities, visual disabilities, 12. *See also* accessibility
disappearing masks, 207-208
displayFrame function, 175-177
    for-in loops, 176
displaying greeting cards for recipients, 166

downloading Standard font family, 22
downloadWallpaper(), 37
drag and drop behaviors, adding to timeline clips, 173-175
drag function, 172-173
drag method, timeline clips, 173
draggable movie clips and masks, 198
DragSpace, 101
drawBar(), 128-132
drawing
    adding color, 282
    bar charts, 232
    circles, 282
    icons, 290
    lines, 282
    by numbers, preparing, 281
Drawing palette, 290
drawing tools, functions for, 290-293
drawings, erasing, 294
drawingTools(), 291-292
dropLocationOkay, 173-174
dropSpawn, 172-173
DST (daylight saving time), 57
duplicating movie clips, 239
dynamic components, adding to shell interfaces, 109-111
Dynamic Drawing API, 107, 126-132
    shell interfaces
        adding dynamic components, 109-111
        designing, 107-109
dynamic masking, 191
    creating, 200-203
dynamic text, 192
dynamically assigned functions, 73
dynamically generated movie clips, 284-287
dynamically generated text fields, 287-288

E

eCalculate object, 268
eCards. *See* greeting card sites
Editable property, ComboBox, 7
egreetings, displaying cards for recipients, 166
eInit object, 268
email programs, 164-165
embedded video, publishing Flash movies, 277
embedding
    buttons in movie clips, 101
    fonts, outlines, 23
    video, 275

encoding
    video, 274-275
    software, 274
endFill(), 130, 282
endRoll, 253
enforcing color consistency, 108
enterFrame, 21, 193
erasers, clear() method, 282
erasing drawings, 294
error checking data, 164
eSlotInit object, 264
events, on (release) button events, 90
EventStream, 277
Expert mode, switching to, 248
exporting audio and video, 277-278
extending
    Date object with prototype, 50-51
    preloaders, functionality, 28-30
    timelines, for video, 275
extensions, 63
    naming conventions, 247

F

fading movie clips, 219
file extensions, naming conventions, 63
file formats
    publishing Flash movies with embedded video, 277
    videos, 273
files
    .avi, 273
    .flv, 273
    .js, 97
    .php, 222
    MP3s. *See* MP3 players
fill attributes, 130
finding values, 50
Flash movies, publishing with embedded video, 277
Flash UI Components, 8
Flatzee. *See also* games
    dice
        creating, 248-252
        placing on tables, 256-259
        rolling, 253-255
    programming, 247
.flv files, 273
folders
    Components Skins, 8
    Flash UI Components, 8
    saving layers in, 152

VOICES THAT MATTER

VISIT OUR WEB SITE

WWW.NEWRIDERS.COM

On our web site, you'll find information about our other books, authors, tables of contents, and book errata. You will also find information about book registration and how to purchase our books, both domestically and internationally.

EMAIL US

Contact us at: **nrfeedback@newriders.com**

- If you have comments or questions about this book
- To report errors that you have found in this book
- If you have a book proposal to submit or are interested in writing for New Riders
- If you are an expert in a computer topic or technology and are interested in being a technical editor who reviews manuscripts for technical accuracy

Contact us at: **nreducation@newriders.com**

- If you are an instructor from an educational institution who wants to preview New Riders books for classroom use. Email should include your name, title, school, department, address, phone number, office days/hours, text in use, and enrollment, along with your request for desk/examination copies and/or additional information.

Contact us at: **nrmedia@newriders.com**

- If you are a member of the media who is interested in reviewing copies of New Riders books. Send your name, mailing address, and email address, along with the name of the publication or web site you work for.

BULK PURCHASES/CORPORATE SALES

The publisher offers discounts on this book when ordered in quantity for bulk purchases and special sales. For sales within the U.S., please contact: Corporate and Government Sales (800) 382-3419 or **corpsales@pearsontechgroup.com**. Outside of the U.S., please contact: International Sales (317) 581-3793 or **international@pearsontechgroup.com**.

WRITE TO US

New Riders Publishing
201 W. 103rd St.
Indianapolis, IN 46290-1097

CALL/FAX US

Toll-free (800) 571-5840
If outside U.S. (317) 581-3500
Ask for New Riders
FAX: (317) 581-4663

New Riders

WWW.NEWRIDERS.COM

MACROMEDIA®

FLASH™ MX

**Flash Deconstruction:
The Process, Design, and
ActionScript of Juxt
Interactive**
Todd Purgason, Phil Scott
Bonnie Blake, Brian Drake
$45.00, 0735711496

**Flash ActionScript for
Designers: Drag, Slide,
Fade**
Brendan Dawes
$45.00, 0735710473

Flash MX Magic
Matthew David, et al.
$45.00, 0735711607

Inside Flash MX
Jody Keating,
Fig Leaf Software
$49.99, 0735712549

**Skip Intro: Flash
Usability &
Interface Design**
Duncan McAlester,
Michelangelo Capraro
$45.00, 073571178X

**Flash Enabled:
Flash Design and
Development for
Devices**
Phillip Torrone,
Branden Hall,
Glenn Thomas,
Mike Chambers, et al.
$49.99, 0735711771

**Object-Oriented
Programming
with ActionScript**
Branden Hall, Samuel Wan
$39.99, 0735711834

**Flash to the Core:
An Interactive Sketchbook
by Joshua Davis**
Joshua Davis
$45.00, 0735712883

The Flash MX Project
Cheryl Brumbaugh-Duncan
$35.00, 0735712832

ActionScripting in Flash MX
Phillip Kerman
$39.99, 0735712956

**Flash MX Application Design
and Development**
Jessica Speigel
$45.00, 0735712425

The Flash Animator
Sandro Corsaro
$49.99, 0735712824

Flash MX Audio Magic
Brad Kozak, Eric Dolecki,
Craig Swann, Manuel Clement
$39.99, 0735711941

New
Riders

WWW.NEWRIDERS.COM

VOICES
THAT MATTER™